MEAN Web Development

Master real-time web application development using a mean combination of MongoDB, Express, AngularJS, and Node.js

Amos Q. Haviv

PUBLISHING

BIRMINGHAM - MUMBAI

Liran Tal is a top contributor to the open source MEAN.IO and MEAN.JS full-stack JavaScript frameworks. He is also a certified MongoDB developer and a technical reviewer of the yet-to-be-published *MongoDB Cookbook, Packt Publishing* (the name of the book might change in the course of publishing). Being an avid supporter of and contributor to the open source movement, in 2007, he redefined network RADIUS management by establishing daloRADIUS, a world-renowned and industry-leading open source project.

Liran currently works at HP Software as an R&D team leader on a combined technology stack, featuring a Drupal-based collaboration platform, Java, Node.js, and MongoDB.

At HP Live Network, Liran plays a key role in system architecture design, shaping the technology strategy from planning and development to deployment and maintenance in HP's IaaS cloud. Acting as the technological focal point, he loves mentoring teammates, drives for better code methodology, and seeks out innovative solutions to support business strategies. He has a cum laude (Honors) in his Bachelor's degree in Business and Information Systems Analysis studies and enjoys spending his time with his beloved wife, Tal, and his new born son, Ori. Among other things, his hobbies include playing the guitar, hacking all things on Linux, and continuously experimenting and contributing to open source projects.

Vikram Tiwari is currently working as a MEAN stack developer in SilverPush (SilverEdge, Inc.). Using MEAN, he has developed a frontend tool for a mobile advertising management platform. Along with MEAN stack, he also works on Python, Google App Engine, Redis, DynamoDB, Aerospike, and various Google APIs. In his free time, he contributes to various projects on GitHub and manages the developers' community at New Delhi with Google Developers Group.

Yutaka Yamaguchi is currently working as a frontend MEAN application developer. Prior to this, he worked as a senior manager in the quality assurance area for 7 years. He lives in Tokyo with his wife and their 4-year old son.

He built his first own home page in 1999, which is written with HTML4 by Notepad, without CSS and JavaScript.

He has worked at Six Apart, whose flagship product is the movable type of a social publishing platform dedicated to helping businesses and bloggers manage content and thrive in today's social media landscape.

www.PacktPub.com

Support files, eBooks, discount offers, and more

You might want to visit www.PacktPub.com for support files and downloads related to your book.

Did you know that Packt offers eBook versions of every book published, with PDF and ePub files available? You can upgrade to the eBook version at www.PacktPub.com and as a print book customer, you are entitled to a discount on the eBook copy. Get in touch with us at service@packtpub.com for more details.

At www.PacktPub.com, you can also read a collection of free technical articles, sign up for a range of free newsletters and receive exclusive discounts and offers on Packt books and eBooks.

http://PacktLib.PacktPub.com

Do you need instant solutions to your IT questions? PacktLib is Packt's online digital book library. Here, you can access, read and search across Packt's entire library of books.

Why subscribe?

- Fully searchable across every book published by Packt
- Copy and paste, print and bookmark content
- On demand and accessible via web browser

Free access for Packt account holders

If you have an account with Packt at www.PacktPub.com, you can use this to access PacktLib today and view nine entirely free books. Simply use your login credentials for immediate access.

Table of Contents

Preface

Back in the spring of 1995, web browsers were very different from present day web browsers. It had been 4 years since the release of World Wide Web (the first internet browser written by Tim Berners-Lee), 2 years since the initial release of Mosaic, and Internet Explorer 1.0 was a few months months away from release. The World Wide Web began to show signs of popularity, and though some of the big companies showed interest in the field, the main disruptor back then was a small company named Netscape.

Netscape's already popular browser Netscape Navigator, was in the works for its second version, when the client engineering team and co-founder Marc Anderseen decided that Navigator 2.0 should embed a programming language. The task was assigned to a software engineer named Branden Eich, who completed it in 10 days between May 6 and May 15, 1995, naming the language Mocha, then LiveScript, and eventually JavaScript.

Netscape Navigator 2.0 was released in September 1995 and transformed the way we perceived the web browser. By August 1996, Internet Explorer 3.0 introduced its own implementation of JavaScript, and in November of that year, Netscape had announced that they had submitted JavaScript to ECMA for standardization. In June 1997, the ECMA-262 specification was published, making JavaScript the de facto standard programming language for the Web.

For years, JavaScript was denigrated by many as the programming language for amateurs. JavaScript's architecture, fragmented implementation, and original "amateur" audience made professional programmers dismiss it. But then AJAX was introduced, and when Google released their Gmail and Google Maps applications in the mid-2000s, it suddenly became clear that AJAX technology could transform websites into web applications. This inspired the new generation of web developers to take JavaScript development to next level.

What began with the first generation of utility libraries, such as jQuery and Prototype, soon got boosted by Google's next great contribution, the Chrome browser and its V8 JavaScript engine, released in end of 2008. The V8 engine, with its JIT compiling capabilities, greatly enhanced JavaScript performance. This led to a new era in JavaScript development.

2009 was JavaScript's *annus mirabilis*; suddenly, platforms such as Node.js enabled developers to run JavaScript on the server, databases such as MongoDB popularized and simplified the use of JSON storage, and frameworks such as AngularJS started making use of the powerful new browsers. Almost 20 years after its original debut, JavaScript is now everywhere. What used to be an "amateur" programming language, capable of executing small scripts, is now one of the most popular programming languages in the world. The rise of open source collaboration tools, along with the devoted involvement of talented engineers, created one of the richest communities in the world, and the seeds planted by many contributors are now flourishing in a burst of sheer creativity.

The practical implications are enormous. What was once a fragmented team of developers, each an expert in his own domain, can now become a homogeneous team capable of developing leaner, more agile software together using a single language across all layers.

There are many full-stack JavaScript frameworks out there, some built by great teams, some address important issues, but none of them are as open and modular as the MEAN stack. The idea is simple, we'll take MongoDB as the database, Express as the web framework, AngularJS as the frontend framework, and Node.js as the platform, and combine them together in a modular approach that will ensure the flexibility needed in modern software development. MEAN's approach relies on the communities around each of the open source modules keeping it updated and stable, ensuring that if one of the modules becomes useless, we can just seamlessly replace it with a better-suited one.

I would like to welcome you to the JavaScript revolution and assure you I will do my best to help you become a full-stack JavaScript developer.

In this book, we'll help you set up your environment and explain how to connect the different MEAN components together using the best modules. You'll be introduced to the best practices of maintaining your code clear and simple and how to avoid common pitfalls. We'll walk through building your authentication layer and adding your first entity. You'll learn how to leverage JavaScript nonblocking architecture in building real-time communication between your server and client applications. Finally, we'll show you how to cover your code with the proper tests and what tools to use to automate your development process.

What this book covers

Chapter 1, Introduction to MEAN, introduce you to the MEAN stack and shows you how to install the different prerequisites on each OS.

Chapter 2, Getting Started with Node.js, explains the basics of Node.js and how it is used in web application development.

Chapter 3, Building an Express Web Application, explains how to create and structure an Express application by implementing the MVC pattern.

Chapter 4, Introduction to MongoDB, explains the basics of MongoDB and how it can be used to store your application data.

Chapter 5, Introduction to Mongoose, shows how to use a Mongoose to connect an Express application with a MongoDB database.

Chapter 6, Managing User Authentication Using Passport, explains how to manage your users' authentication and offer them diverse login options.

Chapter 7, Introduction to AngularJS, explains how to implement an AngularJS application in conjunction with your Express application.

Chapter 8, Creating a MEAN CRUD Module, explains how to write and use your MEAN application's entities.

Chapter 9, Adding Real-time Functionality Using Socket.io, shows you how to create and use real-time communication between your client and server.

Chapter 10, Testing MEAN Applications, explains how to automatically test the different parts of your MEAN application.

Chapter 11, Automating and Debugging MEAN Applications, explains how to develop your MEAN application more efficiently.

What you need for this book

This book is suitable for beginner and intermediate web developers with basic knowledge in HTML, CSS, and modern JavaScript development.

Who this book is for

Web developers interested in learning how to build modern web applications using MongoDB, Express, AngularJS, and Node.js.

Piracy

Piracy of copyright material on the Internet is an ongoing problem across all media. At Packt, we take the protection of our copyright and licenses very seriously. If you come across any illegal copies of our works, in any form, on the Internet, please provide us with the location address or website name immediately so that we can pursue a remedy.

Please contact us at copyright@packtpub.com with a link to the suspected pirated material.

We appreciate your help in protecting our authors, and our ability to bring you valuable content.

Questions

You can contact us at questions@packtpub.com if you are having a problem with any aspect of the book, and we will do our best to address it.

1
Introduction to MEAN

The MEAN stack is a powerful, full-stack JavaScript solution that comprises four major building blocks: MongoDB as the database, Express as the web server framework, AngularJS as the web client framework, and Node.js as the server platform. These building blocks are being developed by different teams and involve a substantial community of developers and advocates pushing forward the development and documentation of each component. The main strength of the stack lies in its centralization of JavaScript as the main programming language. However, the problem of connecting these tools together can lay the foundation for scaling and architecture issues, which can dramatically affect your development process.

In this book, I will try to present the best practices and known issues of building a MEAN application, but before you begin with actual MEAN development, you will first need to set up your environment. This chapter will cover a bit of a programming overview but mostly present the proper ways of installing the basic perquisites of a MEAN application. By the end of this chapter, you'll learn how to install and configure MongoDB and Node.js on all the common operating systems and how to use Node's package manager. In this chapter, we're going to cover the following topics:

- Introduction to the MEAN stack architecture
- Installing and running MongoDB on Windows, Linux, and Mac OS X
- Installing and running Node.js on Windows, Linux, and Mac OS X
- Introduction to **Node.js Package Manager** (**NPM**) and how to use it to install Node modules

Three-tier web application development

Most web applications are built in a three-tier architecture that consists of three important layers: data, logic, and presentation. In web applications, the application structure usually breaks down to database, server, and client, while in modern web development, it can also be broken into database, server logic, client logic, and client UI.

A popular paradigm of implementing this model is the MVC architectural pattern. In the MVC paradigm, the logic, data, and visualization are separated into three types of objects, each handling its own tasks. The **View** handles the visual part, taking care of user interaction. The **Controller** responds to system and user events, commanding the Model and View to change appropriately. The **Model** handles data manipulation, responding to requests for information or changing its state according to the Controller's instructions. A simple visual representation of MVC is shown in the following diagram:

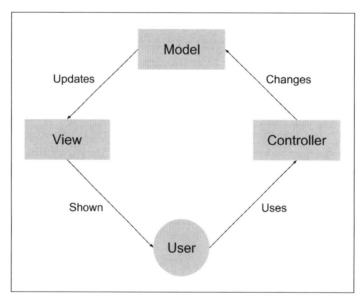

Common MVC architecture communication

In the 25 years of web development, many technology stacks became popular building three-tier web applications; among those now ubiquitous stacks, you can find the LAMP stack, the .NET stack, and a rich variety of other frameworks and tools. The main problem with these stacks is that each tier demands a knowledge base that usually exceeds the abilities of a single developer, making teams bigger than they should be, less productive, and exposed to unexpected risks.

The evolution of JavaScript

JavaScript is an interpreted computer programming language that was built for the Web. First implemented by the Netscape Navigator web browser, it became the programming language that web browsers use to execute client-side logic. In the mid 2000s, the shift from websites to web applications, along with the release of faster browsers, gradually created a community of JavaScript developers writing more complex applications. These developers started creating libraries and tools that shortened development cycles, giving birth to a new generation of even more advanced web applications, which in turn created a continuous demand for better browsers. This cycle went on for a few years, where the vendors kept improving their browsers and JavaScript developers kept pushing the boundaries. The real revolution began in 2008, when Google released its Chrome browser, along with its fast JIT-compiling V8 JavaScript engine. Google's V8 engine made JavaScript run so much faster that it completely transformed web application development. More importantly, the release of the engine's source code allowed developers to start reimagining JavaScript outside of the browser. One of the first products of this revolution was Node.js.

After looking into other options for a while, programmer Ryan Dahl found that V8 engine fit his non-blocking I/O experiment called Node.js. The idea was simple: help developers build non-blocking units of code to allow better use of system resources and create more responsive applications. The result was a minimal yet powerful platform, which utilized JavaScript's non-blocking nature outside of the browser. Node's elegant module system enabled developers to freely extend the platform using third-party modules to achieve almost any functionality. The reaction by the online community was a creation of various tools from modern web frameworks to robotics server platforms. However, server-side JavaScript was only the beginning.

When Dwight Merriman and Eliot Horowitz set out to build their scalable hosting solution back in 2007, they already had a lot of experience with building web applications. However, the platform they built did not succeed as planned, so in 2009 they decided to take it apart and open source its components, including a V8-based database called MongoDB. Derived from the word humongous, MongoDB was a scalable NoSQL database that used a JSON-like data model with dynamic schemas. MongoDB gained a lot of traction right away by giving developers the flexibility they needed when dealing with complex data, while providing RDBMS features such as advanced queries and easy scaling—features that eventually made MongoDB one of the leading NoSQL solutions. JavaScript broke another boundary. But the JavaScript revolutionaries haven't forgotten where it all began; in fact, the popularization of modern browsers created a new wave of JavaScript frontend frameworks.

Back in 2009, while building their JSON as a platform service, developers Miško Hevery and Adam Abrons noticed that the common JavaScript libraries weren't enough. The nature of their rich web application raised the need for a more structured framework that would reduce grunt work and maintain an organized code base. Abandoning the original idea, they decided to focus on the development of their frontend framework and open sourced the project, naming it AngularJS. The idea was to bridge the gap between JavaScript and HTML and help popularize single page application development. The result was a rich web framework, which presented frontend web developers with concepts such as two-way data binding, cross-component dependency injection, and MVC-based components. AngularJS along with other MVC frameworks revolutionized web development by transforming the once unmaintainable frontend code base into a structured code base that can support more advanced development paradigms such as TDD.

The rise of open source collaboration tools, along with the devoted involvement of these talented engineers, created one of the richest communities in the world. More importantly, these major advancements allowed the development of three-tier web applications to be unified under JavaScript as the programming language across all three layers — an idea that is commonly referred to as the full-stack JavaScript. The MEAN stack is just a single example of this idea.

Introducing MEAN

MEAN is an abbreviation for MongoDB, Express, AngularJS, and Node.js. The concept behind it is to use only JavaScript - driven solutions to cover the different parts of your application. The advantages are great and are as follows:

- A single language is used throughout the application
- All the parts of the application can support and often enforce the use of the MVC architecture
- Serialization and deserialization of data structures is no longer needed because data marshaling is done using JSON objects

However, there are still a few important questions that remain unanswered:

- How do you connect all the components together?
- Node.js has a huge ecosystem of modules, so which modules should you use?
- JavaScript is paradigm agnostic, so how can you maintain the MVC application structure?
- JSON is a schema-less data structure, so how and when should you model your data?

- How do you handle user authentication?
- How should you use the Node.js non-blocking architecture to support real-time interactions?
- How can you test your MEAN application code base?
- What kind of JavaScript development tools can you use to expedite your MEAN application development process?

In this book, I'll try to answer these questions and many more, but before we can go any further, you will first need to install the basic prerequisites.

Installing MongoDB

For MongoDB's stable versions, the official MongoDB website supplies linked binaries that provide the easiest way to install MongoDB on Linux, Mac OS X, and Windows. Notice that you need to download the right architecture version for your operating system. If you use Windows or Linux, make sure to download either the 32-bit or 64-bit version according to your system architecture. Mac users are safe to download the 64-bit version.

 The MongoDB versioning scheme works in such a way that only even version numbers mark stable releases, and so versions 2.2.x and 2.4.x are stable, while 2.1.x and 2.3.x are unstable releases and should not be used in production. The latest stable version of MongoDB is 2.6.x.

When you visit the download page at http://mongodb.org/downloads, you'll be offered a download of an archive containing the binaries you need to install MongoDB. After downloading and extracting the archive file, you will need to locate the mongod binary, which is usually located in the bin folder. The mongod process runs the main MongoDB server process, which can be used as a standalone server or a single node of a MongoDB replica set. In our case, we will use MongoDB as a standalone server. The mongod process requires a folder to store the database files in (the default folder is /data/db) and a port to listen to (the default port is 27017). In the following subsections, we'll go over the setup steps for each operating system; we'll begin with the common Windows installation process.

 It is recommended that you learn more about MongoDB by visiting the official documentation at https://mongodb.org.

Installing MongoDB on Windows

Once you have downloaded the right version, unpack the archive file, and move the folder to `C:\mongodb`. MongoDB uses a default folder to store its files. On Windows, the default location is `C:\data\db`, so in the command prompt, go to `C:\` and issue the following command:

```
> md data\db
```

 You can tell the `mongod` service to use an alternative path for the data files using the `--dbpath` command-line flag.

Once you've moved the MongoDB files to the right folder and finished creating the data folders, you'll get two options while running the main MongoDB service.

Running MongoDB manually

To run MongoDB manually, you will need to run the `mongod` binary. So, open the command prompt and issue the following command:

```
> C:\mongodb\bin\mongod.exe
```

The preceding command will run the main MongoDB service that starts listening to the default `27017` port. If everything goes well, you should see a console output similar to the following screenshot.

```
C:\Windows\system32\cmd.exe - C:\mongodb\bin\mongod.exe

c:\>c:\mongodb\bin\mongod.exe
C:\mongodb\bin\mongod.exe --help for help and startup options
2014-07-05T12:40:29.140+0300
2014-07-05T12:40:29.140+0300 warning: 32-bit servers don't have journaling enabled by defa
ult. Please use --journal if you want durability.
2014-07-05T12:40:29.140+0300
2014-07-05T12:40:29.140+0300 [initandlisten] MongoDB starting : pid=976 port=27017 dbpath=
\data\db\ 32-bit host=IE9Win7
2014-07-05T12:40:29.140+0300 [initandlisten]
2014-07-05T12:40:29.140+0300 [initandlisten] ** NOTE: This is a 32 bit MongoDB binary.
2014-07-05T12:40:29.140+0300 [initandlisten] **       32 bit builds are limited to less th
an 2GB of data (or less with --journal).
2014-07-05T12:40:29.140+0300 [initandlisten] **       Note that journaling defaults to off
 for 32 bit and is currently off.
2014-07-05T12:40:29.140+0300 [initandlisten] **       See http://dochub.mongodb.org/core/3
2bit
2014-07-05T12:40:29.140+0300 [initandlisten]
2014-07-05T12:40:29.140+0300 [initandlisten] targetMinOS: Windows XP SP3
2014-07-05T12:40:29.140+0300 [initandlisten] db version v2.6.3
2014-07-05T12:40:29.140+0300 [initandlisten] git version: 255f67a66f9603c59380b2a389e38691
0bbb52cb
2014-07-05T12:40:29.140+0300 [initandlisten] build info: windows sys.getwindowsversion(maj
or=6, minor=1, build=7601, platform=2, service_pack='Service Pack 1') BOOST_LIB_VERSION=1_
49
2014-07-05T12:40:29.140+0300 [initandlisten] allocator: system
2014-07-05T12:40:29.140+0300 [initandlisten] options: {}
2014-07-05T12:40:29.156+0300 [initandlisten] waiting for connections on port 27017
```

Running the MongoDB server on Windows

Depending on the Windows security level, a security alert dialog, which notifies you about the blocking of some service features, will be issued. If this occurs, select a private network and click on **Allow Access**.

 You should be aware that the MongoDB service is self-contained, so you can alternatively run it from any folder of your choice.

Running MongoDB as a Windows Service

The more popular approach is running MongoDB automatically after every reboot cycle. Before you begin setting up MongoDB as a Windows Service, it's considered good practice to specify a path for the MongoDB log and configuration files. Start by creating a folder for these files by running the following command in your command prompt:

```
> md C:\mongodb\log
```

Then, you'll be able to create a configuration file using the `--logpath` command-line flag, so in the command prompt, issue the following command:

```
> echo logpath=C:\mongodb\log\mongo.log > C:\mongodb\mongod.cfg
```

When you have your configuration file in place, open a new command prompt window with administrative privileges by right-clicking on the command prompt icon and clicking on **Run as administrator**. In the new command prompt window, install the MongoDB service by running the following command:

```
> sc.exe create MongoDB binPath= "\"C:\mongodb\bin\mongod.exe\" --service
--config=\"C:\mongodb\mongod.cfg\"" DisplayName= "MongoDB 2.6" start=
"auto"
```

If the service was successfully created, you will get the following log message:

```
[SC] CreateService SUCCESS
```

Notice that the install process will only succeed if your configuration file is set correctly and contains the `logpath` option. After installing your MongoDB service, you can run it by executing the following command in the administrative command prompt window:

```
> net start MongoDB
```

Downloading the example code

You can download the example code files for all the Packt books you have purchased from your account at http://www.packtpub.com. If you purchased this book elsewhere, you can visit http://www.packtpub.com/support and register to have the files e-mailed to you.

Be aware that the MongoDB configuration file can be modified to accommodate your needs. You can learn more about it by visiting http://docs.mongodb.org/manual/reference/configuration-options/.

Installing MongoDB on Mac OS X and Linux

In this section, you'll learn the different ways of installing MongoDB on Unix-based operating systems. Let's begin with the simplest way to install MongoDB, which involves downloading MongoDB's precompiled binaries.

Installing MongoDB from binaries

You can download the right version of MongoDB using the download page at http://www.mongodb.org/downloads. Alternatively, you can do this via CURL by executing the following command:

```
$ curl -O http://downloads.mongodb.org/osx/mongodb-osx-x86_64-2.6.4.tgz
```

Notice that we have downloaded the Mac OS X 64-bit version, so make sure you alter the command to fit the version suitable for your machine. After the downloading process is over, unpack the file by issuing the following command in your command-line tool:

```
$ tar -zxvf mongodb-osx-x86_64-2.6.4.tgz
```

Now, change the name of the extracted folder to a simpler folder name by running the following command:

```
$ mv mongodb-osx-x86_64-2.6.4 mongodb
```

MongoDB uses a default folder to store its files. On Linux and Mac OS X, the default location is /data/db, so in your command-line tool run the following command:

```
$ mkdir -p /data/db
```

You may experience some troubles creating this folder. This is usually a permission issue, so use sudo or super user when running the preceding command.

The preceding command will create the data and db folders because the -p flag creates parent folders as well. Notice that the default folder is located outside of your home folder, so do make sure you set the folder permission by running the following command:

```
$ chown -R $USER /data/db
```

Now that you have everything prepared, use your command-line tool and go to the bin folder to run the mongod service as follows:

```
$ cd mongodb/bin
```

```
$ mongod
```

This will run the main MongoDB service, which will start listening to the default 27017 port. If everything goes well, you should see a console output similar to the following screenshot:

```
● ● ●                         bin — mongod — 80×24
Amoss-MacBook-Pro:bin Amos$ mongod
mongod --help for help and startup options
2014-07-07T23:31:48.598+0300 [initandlisten] MongoDB starting : pid=46137 port=2
7017 dbpath=/data/db 64-bit host=Amoss-MacBook-Pro.local
2014-07-07T23:31:48.598+0300 [initandlisten]
2014-07-07T23:31:48.598+0300 [initandlisten] ** WARNING: soft rlimits too low. N
umber of files is 256, should be at least 1000
2014-07-07T23:31:48.598+0300 [initandlisten] db version v2.6.3
2014-07-07T23:31:48.598+0300 [initandlisten] git version: nogitversion
2014-07-07T23:31:48.598+0300 [initandlisten] build info: Darwin minimavericks.lo
cal 13.2.0 Darwin Kernel Version 13.2.0: Thu Apr 17 23:03:13 PDT 2014; root:xnu-
2422.100.13~1/RELEASE_X86_64 x86_64 BOOST_LIB_VERSION=1_49
2014-07-07T23:31:48.598+0300 [initandlisten] allocator: tcmalloc
2014-07-07T23:31:48.598+0300 [initandlisten] options: {}
2014-07-07T23:31:48.599+0300 [initandlisten] journal dir=/data/db/journal
2014-07-07T23:31:48.599+0300 [initandlisten] recover : no journal files present,
 no recovery needed
2014-07-07T23:31:48.632+0300 [initandlisten] waiting for connections on port 270
17
```

Running the MongoDB server on Mac OS X

Install MongoDB using a package manager

Sometimes the easiest way to install MongoDB is by using a package manager. The downside is that some package managers are falling behind in supporting the latest version. Luckily, the team behind MongoDB also maintains the official packages for RedHat, Debian, and Ubuntu, as well as a Hombrew package for Mac OS X. Note that you'll have to configure your package manager repository to include the MongoDB servers to download the official packages.

To install MongoDB on Red Hat Enterprise, CentOS, or Fedora using Yum, follow the instructions at `http://docs.mongodb.org/manual/tutorial/install-mongodb-on-red-hat-centos-or-fedora-linux/`.

To install MongoDB on Ubuntu using APT, follow the instructions at `http://docs.mongodb.org/manual/tutorial/install-mongodb-on-ubuntu/`.

To install MongoDB on Debian using APT, follow the instructions at `http://docs.mongodb.org/manual/tutorial/install-mongodb-on-debian/`.

To install MongoDB on Mac OS X using Homebrew, follow the instructions at `http://docs.mongodb.org/manual/tutorial/install-mongodb-on-os-x/`.

Using the MongoDB shell

MongoDB archive file includes the MongoDB shell, which allows to you to interact with your server instance using the command line. To start the shell, navigate to the MongoDB `bin` folder and run the `mongo` service as follows:

```
$ cd mongodb/bin
```

```
$ mongo
```

If you successfully installed MongoDB, the shell will automatically connect to your local instance, using the `test` database. You should see a console output similar to the following screenshot:

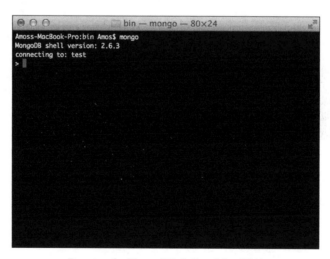

Running the MongoDB shell on Mac OS X

To test your database, run the following command:

```
> db.articles.insert({title: "Hello World"})
```

The preceding command will create a new article collection and insert a JSON object containing a title property. To retrieve the `article` object, execute the following command:

```
> db.articles.find()
```

The console will output the following message:

```
{ _id : ObjectId("52d02240e4b01d67d71ad577"), title: "Hello World " }
```

Congratulations! This means your MongoDB instance is working properly and you have successfully managed to interact with it using the MongoDB shell. In the upcoming chapters, you'll learn more about MongoDB and how to use the MongoDB shell.

Installing Node.js

For the stable versions, the official Node.js website supplies linked binaries that provide the easiest way to install Node.js on Linux, Mac OS X, and Windows. Note that you need to download the right architecture version for your operating system. If you use Windows or Linux, make sure to download either the 32-bit or 64-bit version according to your system architecture. Mac users are safe to download the 64-bit version.

> The Node.js version scheme works in a way similar to that of MongoDB, where even version numbers mark stable releases, and so versions 0.8.x and 0.10.x are stable, while 0.9.x and 0.11.x are unstable releases and should not be used in production. The latest stable version of Node.js is 0.10.x.

Installing Node.js on Windows

Installing Node.js on a Windows machine is a simple task that can be easily accomplished using the standalone installer. To begin with, navigate to the `http://nodejs.org/download/` page and download the right `.msi` file. Notice there are 32-bit and 64-bit versions, so make sure you download the right one for your system.

After downloading the installer, run it. If you get any security dialog boxes, just click on the **Run** button and the installation wizard should start. You will be prompted with an installation screen similar to the following screenshot:

Node.js Windows installation wizard

Once you click on the **Next** button, the installation should begin. A few moments later, you'll see a confirmation screen similar to the following screenshot, telling you Node.js was successfully installed:

Node.js Windows installation confirmation

Installing Node.js on Mac OS X

Installing Node.js on Mac OS X is a simple task that can be easily accomplished using the standalone installer. Start by navigating to the `http://nodejs.org/download/` page and download the `.pkg` file.

After downloading the installer, run it and you will be prompted with an installation screen similar to the following screenshot:

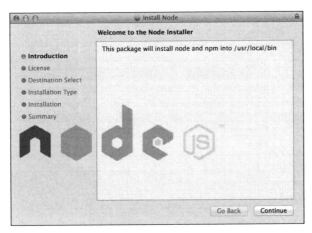

Node.js Mac OS X Installation Wizard

Click on **Continue** and the installation process should begin. The installer will ask you to confirm the license agreement and then offer you to select the folder destination. Choose the option most suitable for you before clicking on the **Continue** button again. The installer will then ask you to confirm the installation information and ask you for your user password. A few moments later, you'll see a confirmation screen similar to the following screenshot, telling you that Node.js was successfully installed:

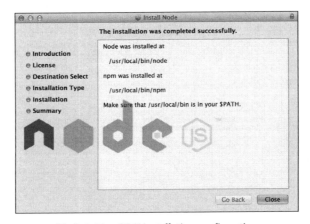

Node.js Mac OS X installation confirmation

Installing Node.js on Linux

To install Node.js on a Linux machine, you'll have to use the `tarball` file from the official website. The best way of doing so is to download the latest version and then build and install the source code using the `make` command. Start by navigating to the `http://nodejs.org/download/` page, and download the suitable `.tar.gz` file. Then, expand the file and install Node.js by issuing the following commands:

```
$ tar -zxf node-v0.10.31.tar.gz
$ cd node-v0.10.31
$ ./configure && make && sudo make install
```

If everything goes well, this will install Node.js on your machine. Note that these commands are for the Node.js 0.10.31 version, so remember to replace the version number to the version you downloaded. If you encounter any problems, the team behind Node.js has created a set of alternative installation options for you, documented at `https://github.com/joyent/node/wiki/installation`.

 It is recommended that you learn more about Node.js by visiting the official documentation at `https://nodejs.org`.

Running Node.js

After you successfully installed Node.js, you will now be able to start experimenting with it using the provided **command-line interface (CLI)**. Go to your command-line tool and execute the following command:

```
$ node
```

This will start the Node.js CLI, which will wait for a JavaScript input. To test the installation, run the following command:

```
> console.log('Node is up and running!');
Node is up and running!
undefined
```

This is nice, but you should also try to execute a JavaScript file. Start by creating a file named `application.js` that contains the following code:

```
console.log('Node is up and running!');
```

To run it, you'll have to pass the file name as the first argument to Node CLI by issuing the following command:

```
$ node application.js
Node is up and running!
```

Congratulations! You have just created your first Node.js application. To stop the CLI, press *CTRL + D* or *CTRL + C*.

Introducing NPM

Node.js is a platform, which means its features and APIs are kept to a minimum. To achieve more complex functionality, it uses a module system that allows you to extend the platform. The best way to install, update, and remove Node.js modules is using the NPM. NPM has the following main features:

- A registry of packages to browse, download, and install third-party modules
- A CLI tool to manage local and global packages

Conveniently, NPM is installed during the Node.js installation process, so let's quickly jump in and learn how to use it.

Using NPM

To understand how NPM works, we're going to install the Express web framework module, which you'll use in the upcoming chapters. NPM is a robust package manager, which keeps a centralized registry for public modules. To browse the available public packages, visit the official website at `https://npmjs.org/`.

Most of the packages in the registry are open source and contributed by the Node.js community developers. When developing an open source module, the package author can decide to publish it to the central registry, allowing other developers to download and use it in their projects. In the package configuration file, the author will choose a name that will later be used as a unique identifier to download that package.

[It is recommended you learn more about Node.js by visiting the official documentation at `https://npmjs.org`.]

Managing dependencies using the package.json file

Installing a single package is nice, but pretty soon, your application will need to use several packages, and so you'll need a better way to manage these package dependencies. For this purpose, NPM allows you to use a configuration file named `package.json` in the root folder of your application. In your `package.json` file, you'll be able to define various metadata properties of your application, including properties such as the name, version, and author of your application. This is also where you define your application dependencies.

The `package.json` file is basically a JSON file that contains the different attributes you'll need to describe your application properties.

An application using the latest Express and Grunt packages will have a `package.json` file as follows:

```
{
  "name" : "MEAN",
  "version" : "0.0.1",
  "dependencies" : {
    "express" : "latest",
    "grunt" : "latest"
  }
}
```

 Your application name and version properties are required, so removing these properties will prevent NPM from working properly.

Creating a package.json file

While you can manually create a `package.json` file, an easier approach would be to use the `npm init` command. To do so, use your command-line tool and issue the following command:

```
$ npm init
```

NPM will ask you a few questions about your application and will automatically create a new `package.json` file for you. A sample process should look similar to the following screenshot:

```
● ○ ○                    ⬜ mean — bash — 80×43                         ↗
Amoss-MacBook-Pro:mean Amos$ npm init
This utility will walk you through creating a package.json file.
It only covers the most common items, and tries to guess sane defaults.

See `npm help json` for definitive documentation on these fields
and exactly what they do.

Use `npm install <pkg> --save` afterwards to install a package and
save it as a dependency in the package.json file.

Press ^C at any time to quit.
name: (mean) MEAN
version: (0.0.0) 0.0.1
description: My First MEAN Application
entry point: (index.js) server.js
test command:
git repository:
keywords: MongoDB, Express, AngularJS, Node.js
author: Amos Haviv
license: (ISC) MIT
About to write to /Users/Amos/Projects/SportsTopNews/mean/package.json:

{
  "name": "MEAN",
  "version": "0.0.1",
  "description": "My First MEAN Application",
  "main": "server.js",
  "scripts": {
    "test": "echo \"Error: no test specified\" && exit 1"
  },
  "keywords": [
    "MongoDB",
    "Express",
    "AngularJS",
    "Node.js"
  ],
  "author": "Amos Haviv",
  "license": "MIT"
}


Is this ok? (yes) yes
Amoss-MacBook-Pro:mean Amos$ █
```

Using NPM init on Mac OS X

After creating your `package.json` file, you'll need to modify it and add a dependencies property. Your final `package.json` file should look like the following code snippet:

```
{
    "name": "MEAN",
    "version": "0.0.1",
    "description": "My First MEAN Application",
    "main": "server.js",
    "scripts": {
      "test": "echo \"Error: no test specified\" && exit 1"
    },
    "keywords": [
      "MongoDB",
      "Express",
      "AngularJS",
      "Node.js"
```

```
  ],
  "author": "Amos Haviv",
  "license": "MIT",
  "dependencies": {
    "express": "latest",
    "grunt": "latest"
  }
}
```

 In the preceding code example, we used the `latest` keyword to tell NPM to install the latest versions of these packages. However, it is highly recommended that you use specific version numbers or range to prevent your application dependencies from changing during development cycles. This is because new package versions might not be backward compatible with older versions, which will cause major issues in your application.

Installing the package.json dependencies

After creating your `package.json` file, you'll be able to install your application dependencies by navigating to your application's root folder and using the `npm install` command as follows:

```
$ npm install
```

NPM will automatically detect your `package.json` file and will install all your application dependencies, placing them under a local `node_modules` folder. An alternative and sometimes better approach to install your dependencies is to use the following `npm update` command:

```
$ npm update
```

This will install any missing packages and will update all of your existing dependencies to their specified version.

Updating the package.json file

Another robust feature of the `npm install` command is the ability to install a new package and save the package information as a dependency in your `package.json` file. This can be accomplished using the `--save` optional flag when installing a specific package. For example, to install the latest version of Express and save it as a dependency, you can issue the following command:

```
$ npm install express --save
```

NPM will install the latest version of Express and will add the express package as a dependency to your package.json file. For clarity reasons, in the upcoming chapters, we'll prefer to manually edit the package.json file; however, this useful feature can come in pretty handy in your daily development cycles.

 It is recommended that you learn more about NPM's vast configuration options by visiting the official documentation at https://npmjs.org/doc/json.html.

Summary

In this chapter, you learned how to install MongoDB and how to connect to your local database instance using the MongoDB shell. You also learned how to install Node.js and use the Node.js CLI. You learned about NPM and discovered how to use it to download and install Node.js packages. You also learned how to easily manage your application dependencies using the package.json file. In the next chapter, we'll discuss some Node.js basics and you'll build your first Node.js web application.

As simple as this example is, it illustrates well how JavaScript uses events to execute a set of commands. Since the browser is single-threaded, using synchronous programming in this example would freeze everything else in the page, which would make every web page extremely unresponsive and impair the web experience in general. Thankfully, this is not how it works. The browser manages a single thread to run the entire JavaScript code using an inner loop, commonly referred to as the event loop. The event loop is a single-threaded loop that the browser runs infinitely. Every time an event is emitted, the browser adds it to an event queue. The loop will then grab the next event from the queue in order to execute the event handlers registered to that event. After all of the event handlers are executed, the loop grabs the next event, executes its handlers, grabs the next event, and so on. You can see a visual representation of this process in the following diagram:

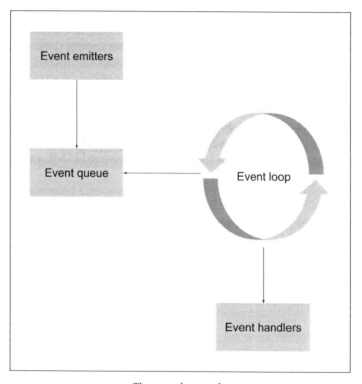

The event loop cycle

While the browser usually deals with user-generated events (such as button clicks), Node.js has to deal with various types of events that are generated from different sources.

Node.js event-driven programming

When developing web server logic, you will probably notice a lot of your system resources are wasted on blocking code. For instance, let's observe the following PHP database interactions:

```
$output = mysql_query('SELECT * FROM Users');
echo($output);
```

Our server will try querying the database that will then perform the `select` statement and return the result to the PHP code, which will eventually output the data as a response. The preceding code blocks any other operation until it gets the result from the database. This means the process, or more commonly, the thread, will stay idle, consuming system resources while it waits for other processes.

To solve this issue, many web platforms have implemented a thread pool system that usually issues a single thread per connection. This kind of multithreading may seem intuitive at first, but has some significant disadvantages, as follows:

* Managing threads becomes a complex task
* System resources are wasted on idle threads
* Scaling these kinds of applications cannot be done easily

This is tolerable while developing one-sided web applications, where the browser makes a quick request that ends with a server response. But, what happens when you want to build real-time applications that keep a long-living connection between the browser and the server? To understand the real-life consequences of these design choices, take a look at the following graphs. They present a famous performance comparison between Apache, which is a blocking web server, and NGINX, which uses a non-blocking event loop. The following screenshot shows concurrent request handling in Apache versus Nginx (`http://blog.webfaction.com/2008/12/a-little-holiday-present-10000-reqssec-with-nginx-2/`):

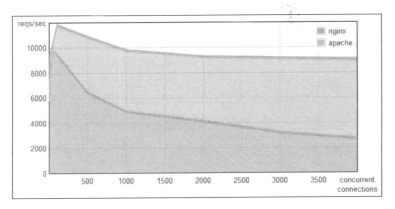

In the preceding screenshot, you can see how Apache's request handling ability is degrading much faster than Nginx's. But, an even clearer impact can be seen in the following screenshot, where you can witness how Nginx's event loop architecture affects memory consumption:

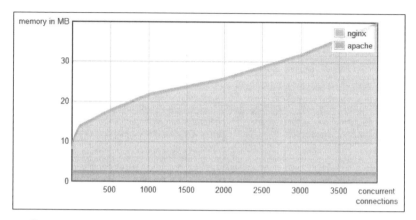

Concurrent connections impact on memory allocation in Apache versus Nginx
(http://blog.webfaction.com/2008/12/a-little-holiday-present-10000-reqssec-with-nginx-2/)

As you can see from the results, using event-driven architecture will help you dramatically reduce the load on your server while leveraging JavaScript's asynchronous behavior in building your web application. This approach is made possible thanks to a simple design pattern, which is called *closure* by JavaScript developers.

JavaScript closures

Closures are functions that refer to variables from their parent environment. Using the closure pattern enables variables from the parent() function to remain bound to the closure. Let's take a look at the following example:

```
function parent() {
    var message = "Hello World";

    function child() {
        alert (message);
    }

    child();
}

parent();
```

In the preceding example, you can see how the child() function has access to a variable defined in the parent() function. But this is a simple example, so let's see a more interesting one:

```
function parent() {
   var message = 'Hello World';

  function child() {
    alert (message);
    }

   return child;
}

var childFN = parent()
childFN();
```

This time, the parent() function returned the child() function, and the child() function is called after the parent() function has already been executed. This is counterintuitive to some developers because usually the parent() function's local variables should only exist while the function is being executed. This is what closures are all about! A closure is not only the function, but also the environment in which the function was created. In this case, the childFN() is a closure object that consists of the child() function and the environment variables that existed when the closure was created, including the message variable.

Closures are very important in asynchronous programming because JavaScript functions are first-class objects that can be passed as arguments to other functions. This means that you can create a callback function and pass it as an argument to an event handler. When the event will be emitted, the function will be invoked, and it will be able to manipulate any variable that existed when the callback function was created even if its parent function was already executed. This means that using the closure pattern will help you utilize event-driven programming without the need to pass the scope state to the event handler.

Node modules

JavaScript has turned out to be a powerful language with some unique features that enable efficient yet maintainable programming. Its closure pattern and event-driven behavior have proven to be very helpful in real-life scenarios, but like all programming languages, it isn't perfect, and one of its major design flaws is the sharing of a single global namespace.

To understand the problem, we need to go back to JavaScript's browser origins. In the browser, when you load a script into your web page, the engine will inject its code into an address space that is shared by all the other scripts. This means that when you assign a variable in one script, you can accidently overwrite another variable already defined in a previous script. While this could work with a small code base, it can easily cause conflicts in larger applications, as errors will be difficult to trace. It could have been a major threat for Node.js evolution as a platform, but luckily a solution was found in the CommonJS modules standard.

CommonJS modules

CommonJS is a project started in 2009 to standardize the way of working with JavaScript outside the browser. The project has evolved since then to support a variety of JavaScript issues, including the global namespace issue, which was solved through a simple specification of how to write and include isolated JavaScript modules.

The CommonJS standards specify the following three key components when working with modules:

- `require()`: This method is used to load the module into your code.
- `exports`: This object is contained in each module and allows you to expose pieces of your code when the module is loaded.
- `module`: This object was originally used to provide metadata information about the module. It also contains the pointer of an `exports` object as a property. However, the popular implementation of the `exports` object as a standalone object literally changed the use case of the `module` object.

In Node's CommonJS module implementation, each module is written in a single JavaScript file and has an isolated scope that holds its own variables. The author of the module can expose any functionality through the `exports` object. To understand it better, let's say we created a module file named `hello.js` that contains the following code snippet:

```
var message = 'Hello';

exports.sayHello = function(){
    console.log(message);
}
```

Also, let's say we created an application file named `server.js`, which contains the following lines of code:

```
var hello = require('./hello');
hello.sayHello();
```

In the preceding example, you have the `hello` module, which contains a variable named `message`. The `message` variable is self-contained in the `hello` module, which only exposes the `sayHello()` method by defining it as a property of the `exports` object. Then, the application file loads the `hello` module using the `require()` method, which will allow it to call the `sayHello()` method of the `hello` module.

A different approach to creating modules is exposing a single function using the `module.exports` pointer. To understand this better, let's revise the preceding example. A modified `hello.js` file should look as follows:

```
module.exports = function() {
    var message = 'Hello';

    console.log(message);
}
```

Then, the module is loaded in the `server.js` file as follows:

```
var hello = require('./hello');
hello();
```

In the preceding example, the application file uses the `hello` module directly as a function instead of using the `sayHello()` method as a property of the `hello` module.

The CommonJS module standard allows the endless extension of the Node.js platform while preventing the pollution of Node's core; without it, the Node.js platform would become a mess of conflicts. However, not all modules are the same, and while developing a Node application, you will encounter several types of modules.

 You can omit the .js extension when requiring modules. Node will automatically look for a folder with that name, and if it doesn't find one, it will look for an applicable .js file.

Node.js core modules

Core modules are modules that were compiled into the Node binary. They come prebundled with Node and are documented in great detail in its documentation. The core modules provide most of the basic functionalities of Node, including filesystem access, HTTP and HTTPS interfaces, and much more. To load a core module, you just need to use the require method in your JavaScript file. An example code, using the fs core module to read the content of the environment hosts file, would look like the following code snippet:

```
fs = require('fs');

fs.readFile('/etc/hosts', 'utf8', function (err, data) {
  if (err) {
    return console.log(err);
  }

  console.log(data);
});
```

When you require the fs module, Node will find it in the core modules folder. You'll then be able to use the fs.readFile() method to read the file's content and print it in the command-line output.

 To learn more about Node's core modules, it is recommended that you visit the official documentation at http://nodejs.org/api/.

Node.js third-party modules

In the previous chapter, you learned how to use NPM to install third-party modules. As you probably remember, NPM installs these modules in a folder named node_ modules under the root folder of your application. To use third-party modules, you can just require them as you would normally require a core module. Node will first look for the module in the core modules folder and then try to load the module from the module folder inside the node_modules folder. For instance, to use the express module, your code should look like the following code snippet:

```
var express = require('express');
var app = express();
```

Node will then look for the express module in the node_modules folder and load it into your application file, where you'll be able to use it as a method to generate the express application object.

Node.js file modules

In previous examples, you saw how Node loads modules directly from files. These examples describe a scenario where the files reside in the same folder. However, you can also place your modules inside a folder and load them by providing the folder path. Let's say you moved your hello module to a modules folder. The application file would have to change, so Node would look for the module in the new relative path:

```
var hello = require('./modules/hello');
```

Note that the path can also be an absolute path, as follows:

```
var hello = require('/home/projects/first-example/modules/hello');
```

Node will then look for the hello module in that path.

Node.js folder modules

Although this is not common with developers that aren't writing third-party Node modules, Node also supports the loading of folder modules. Requiring folder modules is done in the same way as file modules, as follows:

```
var hello = require('./modules/hello');
```

Now, if a folder named `hello` exists, Node will go through that folder looking for a `package.json` file. If Node finds a `package.json` file, it will try parsing it, looking for the `main` property, with a `package.json` file that looks like the following code snippet:

```
{
    "name" : "hello",
    "version" : "1.0.0",
    "main" : "./hello-module.js"
}
```

Node will try to load the `./hello/hello-module.js` file. If the `package.json` file doesn't exist or the `main` property isn't defined, Node will automatically try to load the `./hello/index.js` file.

Node.js modules have been found to be a great solution to write complex JavaScript applications. They have helped developers organize their code better, while NPM and its third-party modules registry helped them to find and install one of the many third-party modules created by the community. Ryan Dahl's dream of building a better web framework ended up as a platform that supports a huge variety of solutions. But the dream was not abandoned; it was just implemented as a third-party module named `express`.

Developing Node.js web applications

Node.js is a platform that supports various types of applications, but the most popular kind is the development of web applications. Node's style of coding depends on the community to extend the platform through third-party modules; these modules are then built upon to create new modules, and so on. Companies and single developers around the globe are participating in this process by creating modules that wrap the basic Node APIs and deliver a better starting point for application development.

There are many modules to support web application development but none as popular as the Connect module. The Connect module delivers a set of wrappers around the Node.js low-level APIs to enable the development of rich web application frameworks. To understand what Connect is all about, let's begin with a basic example of a basic Node web server. In your working folder, create a file named `server.js`, which contains the following code snippet:

```
var http = require('http');

http.createServer(function(req, res) {
    res.writeHead(200, {
```

```
      'Content-Type': 'text/plain'
  });
  res.end('Hello World');
}).listen(3000);

  console.log('Server running at http://localhost:3000/');
```

To start your web server, use your command-line tool, and navigate to your working folder. Then, run the node CLI tool and run the `server.js` file as follows:

$ node server

Now open `http://localhost:3000` in your browser, and you'll see the **Hello World** response.

So how does this work? In this example, the `http` module is used to create a small web server listening to the `3000` port. You begin by requiring the `http` module and use the `createServer()` method to return a new `server` object. The `listen()` method is then used to listen to the `3000` port. Notice the `callback` function that is passed as an argument to the `createServer()` method.

The `callback` function gets called whenever there's an HTTP request sent to the web server. The `server` object will then pass the `req` and `res` arguments, which contain the information and functionality needed to send back an HTTP response. The `callback` function will then do the following two steps:

1. First, it will call the `writeHead()` method of the `response` object. This method is used to set the response HTTP headers. In this example, it will set the `Content-Type` header value to `text/plain`. For instance, when responding with HTML, you just need to replace `text/plain` with `html/plain`.

2. Then, it will call the `end()` method of the response object. This method is used to finalize the response. The `end()` method takes a single string argument that it will use as the HTTP response body. Another common way of writing this is to add a `write()` method before the `end()` method and then call the `end()` method, as follows:

   ```
   res.write('Hello World');
   res.end();
   ```

This simple application illustrates the Node coding style where low-level APIs are used to simply achieve certain functionality. While this is a nice example, running a full web application using the low-level APIs will require you to write a lot of supplementary code to support common requirements. Fortunately, a company called Sencha has already created this scaffolding code for you in the form of a Node module called Connect.

Node will run your application, reporting the server status using the `console.log()` method. You can try reaching your application in the browser by visiting `http://localhost:3000`. However, you should get a response similar to what is shown in the following screenshot:

Connect application's empty response

What this response means is that there isn't any middleware registered to handle the `GET HTTP` request. This means two things:

- You've successfully managed to install and use the Connect module
- It's time for you to write your first Connect middleware

Connect middleware

Connect middleware is just JavaScript function with a unique signature.
Each middleware function is defined with the following three arguments:

- `req`: This is an object that holds the HTTP request information
- `res`: This is an object that holds the HTTP response information and allows you to set the response properties
- `next`: This is the next middleware function defined in the ordered set of Connect middleware

When you have a middleware defined, you'll just have to register it with the Connect application using the app.use() method. Let's revise the previous example to include your first middleware. Change your server.js file to look like the following code snippet:

```
var connect = require('connect');
var app = connect();

var helloWorld = function(req, res, next) {
  res.setHeader('Content-Type', 'text/plain');
  res.end('Hello World');
};
app.use(helloWorld);

app.listen(3000);
console.log('Server running at http://localhost:3000/');
```

Then, start your connect server again by issuing the following command in your command-line tool:

```
$ node server
```

Try visiting http://localhost:3000 again. You will now get a response similar to that in the following screenshot:

Connect application's response

Congratulations, you've just created your first Connect middleware!

Let's recap. First, you added a middleware function named `helloWorld()`, which has three arguments: `req`, `res`, and `next`. In your middleware, you used the `res.setHeader()` method to set the response `Content-Type` header and the `res.end()` method to set the response text. Finally, you used the `app.use()` method to register your middleware with the Connect application.

Understanding the order of Connect middleware

One of Connect's greatest features is the ability to register as many middleware functions as you want. Using the `app.use()` method, you'll be able to set a series of middleware functions that will be executed in a row to achieve maximum flexibility when writing your application. Connect will then pass the next middleware function to the currently executing middleware function using the `next` argument. In each middleware function, you can decide whether to call the next middleware function or stop at the current one. Notice that each Connect middleware function will be executed in **first-in-first-out** (**FIFO**) order using the `next` arguments until there are no more middleware functions to execute or the next middleware function is not called.

To understand this better, we will go back to the previous example and add a `logger` function that will log all the requests made to the server in the command line. To do so, go back to the `server.js` file and update it to look like the following code snippet:

```
var connect = require('connect');
var app = connect();

var logger = function(req, res, next) {
  console.log(req.method, req.url);

  next();
};

var helloWorld = function(req, res, next) {
  res.setHeader('Content-Type', 'text/plain');
  res.end('Hello World');
};

app.use(logger);
app.use(helloWorld);
app.listen(3000);

console.log('Server running at http://localhost:3000/');
```

In the preceding example, you added another middleware called `logger()`. The `logger()` middleware uses the `console.log()` method to simply log the request information to the console. Notice how the `logger()` middleware is registered before the `helloWorld()` middleware. This is important as it determines the order in which each middleware is executed. Another thing to notice is the `next()` call in the `logger()` middleware, which is responsible for calling the `helloWorld()` middleware. Removing the `next()` call would stop the execution of middleware function at the `logger()` middleware, which means that the request would hang forever as the response is never ended by calling the `res.end()` method.

To test your changes, start your connect server again by issuing the following command in your command-line tool:

```
$ node server
```

Then, visit `http://localhost:3000` in your browser and notice the console output in your command-line tool.

Mounting Connect middleware

As you may have noticed, the middleware you registered responds to any request regardless of the request path. This does not comply with modern web application development because responding to different paths is an integral part of all web applications. Fortunately, Connect middleware supports a feature called mounting, which enables you to determine which request path is required for the middleware function to get executed. Mounting is done by adding the path argument to the `app.use()` method. To understand this better, let's revisit our previous example. Modify your `server.js` file to look like the following code snippet:

```
var connect = require('connect');
var app = connect();

var logger = function(req, res, next) {
  console.log(req.method, req.url);

  next();
};

var helloWorld = function(req, res, next) {
  res.setHeader('Content-Type', 'text/plain');
  res.end('Hello World');
};
```

One of his greatest projects is the Express web framework. The Express framework is a small set of common web application features, kept to a minimum in order to maintain the Node.js style. It is built on top of Connect and makes use of its middleware architecture. Its features extend Connect to allow a variety of common web applications' use cases, such as the inclusion of modular HTML template engines, extending the response object to support various data format outputs, a routing system, and much more.

So far, we have used a single `server.js` file to create our application. However, when using Express you'll learn more about better project structure, properly configuring your application, and breaking your application logic into different modules. You'll also learn how to use the EJS template engine, managing sessions, and adding a routing scheme. By the end of this section, you'll have a working application skeleton that you'll use for the rest of the book. Let's begin our journey of creating your first Express application.

Installing Express

Up until now, we used npm to directly install external modules for our Node application. You could, of course, use this approach and install Express by typing the following command:

```
$ npm install express
```

But, directly installing modules isn't really scalable. Think about it for a second: you're going to use many Node modules in your application, transfer it between working environments, and probably share it with other developers. So, installing the project modules this way will soon become a dreadful task. Instead, you should start using the `package.json` file that organizes your project metadata and helps you manage your application dependencies. Begin by creating a new working folder and a new `package.json` file inside it, which contains the following code snippet:

```
{
  "name" : "MEAN",
  "version" : "0.0.3",
  "dependencies" : {
    "express" : "~4.8.8"
  }
}
```

In the `package.json` file, note that you included three properties, the `name` and `version` of your application and the `dependencies` property that defines what modules should be installed before your application can run. To install your application dependencies, use your command-line tool, and navigate to your application folder, and then issue the following command:

```
$ npm install
```

NPM will then install the Express module because it is currently the only dependency defined in your `package.json` file.

Creating your first Express application

After creating your `package.json` file and installing your dependencies, you can now create your first Express application by adding your already familiar `server.js` file with the following lines of code:

```
var express = require('express');
var app = express();

app.use('/', function(req, res) {
  res.send('Hello World');
});

app.listen(3000);
console.log('Server running at http://localhost:3000/');

module.exports = app;
```

You should already recognize most of the code. The first two lines require the Express module and create a new Express application object. Then, we use the `app.use()` method to mount a middleware function with a specific path, and the `app.listen()` method to tell the Express application to listen to the port `3000`. Notice how the `module.exports` object is used to return the application object. This will later help us load and test our Express application.

This new code should also be familiar to you because it resembles the code you used in the previous Connect example. This is because Express wraps the Connect module in several ways. The `app.use()` method is used to mount a middleware function, which will respond to any HTTP request made to the root path. Inside the middleware function, the `res.send()` method is then used to send the response back. The `res.send()` method is basically an Express wrapper that sets the `Content-Type` header according to the `response` object type and then sends a response back using the Connect `res.end()` method.

When passing a buffer to the `res.send()` method, the `Content-Type` header will be set to `application/octet-stream`. When passing a string, it will be set to `text/html` and when passing an object or an array, it will be set to `application/json`.

To run your application, simply execute the following command in your command-line tool:

```
$ node server
```

Congratulations! You have just created your first Express application. You can test it by visiting `http://localhost:3000` in your browser.

The application, request, and response objects

Express presents three major objects that you'll frequently use. The application object is the instance of an Express application you created in the first example and is usually used to configure your application. The request object is a wrapper of Node's HTTP request object and is used to extract information about the currently handled HTTP request. The response object is a wrapper of Node's HTTP response object and is used to set the response data and headers.

The application object

The application object contains the following methods to help you configure your application:

- `app.set(name, value)`: This is used to set environment variables that Express will use in its configuration.

- `app.get(name)`: This is used to get environment variables that Express is using in its configuration.

- `app.engine(ext, callback)`: This is used to define a given template engine to render certain file types, for example, you can tell the EJS template engine to use HTML files as templates like this: `app.engine('html', require('ejs').renderFile)`.

- `app.locals`: This is used to send application-level variables to all rendered templates.

- `app.use([path], callback)`: This is used to create an Express middleware to handle HTTP requests sent to the server. Optionally, you'll be able to mount middleware to respond to certain paths.

- `app.VERB(path, [callback...], callback)`: This is used to define one or more middleware functions to respond to HTTP requests made to a certain path in conjunction with the HTTP verb declared. For instance, when you want to respond to requests that are using the GET verb, then you can just assign the middleware using the `app.get()` method. For POST requests you'll use `app.post()`, and so on.

- `app.route(path).VERB([callback...], callback)`: This is used to define one or more middleware functions to respond to HTTP requests made to a certain unified path in conjunction with multiple HTTP verbs. For instance, when you want to respond to requests that are using the GET and POST verbs, you can just assign the appropriate middleware functions using `app.route(path).get(callback).post(callback)`.

- `app.param([name], callback)`: This is used to attach a certain functionality to any request made to a path that includes a certain routing parameter. For instance, you can map logic to any request that includes the `userId` parameter using `app.param('userId', callback)`.

There are many more application methods and properties you can use, but using these common basic methods enables developers to extend Express in whatever way they find reasonable.

The request object

The request object also provides a handful of helping methods that contain the information you need about the current HTTP request. The key properties and methods of the request object are as follows:

- `req.query`: This is an object containing the parsed query-string parameters.

- `req.params`: This is an object containing the parsed routing parameters.

- `req.body`: This is an object used to retrieve the parsed request body. This property is included in the `bodyParser()` middleware.

- `req.param(name)`: This is used to retrieve a value of a request parameter. Note that the parameter can be a query-string parameter, a routing parameter, or a property from a JSON request body.

- `req.path`, `req.host`, and `req.ip`: These are used to retrieve the current request path, host name, and remote IP.

- `req.cookies`: This is used in conjunction with the `cookieParser()` middleware to retrieve the cookies sent by the user-agent.

The request object contains many more methods and properties that we'll discuss later in this book, but these methods are what you'll usually use in a common web application.

The response object

The response object is frequently used when developing an Express application because any request sent to the server will be handled and responded using the response object methods. It has several key methods, which are as follows:

- `res.status(code)`: This is used to set the response HTTP status code.

- `res.set(field, [value])`: This is used to set the response HTTP header.

- `res.cookie(name, value, [options])`: This is used to set a response cookie. The `options` argument is used to pass an object defining common cookie configuration, such as the `maxAge` property.

- `res.redirect([status], url)`: This is used to redirect the request to a given URL. Note that you can add an HTTP status code to the response. When not passing a status code, it will be defaulted to 302 Found.

- `res.send([body|status], [body])`: This is used for non-streaming responses. This method does a lot of background work, such as setting the `Content-Type` and `Content-Length` headers, and responding with the proper cache headers.

- `res.json([status|body], [body])`: This is identical to the `res.send()` method when sending an object or array. Most of the times, it is used as syntactic sugar, but sometimes you may need to use it to force a JSON response to non-objects, such as null or undefined.

- `res.render(view, [locals], callback)`: This is used to render a view and send an HTML response.

The response object also contains many more methods and properties to handle different response scenarios, which you'll learn about later in this book.

External middleware

The Express core is minimal, yet the team behind it provides various predefined middleware to handle common web development features. These types of middleware vary in size and functionality and extend Express to provide a better framework support. The popular Express middleware are as follows:

- `Morgan`: This is an HTTP request logger middleware.
- `body-parser`: This is a body-parsing middleware that is used to parse the request body, and it supports various request types.
- `method-override`: This is a middleware that provides HTTP verb support such as `PUT` or `DELETE` in places where the client doesn't support it.
- `Compression`: This is a compression middleware that is used to compress the response data using `gzip/deflate`.
- `express.static`: This middleware used to serve static files.
- `cookie-parser`: This is a cookie-parsing middleware that populates the `req.cookies` object.
- `Session`: This is a session middleware used to support persistent sessions.

There are many more types of Express middleware that enable you to shorten your development time, and even a larger number of third-party middleware.

 To learn more about the Connect and Express middleware, visit the Connect module's official repository page at `https://github.com/senchalabs/connect#middleware`. If you'd like to browse the third-party middleware collection, visit Connect's wiki page at `https://github.com/senchalabs/connect/wiki`.

Implementing the MVC pattern

The Express framework is pattern agnostic, which means it doesn't support any predefined syntax or structure as do some other web frameworks. Applying the MVC pattern to your Express application means that you can create specific folders where you place your JavaScript files in a certain logical order. All those files are basically CommonJS modules that function as logical units. For instance, models will be CommonJS modules containing a definition of Mongoose models placed in the `models` folder, views will be HTML or other template files placed in the `views` folder, and controllers will be CommonJS modules with functional methods placed in the `controllers` folder. To illustrate this better, it's time to discuss the different types of an application structure.

Application folder structure

We previously discussed better practices while developing a real application, where we recommended the use of the `package.json` file over directly installing your modules. However, this was only the beginning; once you continue developing your application, you'll soon find yourself wondering how you should arrange your project files and break them into logical units of code. JavaScript, in general, and consequently the Express framework, are agnostic about the structure of your application as you can easily place your entire application in a single JavaScript file. This is because no one expected JavaScript to be a full-stack programming language, but it doesn't mean you shouldn't dedicate special attention to organizing your project. Since the MEAN stack can be used to build all sorts of applications that vary in size and complexity, it is also possible to handle the project structure in various ways. The decision is often directly related to the estimated complexity of your application. For instance, simple projects may require a leaner folder structure, which has the advantage of being clearer and easier to manage, while complex projects will often require a more complex structure and a better breakdown of the logic since it will include many features and a bigger team working on the project. To simplify this discussion, it would be reasonable to divide it into two major approaches: a horizontal structure for smaller projects and a vertical structure for feature-rich applications. Let's begin with a simple horizontal structure.

Horizontal folder structure

A horizontal project structure is based on the division of folders and files by their functional role rather than by the feature they implement, which means that all the application files are placed inside a main application folder that contains an MVC folder structure. This also means that there is a single `controllers` folder that contains all of the application controllers, a single `models` folder that contains all of the application models, and so on. An example of the horizontal application structure is as follows:

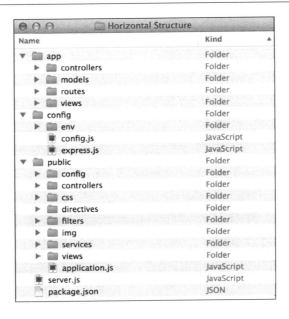

Let's review the folder structure:

- The `app` folder is where you keep your Express application logic and is divided into the following folders that represent a separation of functionality to comply with the MVC pattern:
    - The `controllers` folder is where you keep your Express application controllers
    - The `models` folder is where you keep your Express application models
    - The `routes` folder is where you keep your Express application routing middleware
    - The `views` folder is where you keep your Express application views

- The `config` folder is where you keep your Express application configuration files. In time you'll add more modules to your application and each module will be configured in a dedicated JavaScript file, which is placed inside this folder. Currently, it contains several files and folders, which are as follows:
    - The `env` folder is where you'll keep your Express application environment configuration files
    - The `config.js` file is where you'll configure your Express application
    - The `express.js` file is where you'll initialize your Express application

- The `public` folder is where you keep your static client-side files and is divided into the following folders that represent a separation of functionality to comply with the MVC pattern:

  - The `config` folder is where you keep your AngularJS application configuration files
  - The `controllers` folder is where you keep your AngularJS application controllers
  - The `css` folder is where you keep your CSS files
  - The `directives` folder is where you keep your AngularJS application directives
  - The `filters` folder is where you keep your AngularJS application filters
  - The `img` folder is where you keep your image files
  - The `views` folder is where you keep your AngularJS application views
  - The `application.js` file is where you initialize your AngularJS application

- The `package.json` file is the metadata file that helps you to organize your application dependencies.

- The `server.js` file is the main file of your Node.js application, and it will load the `express.js` file as a module to bootstrap your Express application.

As you can see, the horizontal folder structure is very useful for small projects where the number of features is limited, and so files can be conveniently placed inside folders that represent their general roles. Nevertheless, to handle large projects, where you'll have many files that handle certain features, it might be too simplistic. In that case, each folder could be overloaded with too many files, and you'll get lost in the chaos. A better approach would be to use a vertical folder structure.

Vertical folder structure

A vertical project structure is based on the division of folders and files by the feature they implement, which means each feature has its own autonomous folder that contains an MVC folder structure. An example of the vertical application structure is as follows:

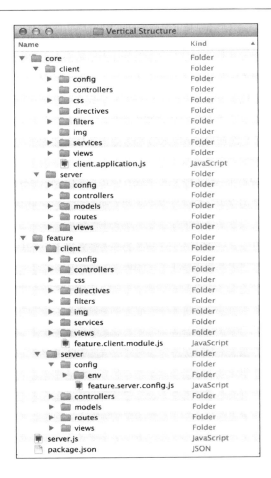

As you can see, each feature has its own application-like folder structure. In this example, we have the core feature folder that contains the main application files and the `feature` folder that include the feature's files. An example feature would be a user management feature that includes the authentication and authorization logic. To understand this better, let's review a single feature's folder structure:

- The `server` folder is where you keep your feature's server logic and is divided into the following folders that represent a separation of functionality to comply with the MVC pattern:
    - The `controllers` folder is where you keep your feature's Express controllers
    - The `models` folder is where you keep your feature's Express models
    - The `routes` folder is where you keep your feature's Express routing middleware

```
      next();
    } else {
      res.send('What is your name?');
    }
};

var sayHello = function(req, res, next) {
  res.send('Hello ' + req.param('name'));
};

var app = express();
app.get('/', hasName, sayHello);

app.listen(3000);
console.log('Server running at http://localhost:3000/');
```

In the preceding code, there are two middleware functions named hasName() and sayHello(). The hasName() middleware is looking for the name parameter; if it finds a defined name parameter, it will call the next middleware function using the next argument. Otherwise, the hasName() middleware will handle the response by itself. In this case, the next middleware function would be the sayHello() middleware function. This is possible because we've added the middleware function in a row using the app.get() method. It is also worth noticing the order of the middleware functions because it determines which middleware function is executed first.

This example demonstrates well how routing middleware can be used to perform different validations when determining what the response should be. You can of course leverage this functionality to perform other tasks, such as validating user authentication and resources' authorization. For now though, let's just continue with our example.

Adding the routing file

The next file you're going to create is your first routing file. In the app/routes folder, create a file named index.server.routes.js with the following code snippet:

```
module.exports = function(app) {
    var index = require('../controllers/index.server.controller');
    app.get('/', index.render);
};
```

Here you did a few things: first, you used the CommonJS module pattern again. As you may recall the CommonJS module pattern supports both the exporting of several functions like you did with your controller and the use of a single module function like you did here. Next, you required your `index` controller and used its `render()` method as a middleware to GET requests made to the root path.

> The routing module function accepts a single argument called `app`, so when you call this function, you'll need to pass it the instance of the Express application.

All that you have left to do is to create the Express application object and bootstrap it using the controller and routing modules you just created. To do so, go to the `config` folder and create a file named `express.js` with the following code snippet:

```
var express = require('express');

module.exports = function() {
  var app = express();
  require('../app/routes/index.server.routes.js')(app);
  return app;
};
```

In the preceding code snippet, you required the Express module then used the CommonJS module pattern to define a module function that initializes the Express application. First, it creates a new instance of an Express application, and then it requires your routing file and calls it as a function passing it the application instance as an argument. The routing file will use the application instance to create a new routing configuration and will call the controller's `render()` method. The `module` function ends by returning the application instance.

> The `express.js` file is where we configure our Express application. This is where we add everything related to the Express configuration.

To finalize your application, you'll need to create a file named `server.js` in the root folder and copy the following code:

```
var express = require('./config/express');

var app = express();
app.listen(3000);
module.exports = app;

console.log('Server running at http://localhost:3000/');
```

This is it! In the main application file, you connected all the loose ends by requiring the Express configuration module and then using it to retrieve your application object instance, and listen to the 3000 port.

To start your application, navigate to your application's root folder using your command-line tool, and install your application dependencies using npm, as follows:

```
$ npm install
```

Once the installation process is over, all you have to do is start your application using Node's command-line tool:

```
$ node server
```

Your Express application should now run! To test it, navigate to http://localhost:3000.

In this example, you learned how to properly build your Express application. It is important that you notice the different ways you used the CommonJS module pattern to create your files and require them across the application. This pattern will often repeat itself in this book.

Configuring an Express application

Express comes with a pretty simple configuration system, which enables you to add certain functionality to your Express application. Although there are predefined configuration options that you can change to manipulate the way it works, you can also add your own key/value configuration options for any other usage. Another robust feature of Express is the ability to configure your application based on the environment it's running on. For instance, you may want to use the Express logger in your development environment and not in production, while compressing your responses body might seem like a good idea when running in a production environment.

To achieve this, you will need to use the process.env property. The process.env is a global variable that allows you to access predefined environment variables, and the most common one is the NODE_ENV environment variable. The NODE_ENV environment variable is often used for environment-specific configurations. To understand this better, let's go back to the previous example and add some external middleware. To use these middleware, you will first need to download and install them as your project dependencies.

To do so, edit your `package.json` file to look like the following code snippet:

```
{
  "name": "MEAN",
  "version": "0.0.3",
  "dependencies": {
    "express": "~4.8.8",
    "morgan": "~1.3.0",
    "compression": "~1.0.11",
    "body-parser": "~1.8.0",
    "method-override": "~2.2.0"
  }
}
```

As we previously stated, the `morgan` module provides a simple logger middleware, the `compression` module will provides response compression, the `body-parser` module provides several middleware to handle request data, and the `method-override` module provides DELETE and PUT HTTP verbs legacy support. To use these modules, you will need to modify your `config/express.js` file to look like the following code snippet:

```
var express = require('express'),
  morgan = require('morgan'),
  compress = require('compression'),
  bodyParser = require('body-parser'),
  methodOverride = require('method-override');

module.exports = function() {
  var app = express();

  if (process.env.NODE_ENV === 'development') {
    app.use(morgan('dev'));
  } else if (process.env.NODE_ENV === 'production') {
    app.use(compress());
  }

  app.use(bodyParser.urlencoded({
    extended: true
  }));
  app.use(bodyParser.json());
  app.use(methodOverride());

  require('../app/routes/index.server.routes.js')(app);

  return app;
};
```

As you can see, we just used the `process.env.NODE_ENV` variable to determine our environment and configure the Express application accordingly. We simply used the `app.use()` method to load the `morgan()` middleware in a development environment and the `compress()` middleware in a production environment. The `bodyParser.urlencoded()`, `bodyParser.json()`, and `methodOverride()` middleware will always load, regardless of the environment.

To finalize your configuration, you'll need to change your `server.js` file to look like the following code snippet:

```
process.env.NODE_ENV = process.env.NODE_ENV || 'development';

var express = require('./config/express');

var app = express();
app.listen(3000);
module.exports = app;

console.log('Server running at http://localhost:3000/');
```

Notice how the `process.env.NODE_ENV` variable is set to the default `'development'` value if it doesn't exist. This is because, often, the NODE_ENV environment variable is not properly set.

> It is recommended that you set the NODE_ENV environment variable in your operating system prior to running your application.
>
> In a Windows environment, this can be done by executing the following command in your command prompt:
>
> `> set NODE_ENV=development`
>
> While in a Unix-based environment, you should simply use the following export command:
>
> `$ export NODE_ENV=development`

To test your changes, navigate to your application's root folder using your command-line tool and install your application dependencies using npm, as follows:

```
$ npm install
```

Once the installation process is over, all you have to do is start your application using Node's command-line tool:

```
$ node server
```

Your Express application should now run! To test it, navigate to `http://localhost:3000`, and you'll be able to see the logger in action in your command-line output. However, the `process.env.NODE_ENV` environment variable can be used even more sophisticatedly when dealing with more complex configuration options.

Environment configuration files

During your application development, you will often need to configure third-party modules to run differently in various environments. For instance, when you connect to your MongoDB server, you'll probably use different connection strings in your development and production environments. Doing so in the current setting will probably cause your code to be filled with endless `if` statements, which will generally be harder to maintain. To solve this issue, you can manage a set of environment configuration files that holds these properties. You will then be able to use the `process.env.NODE_ENV` environment variable to determine which configuration file to load, thus keeping your code shorter and easier to maintain. Let's begin by creating a configuration file for our default development environment. To do so, create a new file inside your `config/env` folder and call it `development.js`. Inside your new file, paste the following lines of code:

```
module.exports = {
    // Development configuration options
};
```

As you can see, your configuration file is currently just an empty CommonJS module initialization; don't worry about it, we'll soon add the first configuration option, but first, we'll need to manage the configuration files loading. To do so, go to your application `config` folder and create a new file named `config.js`. Inside your new file, paste the following lines of code:

```
module.exports = require('./env/' + process.env.NODE_ENV + '.js');
```

As you can see, this file simply loads the correct configuration file according to the `process.env.NODE_ENV` environment variable. In the upcoming chapters, we'll use this file, which will load the correct environment configuration file for us. To manage other environment configurations, you'll just need to add a dedicated environment configuration file and properly set the `NODE_ENV` environment variable.

Rendering views

A very common feature of web frameworks is the ability to render views. The basic concept is passing your data to a template engine that will render the final view usually in HTML. In the MVC pattern, your controller uses the model to retrieve the data portion and the view template to render the HTML output as described in the next diagram. The Express extendable approach allows the usage of many Node.js template engines to achieve this functionality. In this section, we'll use the EJS template engine, but you can later replace it with other template engines. The following diagram shows the MVC pattern in rendering application views:

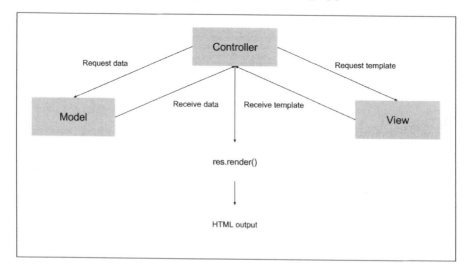

Express has two methods for rendering views: `app.render()`, which is used to render the view and then pass the HTML to a callback function, and the more common `res.render()`, which renders the view locally and sends the HTML as a response. You'll use `res.render()` more frequently because you usually want to output the HTML as a response. However, if, for an instance, you'd like your application to send HTML e-mails, you will probably use `app.render()`. Before we begin exploring the `res.render()` method, let's first configure our view system.

Configuring the view system

In order to configure the Express view system, you will need to use the EJS template engine. Let's get back to our example and install the EJS module. You should begin by changing your `package.json` file to look like the following code snippet:

```
{
  "name": "MEAN",
  "version": "0.0.3",
  "dependencies": {
    "express": "~4.8.8",
    "morgan": "~1.3.0",
    "compression": "~1.0.11",
    "body-parser": "~1.8.0",
    "method-override": "~2.2.0",
    "ejs": "~1.0.0"
  }
}
```

Now install the EJS module by navigating in the command line to your project's root folder and issue the following command:

```
$ npm update
```

After NPM finishes installing the EJS module, you'll be able to configure Express to use it as the default template engine. To configure your Express application, go back to the `config/express.js` file and change it to look like the following lines of code:

```
var express = require('express'),
  morgan = require('morgan'),
  compress = require('compression'),
  bodyParser = require('body-parser'),
  methodOverride = require('method-override');

module.exports = function() {
  var app = express();
  if (process.env.NODE_ENV === 'development') {
    app.use(morgan('dev'));
  } else if (process.env.NODE_ENV === 'production') {
    app.use(compress());
  }

  app.use(bodyParser.urlencoded({
    extended: true
  }));
```

```
    app.use(bodyParser.json());
    app.use(methodOverride());

    app.set('views', './app/views');
    app.set('view engine', 'ejs');

    require('../app/routes/index.server.routes.js')(app);

    return app;
};
```

Notice how we use the `app.set()` method to configure the Express application views folder and template engine. Let's create your first view.

Rendering EJS views

EJS views basically consist of HTML code mixed with EJS tags. EJS templates will reside in the `app/views` folder and will have the `.ejs` extension. When you'll use the `res.render()` method, the EJS engine will look for the template in the `views` folder, and if it finds a complying template, it will render the HTML output. To create your first EJS view, go to your `app/views` folder, and create a new file named `index.ejs` that contains the following HTML code snippet:

```
<!DOCTYPE html>
<html>
  <head>
    <title><%= title %></title>
  </head>
  <body>
    <h1><%= title %></h1>
  </body>
</html>
```

This code should be mostly familiar to you except for the `<%= %>` tag. These tags are the way to tell the EJS template engine where to render the template variables—in this case, the `title` variable. All you have left to do is configure your controller to render this template and automatically output it as an HTML response. To do so, go back to your `app/controllers/index.server.controller.js` file, and change it to look like the following code snippet:

```
exports.render = function(req, res) {
  res.render('index', {
    title: 'Hello World'
  })
};
```

Notice the way the `res.render()` method is used. The first argument is the name of your EJS template without the `.ejs` extension, and the second argument is an object containing your template variables. The `res.render()` method will use the EJS template engine to look for the file in the `views` folder that we set in the `config/express.js` file and will then render the view using the template variables. To test your changes, use your command-line tool and issue the following command:

```
$ node server
```

Well done, you have just created your first EJS view! Test your application by visiting `http://localhost:3000` where you'll be able to see the rendered HTML.

EJS views are simple to maintain and provides an easy way to create your application views. We'll elaborate a bit more on EJS templates later in this book; however, not as much as you would expect because in MEAN applications, most of the HTML rendering is done in the client side using AngularJS.

Serving static files

In any web application, there is always a need to serve static files. Fortunately, Express comes prebundled with the `express.static()` middleware, which provides this feature. To add static file support to the previous example, just make the following changes in your `config/express.js` file:

```
var express = require('express'),
  morgan = require('morgan'),
  compress = require('compression'),
  bodyParser = require('body-parser'),
  methodOverride = require('method-override');
module.exports = function() {
  var app = express();

  if (process.env.NODE_ENV === 'development') {
    app.use(morgan('dev'));
  } else if (process.env.NODE_ENV === 'production') {
    app.use(compress());
  }

  app.use(bodyParser.urlencoded({
    extended: true
  }));
  app.use(bodyParser.json());
  app.use(methodOverride());
```

```
    app.set('views', './app/views');
    app.set('view engine', 'ejs');

    require('../app/routes/index.server.routes.js')(app);

    app.use(express.static('./public'));

    return app;
};
```

The `express.static()` middleware takes one argument to determine the location of the static folder. Notice how the `express.static()` middleware is placed below the call for the routing file. This order matters because if it were above it, Express would first try to look for HTTP request paths in the static files folder. This would make the response a lot slower as it would have to wait for a filesystem I/O operation.

To test your static middleware, add an image named `logo.png` to the `public/img` folder and then make the following changes in your `app/views/index.ejs` file:

```
<!DOCTYPE html>
<html>
  <head>
    <title><%= title %></title>
  </head>
  <body>
    <img src="img/logo.png" alt="Logo">
    <h1><%= title %></h1>
  </body>
</html>
```

Now run your application using node's command-line tool:

```
$ node server
```

To test the result, visit `http://localhost:3000` in your browser and watch how Express is serving your image as a static file.

Configuring sessions

Sessions are a common web application pattern that allows you to keep track of the user's behavior when they visit your application. To add this functionality, you will need to install and configure the `express-session` middleware. To do so, start by modifying your `package.json` file like this:

```
{
  "name": "MEAN",
  "version": "0.0.3",
  "dependencies": {
    "express": "~4.8.8",
    "morgan": "~1.3.0",
    "compression": "~1.0.11",
    "body-parser": "~1.8.0",
    "method-override": "~2.2.0",
    "express-session": "~1.7.6",
    "ejs": "~1.0.0"
  }
}
```

Then, install the `express-session` module by navigating to your project's root folder in the command line and issuing the following command:

```
$ npm update
```

Once the installation process is finished, you'll be able to configure your Express application to use the `express-session` module. The `express-session` module will use a cookie-stored, signed identifier to identify the current user. To sign the session identifier, it will use a secret string, which will help prevent malicious session tampering. For security reasons, it is recommended that the cookie secret be different for each environment, which means this would be an appropriate place to use our environment configuration file. To do so, change the `config/env/development.js` file to look like the following code snippet:

```
module.exports = {
  sessionSecret: 'developmentSessionSecret'
};
```

Since it is just an example, feel free to change the secret string. For other environments, just add the `sessionSecret` property in their environment configuration files. To use the configuration file and configure your Express application, go back to your `config/express.js` file and change it to look like the following code snippet:

```javascript
var config = require('./config'),
  express = require('express'),
  morgan = require('morgan'),
  compress = require('compression'),
  bodyParser = require('body-parser'),
  methodOverride = require('method-override'),
  session = require('express-session');

module.exports = function() {
  var app = express();

  if (process.env.NODE_ENV === 'development') {
    app.use(morgan('dev'));
  } else if (process.env.NODE_ENV === 'production') {
    app.use(compress());
  }

  app.use(bodyParser.urlencoded({
    extended: true
  }));
  app.use(bodyParser.json());
  app.use(methodOverride());

  app.use(session({
    saveUninitialized: true,
    resave: true,
    secret: config.sessionSecret
  }));

  app.set('views', './app/views');
  app.set('view engine', 'ejs');

  require('../app/routes/index.server.routes.js')(app);

  app.use(express.static('./public'));

  return app;
};
```

Notice how the configuration object is passed to the `express.session()` middleware. In this configuration object, the `secret` property is defined using the configuration file you previously modified. The `session` middleware adds a `session` object to all request objects in your application. Using this `session` object, you can set or get any property that you wish to use in the current session. To test the session, change the `app/controller/index.server.controller.js` file as follows:

```
exports.render = function(req, res) {
  if (req.session.lastVisit) {
    console.log(req.session.lastVisit);
  }

  req.session.lastVisit = new Date();

  res.render('index', {
    title: 'Hello World'
  });
};
```

What you did here is basically record the time of the last user request. The controller checks whether the `lastVisit` property was set in the `session` object, and if so, outputs the last visit date to the console. It then sets the `lastVisit` property to the current time. To test your changes, use node's command-line tool to run your application, as follows:

```
$ node server
```

Now test your application by visiting `http://localhost:3000` in your browser and watching the command-line output.

Summary

In this chapter, you created your first Express application and learned how to properly configure it. You arranged your files and folders in an organized structure and discovered alternative folder structures. You also created your first Express controller and learned how to call its methods using Express' routing mechanism. You rendered your first EJS view and learned how to serve static files. You also learned how to use `express-session` to track your users' behavior. In the next chapter, you'll learn how to save your application's persistent data using MongoDB.

4
Introduction to MongoDB

MongoDB is an exciting new breed of database. The leader of the NoSQL movement is emerging as one of the most useful database solutions in the world. Designed with web applications in mind, Mongo's high throughput, unique BSON data model, and easily scalable architecture provides web developers with better tools to store their persistent data. But the move from relational databases to NoSQL solutions can be an overwhelming task, which can be easily simplified by understanding MongoDB's design goals. In this chapter, we'll cover the following topics:

- Understanding the NoSQL movement and MongoDB design goals
- MongoDB BSON data structure
- MongoDB collections and documents
- MongoDB query language
- Working with the MongoDB shell

Introduction to NoSQL

In the past couple of years, web application development usually required the usage of a relational database to store persistent data. Most developers are already pretty comfortable with using one of the many SQL solutions. So, the approach of storing a normalized data model using a mature relational database became the standard. Object-relational mappers started to crop up, giving developers proper solutions to marshal their data between the different parts of their application. But as the Web grew larger, more scaling problems were presented to a larger base of developers. To solve this problem, the community created a variety of key-value storage solutions that were designed for better availability, simple querying, and horizontal scaling. This new kind of data store became more and more robust, offering many of the features of the relational databases. During this evolution, different storage design patterns emerged, including key-value storage, column storage, object storage, and the most popular one, document storage.

In a common relational database, your data is stored in different tables, often connected using a primary to foreign key relation. Your program will later reconstruct the model using various SQL statements to arrange the data in some kind of hierarchical object representation. Document-oriented databases handle data differently. Instead of using tables, they store hierarchical documents in standard formats, such as JSON and XML.

To understand this better, let's have a look at an example of a typical blog post. To construct this blog post model using a SQL solution, you'll probably have to use at least two tables. The first one would contain post information while the second would contain post comments. A sample table structure can be seen in the following diagram:

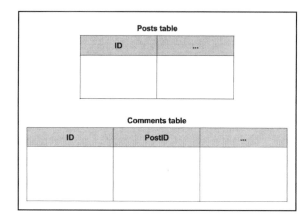

In your application, you'll use an object-relational mapping library or direct SQL statements to select the blog post record and the post comments records to create your blog post object. However, in a document-based database, the blog post will be stored completely as a single document that can later be queried. For instance, in a database that stores documents in a JSON format, your blog post document would probably look like the following code snippet:

```
{
    "title": "First Blog Post",
    "comments": [

    ]
}
```

This demonstrates the main difference between document-based databases and relational databases. So, while working with relational databases, your data is stored in different tables, with your application assembling objects using table records. Storing your data as holistic documents will allow faster read operations since your application won't have to rebuild the objects with every read. Furthermore, document-oriented databases have other advantages.

While developing your application, you often encounter another problem: model changes. Let's assume you want to add a new property to each blog post. So, you go ahead and change your posts table and then go to your application data layer and add that property to your blog post object. But as your application already contains several blog posts, all existing blog post objects will have to change as well, which means that you'll have to cover your code with extra validation procedures. However, document-based databases are often schemaless, which means you can store different objects in a single collection of objects without changing anything in your database. Although this may sound like a call-for-trouble for some experienced developers, the freedom of schemaless storage has several advantages.

For example, think about an e-commerce application that sells used furniture. Think about your products table for a moment: a chair and a closet might have some common features, such as the type of wood, but a customer might also be interested in the number of doors the closet has. Storing the closet and chair objects in the same table means they could be stored in either a table with a large number of empty columns or using the more practical entity-attribute-value pattern, where another table is used to store key-value attributes. However, using schemaless storage will allow you to define different properties for different objects in the same collection, while still enabling you to query this collection using common properties, such as wood type. This means your application, and not the database, will be in charge of enforcing the data structure, which can help you speed up your development process.

While there are many NoSQL solutions that solve various development issues, usually around caching and scale, the document-oriented databases are rapidly becoming the leaders of the movement. The document-oriented database's ease of use, along with its standalone persistent storage offering, even threatens to replace the traditional SQL solutions in some use cases. And although there are a few document-oriented databases, none are as popular as MongoDB.

Introducing MongoDB

Back in 2007, Dwight Merriman and Eliot Horowitz formed a company named 10gen to create a better platform to host web applications. The idea was to create a hosting as a service that will allow developers to focus on building their application rather than handle hardware management and infrastructure scaling. Soon, they discovered the community wasn't keen on giving up so much of the control over their application's infrastructure. As a result, they released the different parts of the platform as open source projects.

One such project was a document-based database solution called MongoDB. Derived from the word humongous, MongoDB was able to support complex data storage, while maintaining the high-performance approach of other NoSQL stores. The community cheerfully adopted this new paradigm, making MongoDB one of the fastest-growing databases in the world. With more than 150 contributors and over 10,000 commits, it also became one the most popular open source projects.

MongoDB's main goal was to create a new type of database that combined the robustness of a relational database with the fast throughput of distributed key-value data stores. With the scalable platform in mind, it had to support simple horizontal scaling while sustaining the durability of traditional databases. Another key design goal was to support web application development in the form of standard JSON outputs. These two design goals turned out to be MongoDB's greatest advantages over other solutions as these aligned perfectly with other trends in web development, such as the almost ubiquitous use of cloud virtualization hosting or the shift towards horizontal, instead of vertical, scaling.

First dismissed as another NoSQL storage layer over the more viable relational database, MongoDB evolved way beyond the platform where it was born. Its ecosystem grew to support most of the popular programming platforms, with the various community-backed drivers. Along with this, many other tools were formed including different MongoDB clients, profiling and optimization tools, administration and maintenance utilities, as well as a couple of VC-backed hosting services. Even major companies such as eBay and The New York Times began to use MongoDB data storage in their production environment. To understand why developers prefer MongoDB, it's time we dive into some of its key features.

Key features of MongoDB

MongoDB has some key features that helped it become so popular. As we mentioned before, the goal was to create a new breed between traditional database features and the high performance of NoSQL stores. As a result, most of its key features were created to evolve beyond the limitations of other NoSQL solutions while integrating some of the abilities of relational databases. In this section, you'll learn why MongoDB can become your preferred database when approaching modern web application developments.

The BSON format

One of the greatest features of MongoDB is its JSON-like storage format named BSON. Standing for **Binary JSON**, the BSON format is a binary-encoded serialization of JSON-like documents, and it is designed to be more efficient in size and speed, allowing MongoDB's high read/write throughput.

Like JSON, BSON documents are a simple data structure representation of objects and arrays in a key-value format. A document consists of a list of elements, each with a string typed field name and a typed field value. These documents support all of the JSON specific data types along with other data types, such as the Date type.

Another big advantage of the BSON format is the use of the _id field as primary key. The _id field value will usually be a unique identifier type, named ObjectId, that is either generated by the application driver or by the mongod service. In the event the driver fails to provide a _id field with a unique ObjectId, the mongod service will add it automatically using:

- A 4-byte value representing the seconds since the Unix epoch
- A 3-byte machine identifier
- A 2-byte process ID
- A 3-byte counter, starting with a random value

So, a BSON representation of the blog post object from the previous example would look like the following code snippet:

```
{
   "_id": ObjectId("52d02240e4b01d67d71ad577"),
   "title": "First Blog Post",
   "comments": [
   ...
   ]
}
```

The BSON format enables MongoDB to internally index and map document properties and even nested documents, allowing it to scan the collection efficiently and more importantly, to match objects to complex query expressions.

MongoDB ad hoc queries

One of the other MongoDB design goals was to expand the abilities of ordinary key-value stores. The main issue of common key-value stores is their limited query capabilities, which usually means your data is only queryable using the key field, and more complex queries are mostly predefined. To solve this issue, MongoDB drew its inspiration from the relational databases dynamic query language.

Supporting ad hoc queries means that the database will respond to dynamically structured queries out of the box without the need to predefine each query. It is able to do this by indexing BSON documents and using a unique query language. Let's have a look at the following SQL statement example:

```
SELECT * FROM Posts WHERE Title LIKE '%mongo%';
```

This simple statement is asking the database for all the post records with a title containing the word mongo. Replicating this query in MongoDB will be as follows:

```
db.posts.find({ title:/mongo/ });
```

Running this command in the MongoDB shell will return all the posts whose title field contains the word mongo. You'll learn more about the MongoDB query language later in this chapter, but for now it is important to remember that it is almost as query-able as your traditional relational database. The MongoDB query language is great, but it raises the question of how efficiently these queries run when the database gets larger. Like relational databases, MongoDB solves this issue using a mechanism called indexing.

MongoDB indexing

Indexes are a unique data structure that enables the database engine to efficiently resolve queries. When a query is sent to the database, it will have to scan through the entire collection of documents to find those that match the query statement. This way, the database engine processes a large amount of unnecessary data, resulting in poor performance.

To speed up the scan, the database engine can use a predefined index, which maps documents fields and can tell the engine which documents are compatible with this query statement. To understand how indexes work, let's say we want to retrieve all the posts that have more than 10 comments. For instance, if our document is defined as follows:

```
{
   "_id": ObjectId("52d02240e4b01d67d71ad577"),
   "title": "First Blog Post",
   "comments": [

   ],
   "commentsCount": 12
}
```

So, a MongoDB query that requests for documents with more than 10 comments would be as follows

```
db.posts.find({ commentsCount: { $gt: 10 } });
```

To execute this query, MongoDB would have to go through all the posts and check whether the post has commentCount larger than 10. But if a commentCount index was defined, then MongoDB would only have to check which documents have commentCount larger than 10, before retrieving these documents. The following diagram illustrates how a commentCount index would work:

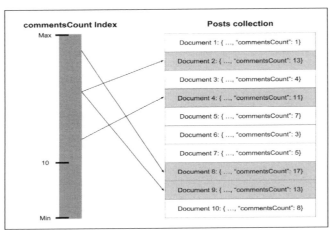

MongoDB replica set

To provide data redundancy and improved availability, MongoDB uses an architecture called replica set. Replication of databases helps protect your data to recover from hardware failure and increase read capacity. A replica set is a set of MongoDB services that host the same dataset. One service is used as the primary and the other services are called secondaries. All of the set instances support read operations, but only the primary instance is in charge of write operations. When a write operation occurs, the primary will inform the secondaries about the changes and make sure they've applied it to their datasets' replication. The following diagram illustrates a common replica set:

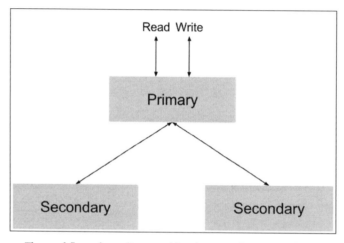

The workflow of a replica set with primary and two secondaries

Another robust feature of the MongoDB replica set is its automatic failover. When one of the set members can't reach the primary instance for more than 10 seconds, the replica set will automatically elect and promote a secondary instance as the new primary. When the old primary comes back online, it will rejoin the replica set as a secondary instance.

Replication is a very robust feature of MongoDB that is derived directly from its platform origin and is one of the main features that makes MongoDB production-ready. However, it is not the only one.

 To learn more about MongoDB replica sets, visit `http://docs.mongodb.org/manual/replication/`.

MongoDB sharding

Scaling is a common problem with a growing web application. The various approaches to solve this issue can be divided into two groups: vertical scaling and horizontal scaling. The differences between the two are illustrated in the following diagram:

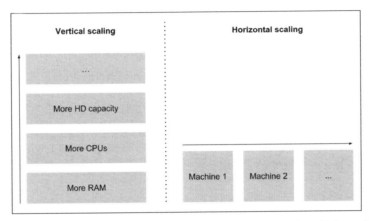

Vertical scaling with a single machine versus horizontal scaling with multiple machines

Vertical scaling is easier and consists of increasing single machine resources, such as RAM and CPU, in order to handle the load. However, it has two major drawbacks: first, at some level, increasing a single machine's resources becomes disproportionately more expensive compared to splitting the load between several smaller machines. Secondly, the popular cloud-hosting providers limit the size of the machine instances you can use. So, scaling your application vertically can only be done up to a certain level.

Horizontal scaling is more complicated and is done using several machines. Each machine will handle a part of the load, providing better overall performance. The problem with horizontal database scaling is how to properly divide the data between different machines and how to manage the read/write operations between them.

Luckily MongoDB supports horizontal scaling, which it refers to as sharding. Sharding is the process of splitting the data between different machines, or shards. Each shard holds a portion of the data and functions as a separate database. The collection of several shards together is what forms a single logical database. Operations are performed through services called query routers, which ask the configuration servers how to delegate each operation to the right shard.

 To learn more about MongoDB sharding, visit `http://docs.mongodb.org/manual/sharding/`.

These features and many others are what make MongoDB so popular. Though there are many good alternatives, MongoDB is becoming more and more ubiquitous among developers and is on its way to becoming the leading NoSQL solution. After this brief overview, it's time we dive in a little deeper.

MongoDB shell

If you followed *Chapter 1, Introduction to MEAN*, you should have a working instance of MongoDB in your local environment. To interact with MongoDB, you'll use the MongoDB shell that you encountered in *Chapter 1, Introduction to MEAN*. The MongoDB shell is a command-line tool that enables the execution of different operations using a JavaScript syntax query language.

In order to explore the different parts of MongoDB, let's start the MongoDB shell by running the mongo executable, as follows:

```
$ mongo
```

If MongoDB has been properly installed, you should see an output similar to what is shown in the following screenshot:

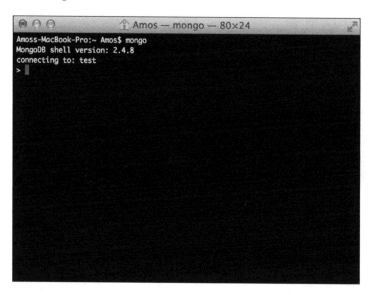

Notice how the shell is telling you the current shell version, and that it has connected to the default test database.

MongoDB databases

Each MongoDB server instance can store several databases. Unless specifically defined, the MongoDB shell will automatically connect to the default `test` database. Let's switch to another database called `mean` by executing the following command:

```
> use mean
```

You'll see a command-line output telling you that the shell switched to the `mean` database. Notice that you didn't need to create the database before using it because in MongoDB, databases and collections are lazily created when you insert your first document. This behavior is consistent with MongoDB's dynamic approach to data. Another way to use a specific database is to run the shell executable with the database name as an argument, as follows:

```
$ mongo mean
```

The shell will then automatically connect to the `mean` database. If you want to list all the other databases in the current MongoDB server, just execute the following command:

```
> show dbs
```

This will show you a list of currently available databases that have at least one document stored.

MongoDB collections

A MongoDB collection is a list of MongoDB documents and is the equivalent of a relational database table. A collection is created when the first document is being inserted. Unlike a table, a collection doesn't enforce any type of schema and can host different structured documents.

To perform operations on a MongoDB collection, you'll need to use the collection methods. Let's create a `posts` collection and insert the first post. In order to do this, execute the following command in the MongoDB shell:

```
> db.posts.insert({"title":"First Post", "user": "bob"})
```

After executing the preceding command, it will automatically create the posts collection and insert the first document. To retrieve the collection documents, execute the following command in the MongoDB shell:

```
> db.posts.find()
```

You should see a command-line output similar to what is shown in the following screenshot:

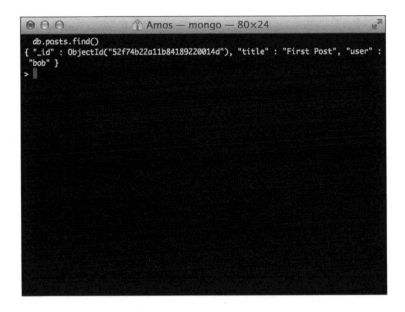

This means that you have successfully created the posts collection and inserted your first document.

To show all available collections, issue the following command in the MongoDB shell:

```
> show collections
```

The MongoDB shell will output the list of available collections, which in your case are the posts collection and another collection called system.indexes, which holds the list of your database indexes.

If you'd like to delete the posts collection, you will need to execute the drop() command as follows:

```
> db.posts.drop()
```

The shell will inform you that the collection was dropped, by responding with a true output.

MongoDB CRUD operations

Create, read, update, and delete (CRUD) operations, are the basic interactions you perform with a database. To execute CRUD operations over your database entities, MongoDB provides various collection methods.

Creating a new document

You're already familiar with the basic method of creating a new document using the `insert()` method, as you previously did in earlier examples. Besides the `insert()` method, there are two more methods called `update()` and `save()` to create new objects.

Creating a document using insert()

The most common way to create a new document is to use the `insert()` method. The `insert` method takes a single argument that represents the new document. To insert a new post, just issue the following command in the MongoDB shell:

```
> db.posts.insert({"title":"Second Post", "user": "alice"})
```

Creating a document using update()

The `update()` method is usually used to update an existing document. You can also use it to create a new document, if no document matches the query criteria, using the following upsert flag:

```
> db.posts.update({
    "user": "alice"
}, {
    "title": "Second Post",
    "user": "alice"
}, {
    upsert: true
})
```

In the preceding example, MongoDB will look for a post created by `alice` and try to update it. Considering the fact that the `posts` collection doesn't have a post created by `alice` and the fact you have used the `upsert` flag, MongoDB will not find an appropriate document to update and will create a new document instead.

Creating a document using save()

Another way of creating a new document is by calling the `save()` method, passing it a document that either doesn't have an `_id` field or has an `_id` field that doesn't exist in the collection:

```
> db.posts.save({"title":"Second Post", "user": "alice"})
```

This will have the same effect as the `update()` method and will create a new document instead of updating an existing one.

Reading documents

The `find()` method is used to retrieve a list of documents from a MongoDB collection. Using the `find()` method, you can either request for all the documents in a collection or use a query to retrieve specific documents.

Finding all the collection documents

To retrieve all the documents in the `posts` collection, you should either pass an empty query to the `find()` method or not pass any arguments at all. The following query will retrieve all the documents in the posts collection:

```
> db.posts.find()
```

Furthermore, performing the same operation can also be done using the following query:

```
> db.posts.find({})
```

These two queries are basically the same and will return all the documents in the `posts` collection.

Using an equality statement

To retrieve a specific document, you can use an equality condition query that will grab all the documents, which comply with that condition. For instance, to retrieve all the posts created by `alice`, you will need to issue the following command in the shell:

```
> db.posts.find({ "user": "alice" })
```

This will retrieve all the documents that have the `user` property equal to `alice`.

Using query operators

Using an equality statement may not be enough. To build more complex queries, MongoDB supports a variety of query operators. Using query operators, you can look for different sorts of conditions. For example, to retrieve all the posts that were created by either `alice` or `bob`, you can use the following `$in` operator:

```
> db.posts.find({ "user": { $in: ["alice", "bob"] } })
```

> There are plenty of other query operators you can learn about by visiting `http://docs.mongodb.org/manual/reference/operator/query/#query-selectors`.

Building AND/OR queries

When you build a query, you may need to use more than one condition. Like in SQL, you can use AND/OR operators to build multiple condition query statements. To perform an AND query, you simply add the properties you'd like to check to the query object. For instance, take look at the following query:

```
> db.posts.find({ "user": "alice", "commentsCount": { $gt: 10 }  })
```

It is similar to the `find()` query you've previously used but adds another condition that verifies the document's `commentCount` property and will only grab documents that were created by `alice` and have more than 10 comments. An OR query is a bit more complex because it involves the `$or` operator. To understand it better, take a look at another version of the previous example:

```
> db.posts.find( { $or: [{ "user": "alice" }, { "user": "bob" }] })
```

Like the query operators example, this query will also grab all the posts created by either `bob` or `alice`.

Updating existing documents

Using MongoDB, you have the option of updating documents using either the `update()` or `save()` methods.

Updating documents using update()

The update() method takes three arguments to update existing documents. The first argument is the selection criteria that indicate which documents to update, the second argument is the update statement, and the last argument is the options object. For instance, in the following example, the first argument is telling MongoDB to look for all the documents created by alice, the second argument tells it to updates the title field, and the third is forcing it to execute the update operation on all the documents it finds:

```
> db.posts.update({
    "user": "alice"
}, {
    $set: {
      "title": "Second Post"
    }
}, {
    multi: true
})
```

Notice how the multi property has been added to the options object. The update() method's default behavior is to update a single document, so by setting the multi property, you tell the update() method to update all the documents that comply with the selection criteria.

Updating documents using save()

Another way of updating an existing document is by calling the save() method, passing it a document that contains an _id field. For instance, the following command will update an existing document with an _id field that is equal to ObjectId("50691737d386d8fadbd6b01d"):

```
> db.posts.save({
    "_id": ObjectId("50691737d386d8fadbd6b01d"),
    "title": "Second Post",
    "user": "alice"
});
```

It's important to remember that if the save() method is unable to find an appropriate object, it will create a new one instead.

Deleting documents

To remove documents, MongoDB utilizes the `remove()` method. The `remove()` method can accept up to two arguments. The first one is the deletion criteria, and the second is a Boolean argument that indicates whether or not to remove multiple documents.

Deleting all documents

To remove all the documents from a collection, you will need call the `remove()` method with no deletion criteria at all. For example, to remove all the `posts` documents, you'll need to execute the following command:

```
> db.posts.remove()
```

Notice that the `remove()` method is different from the `drop()` method as it will not delete the collection or its indexes. To rebuild your collection with different indexes, it is preferred that you use the `drop()` method.

Deleting multiple documents

To remove multiple documents that match a criteria from a collection, you will need to call the `remove()` method with a deletion criteria. For example, to remove all the posts made by `alice`, you'll need to execute the following command:

```
> db.posts.remove({ "user": "alice" })
```

Note that this will remove all the documents created by `alice`, so be careful when using the `remove()` method.

Deleting a single document

To remove a single document that matches a criteria from a collection, you will need to call the `remove()` method with a deletion criteria and a Boolean stating that you only want to delete a single document. For example, to remove the first post made by `alice`, you'll need to execute the following command:

```
> db.posts.remove({ "user": "alice" }, true)
```

This will remove the first document that was created by `alice` and leave other documents even if they match the deletion criteria.

Summary

In this chapter, you learned about NoSQL databases and how they can be useful for modern web development. You also learned about the emerging leader of the NoSQL movement, MongoDB. You took a deeper dive in understanding the various features that makes MongoDB such a powerful solution and learned about its basic terminology. Finally, you caught a glimpse of MongoDB's powerful query language and how to perform all four CRUD operations. In the next chapter, we'll discuss how to connect Node.js and MongoDB together using the popular Mongoose module.

5
Introduction to Mongoose

Mongoose is a robust Node.js ODM module that adds MongoDB support to your Express application. Mongoose uses schemas to model your entities, offers predefined validation along with custom validations, allows you to define virtual attributes, and uses middleware hooks to intercept operations. The Mongoose design goal is to bridge the gap between the MongoDB schemaless approach and the requirements of real-world application development. In this chapter, you'll go through the following basic features of Mongoose:

- Mongoose schemas and models
- Schema indexes, modifiers, and virtual attributes
- Using the model's methods and perform CRUD operations
- Verifying your data using predefined and custom validators
- Using middleware to intercept the model's methods

Introducing Mongoose

Mongoose is a Node.js module that provides developers with the ability to model objects and save them as MongoDB documents. While MongoDB is a schemaless database, Mongoose offers you the opportunity to enjoy both strict and loose schema approaches when dealing with Mongoose models. Like with any other Node.js module, before you can start using it in your application, you will first need to install it. The examples in this chapter will continue directly from those in the previous chapters; so for this chapter, copy the final example from *Chapter 3, Building an Express Web Application*, and let's start from there.

Installing Mongoose

Once you've installed and verified that your MongoDB local instance is running, you'll be able connect it using the Mongoose module. First, you will need to install Mongoose in your application modules folders, so change your `package.json` file to look like the following code snippet:

```
{
  "name": "MEAN",
  "version": "0.0.5",
  "dependencies": {
    "express": "~4.8.8",
    "morgan": "~1.3.0",
    "compression": "~1.0.11",
    "body-parser": "~1.8.0",
    "method-override": "~2.2.0",
    "express-session": "~1.7.6",
    "ejs": "~1.0.0",
    "mongoose": "~3.8.15"
  }
}
```

To install your application dependencies, go to your application folder and issue the following command in your command-line tool:

```
$ npm install
```

This will install the latest version of Mongoose in your `node_modules` folder. After the installation process has successfully finished, the next step will be to connect to your MongoDB instance.

Connecting to MongoDB

To connect to MongoDB, you will need to use the MongoDB connection URI. The MongoDB connection URI is a string URL that tells the MongoDB drivers how to connect to the database instance. The MongoDB URI is usually constructed as follows:

```
mongodb://username:password@hostname:port/database
```

Since you're connecting to a local instance, you can skip the username and password and use the following URI:

```
mongodb://localhost/mean-book
```

The simplest thing to do is define this connection URI directly in your `config/express.js` configuration file and use the Mongoose module to connect to the database as follows:

```
var uri = 'mongodb://localhost/mean-book';
var db = require('mongoose').connect(uri);
```

However, since you're building a real application, saving the URI directly in the `config/express.js` file is a bad practice. The proper way to store application variables is to use your enviornment configuration file. Go to your `config/env/development.js` file and change it to look like the following code snippet:

```
module.exports = {
  db: 'mongodb://localhost/mean-book',
  sessionSecret: 'developmentSessionSecret'
};
```

Now in your `config` folder, create a new file named `mongoose.js` that contains the following code snippet:

```
var config = require('./config'),
    mongoose = require('mongoose');

module.exports = function() {
  var db = mongoose.connect(config.db);

  return db;
};
```

Notice how you required the Mongoose module and connected to the MongoDB instance using the `db` property of your configuration object. To initialize your Mongoose configuration, go back to your `server.js` file, and change it to look like the following code snippet:

```
process.env.NODE_ENV = process.env.NODE_ENV || 'development';

var mongoose = require('./config/mongoose'),
    express = require('./config/express');

var db = mongoose();
var app = express();
app.listen(3000);

module.exports = app;

console.log('Server running at http://localhost:3000/');
```

That's it, you have installed Mongoose, updated your configuration file, and connected to your MongoDB instance. To start your application, use your command-line tool, and navigate to your application folder to execute the following command:

```
$ node server
```

Your application should be running and connected to the MongoDB local instance.

 If you experience any problems or get this output: `Error: failed to connect to [localhost:27017]`, make sure your MongoDB instance is running properly.

Understanding Mongoose schemas

Connecting to your MongoDB instance was the first step but the real magic of the Mongoose module is the ability to define a document schema. As you already know, MongoDB uses collections to store multiple documents, which aren't required to have the same structure. However, when dealing with objects, it is sometime necessary for documents to be similar. Mongoose uses a `Schema` object to define the document list of properties, each with its own type and constraints, to enforce the document structure. After specifying a schema, you will go on to define a `Model` constructor that you'll use to create instances of MongoDB documents. In this section, you'll learn how to define a user schema and model, and how to use a model instance to create, retrieve, and update user documents.

Creating the user schema and model

To create your first schema, go to the `app/models` folder and create a new file named `user.server.model.js`. In this file, paste the following lines of code:

```
var mongoose = require('mongoose'),
    Schema = mongoose.Schema;

var UserSchema = new Schema({
  firstName: String,
  lastName: String,
  email: String,
  username: String,
  password: String
});

mongoose.model('User', UserSchema);
```

In the preceding code snippet, you did two things: first, you defined your
`UserSchema` object using the `Schema` constructor, and then you used the schema
instance to define your `User` model. Next, you'll learn how to use the `User` model to
perform CRUD operations in your application's logic layer.

Registering the User model

Before you can start using the `User` model, you will need to include the `user.
server.model.js` file in your Mongoose configuration file in order to register
the `User` model. To do so, change your `config/mongoose.js` file to look like the
following code snippet:

```
var config = require('./config'),
    mongoose = require('mongoose');

module.exports = function() {
   var db = mongoose.connect(config.db);

   require('../app/models/user.server.model');

   return db;
};
```

Make sure that your Mongoose configuration file is loaded before any other
configuration in the `server.js` file. This is important since any module that is loaded
after this module will be able to use the `User` model without loading it by itself.

Creating new users using save()

You can start using the `User` model right away, but to keep things organized, it is
better that you create a `Users` controller that will handle all user-related operations.
Under the `app/controllers` folder, create a new file named `users.server.
controller.js` and paste the following lines of code:

```
var User = require('mongoose').model('User');

exports.create = function(req, res, next) {
   var user = new User(req.body);
```

```
       user.save(function(err) {
         if (err) {
           return next(err);
         } else {
           res.json(user);
         }
       });
     };
```

Let's go over this code. First, you used the Mongoose module to call the model method that will return the `User` model you previously defined. Next, you create a controller method named `create()`, which you will later use to create new users. Using the `new` keyword, the `create()` method creates a new model instance, which is populated using the request body. Finally, you call the model instance's `save()` method that either saves the user and outputs the `user` object, or fail, passing the error to the next middleware.

To test your new controller, let's add a set of user-related routes that call the controller's methods. Begin by creating a file named `users.server.routes.js` inside the `app/routes` folder. In this newly created file, paste the following lines of code:

```
var users = require('../../app/controllers/users.server.controller');

module.exports = function(app) {
  app.route('/users').post(users.create);
};
```

Since your Express application will serve mainly as a RESTful API for the AngularJS application, it is a best practice to build your routes according to the REST principles. In this case, the proper way to create a new user is to use an HTTP POST request to the base users route as you defined here. Change your `config/express.js` file to look like the following code snippet:

```
var config = require('./config'),
    express = require('express'),
    morgan = require('morgan'),
    compress = require('compression'),
    bodyParser = require('body-parser'),
    methodOverride = require('method-override'),
    session = require('express-session');

module.exports = function() {
  var app = express();
```

```
if (process.env.NODE_ENV === 'development') {
  app.use(morgan('dev'));
} else if (process.env.NODE_ENV === 'production') {
  app.use(compress());
}

app.use(bodyParser.urlencoded({
  extended: true
}));
app.use(bodyParser.json());
app.use(methodOverride());

app.use(session({
  saveUninitialized: true,
  resave: true,
  secret: config.sessionSecret
}));

app.set('views', './app/views');
app.set('view engine', 'ejs');

require('../app/routes/index.server.routes.js')(app);
require('../app/routes/users.server.routes.js')(app);

app.use(express.static('./public'));

return app;
};
```

That's it! To test it out, go to your root application folder and execute the following command:

```
$ node server
```

Your application should be running. To create a new user, perform an HTTP POST request to the base users route, and make sure the request body includes the following JSON:

```
{
  "firstName": "First",
  "lastName": "Last",
  "email": "user@example.com",
  "username": "username",
  "password": "password"
}
```

Another way to test your application would be to execute the following `curl` command in your command-line tool:

```
$ curl -X POST -H "Content-Type: application/json" -d
'{"firstName":"First", "lastName":"Last","email":"user@example.com","user
name":"username","password":"password"}' localhost:3000/users
```

 You are going to execute many different HTTP requests to test your application. `curl` is a useful tool, but there are several other tools specifically designed for this task; we recommend that you find your favorite one and use it from now on.

Finding multiple user documents using find()

The `find()` method is a model method that retrieves multiple documents stored in the same collection using a query and is a Mongoose implementation of the MongoDB `find()` collection method. To understand this better, add the following `list()` method in your app/controllers/users.server.controller.js file:

```
exports.list = function(req, res, next) {
  User.find({}, function(err, users) {
    if (err) {
      return next(err);
    } else {
      res.json(users);
    }
  });
};
```

Notice how the new `list()` method uses the `find()` method to retrieve an array of all the documents in the users collection. To use the new method you created, you'll need to register a route for it, so go to your app/routes/users.server.routes.js file and change it to look like the following code snippet:

```
var users = require('../../app/controllers/users.server.controller');

module.exports = function(app) {
  app.route('/users')
    .post(users.create)
    .get(users.list);
};
```

All you have left to do is run your application by executing the following command:

```
$ node server
```

Then, you will be able to retrieve a list of your users by visiting
`http://localhost:3000/users` in your browser.

Advanced querying using find()

In the preceding code example, the `find()` method accept two arguments,
a MongoDB query object and a callback function, but it can accept up to four
parameters:

- `Query`: This is a MongoDB query object
- `[Fields]`: This is an optional string object that represents the document
  fields to return
- `[Options]`: This is an optional options object
- `[Callback]`: This is an optional callback function

For instance, to retrieve only the usernames and e-mails of your users, you would
modify your call to look like the following lines of code:

```
User.find({}, 'username email', function(err, users) {
    ...
});
```

Furthermore, you can also pass an options object when calling the `find()` method,
which will manipulate the query result. For instance, to paginate through the `users`
collection and retrieve only a subset of your `users` collection, you can use the `skip`
and `limit` options as follows:

```
User.find({}, 'username email', {
    skip: 10,
    limit: 10
}, function(err, users) {
    ...
});
```

This will return a subset of up to 10 user documents while skipping the first
10 documents.

To learn more about query options, it is recommended that you visit
Mongoose official documentation at `http://mongoosejs.com/docs/api.html`.

Reading a single user document using findOne()

Retrieving a single user document is done using the findOne() method, which is very similar to the find() method, but retrieves only the first document of the subset. To start working with a single user document, we'll have to add two new methods. Add the following lines of code at the end of your app/controllers/users.server.controller.js file:

```
exports.read = function(req, res) {
  res.json(req.user);
};

exports.userByID = function(req, res, next, id) {
  User.findOne({
    _id: id
  }, function(err, user) {
    if (err) {
      return next(err);
    } else {
      req.user = user;
      next();
    }
  });
};
```

The read() method is simple to understand; it is just responding with a JSON representation of the req.user object, but what is creating the req.user object? Well, the userById() method is the one responsible for populating the req.user object. You will use the userById() method as a middleware to deal with the manipulation of single documents when performing read, delete, and update operations. To do so, you will have to modify your app/routes/users.server.routes.js file to look like the following lines of code:

```
var users = require('../../app/controllers/users.server.controller');

module.exports = function(app) {
  app.route('/users')
     .post(users.create)
     .get(users.list);

  app.route('/users/:userId')
     .get(users.read);

  app.param('userId', users.userByID);
};
```

Notice how you added the `users.read()` method with a request path containing `userId`. In Express, adding a colon before a substring in a route definition means that this substring will be handled as a request parameter. To handle the population of the `req.user` object, you use the `app.param()` method that defines a middleware to be executed before any other middleware that uses that parameter. Here, the `users.userById()` method will be executed before any other middleware registered with the `userId` parameter, which in this case is the `users.read()` middleware. This design pattern is useful when building a RESTful API, where you often add request parameters to the routing string.

To test it out, run your application using the following command:

```
$ node server
```

Then, navigate to `http://localhost:3000/users` in your browser, grab one of your users' `_id` values, and navigate to `http://localhost:3000/users/[id]`, replacing the `[id]` part with the user's `_id` value.

Updating an existing user document

The Mongoose model has several available methods to update an existing document. Among those are the `update()`, `findOneAndUpdate()`, and `findByIdAndUpdate()` methods. Each of the methods serves a different level of abstraction, easing the update operation when possible. In our case, and since we already use the `userById()` middleware, the easiest way to update an existing document would be to use the `findByIdAndUpdate()` method. To do so, go back to your `app/controllers/users.server.controller.js` file, and add a new `update()` method:

```
exports.update = function(req, res, next) {
  User.findByIdAndUpdate(req.user.id, req.body, function(err, user) {
    if (err) {
      return next(err);
    } else {
      res.json(user);
    }
  });
};
```

Notice how you used the user's `id` field to find and update the correct document. The next thing you should do is wire your new `update()` method in your users' routing module. Go back to your `app/routes/users.server.routes.js` file and change it to look like the following code snippet:

```
var users = require('../../app/controllers/users.server.controller');

module.exports = function(app) {
  app.route('/users')
      .post(users.create)
      .get(users.list);

  app.route('/users/:userId')
      .get(users.read)
      .put(users.update);

  app.param('userId', users.userByID);
};
```

Notice how you used the route you previously created and just chained the `update()` method using the route's `put()` method. To test your `update()` method, run your application using the following command:

```
$ node server
```

Then, use your favorite REST tool to issue a PUT request, or use `curl` and execute this command, replacing the `[id]` part with a real document's `_id` property:

```
$ curl -X PUT -H "Content-Type: application/json" -d '{"lastName":
"Updated"}' localhost:3000/users/[id]
```

Deleting an existing user document

The Mongoose model has several available methods to remove an existing document. Among those are the `remove()`, `findOneAndRemove()`, and `findByIdAndRemove()` methods. In our case, and since we already use the `userById()` middleware, the easiest way to remove an existing document would be to simply use the `remove()` method. To do so, go back to your `app/controllers/users.server.controller.js` file, and add the following `delete()` method:

```
exports.delete = function(req, res, next) {
  req.user.remove(function(err) {
    if (err) {
      return next(err);
```

```
      } else {
        res.json(req.user);
      }
    })
  };
```

Notice how you use the `user` object to remove the correct document. The next thing you should do is use your new `delete()` method in your users' routing file. Go to your `app/routes/users.server.routes.js` file and change it to look like the following code snippet:

```
var users = require('../../app/controllers/users.server.controller');

module.exports = function(app) {
  app.route('/users')
    .post(users.create)
    .get(users.list);

  app.route('/users/:userId')
    .get(users.read)
    .put(users.update)
    .delete(users.delete);

  app.param('userId', users.userByID);
};
```

Notice how you used the route you previously created and just chained the `delete()` method using the route's `delete()` method. To test your `delete` method, run your application using the following command:

$ node server

Then, use your favorite REST tool to issue a DELETE request, or use `curl` and execute the following command, replacing the `[id]` part with a real document's _id property:

$ curl -X DELETE localhost:3000/users/[id]

This completes the implementation of the four CRUD operations, giving you a brief understanding of the Mongoose model capabilities. However, these methods are just examples of the vast features included with Mongoose. In the next section, you'll learn how to define default values, power your schema fields with modifiers, and validate your data.

Extending your Mongoose schema

Performing data manipulations is great, but to develop complex applications, you will need your ODM module to do more. Luckily, Mongoose supports various other features that help you safely model your documents and keep your data consistent.

Defining default values

Defining default field values is a common feature for data modeling frameworks. You can add this functionality directly in your application's logic layer, but that would be messy and is generally a bad practice. Mongoose offers to define default values at the schema level, helping you organize your code better and guarantee your documents' validity.

Let's say you want to add a `created` date field to your `UserSchema`. The `created` date field should be initialized at creation time and save the time the user document was initially created; a perfect example of when you can utilize a default value. To do so, you'll have to change your `UserSchema`, so go back to your `app/models/user.server.model.js` file and change it to look like the following code snippet:

```
var mongoose = require('mongoose'),
    Schema = mongoose.Schema;

var UserSchema = new Schema({
  firstName: String,
  lastName: String,
  email: String,
  username: String,
  password: String,
  created: {
    type: Date,
    default: Date.now
  }
});

mongoose.model('User', UserSchema);
```

Notice how the `created` field is added and its default value defined. From now on, every new user document will be created with a default creation date that represents the moment the document was created. You should also notice that every user document created prior to this schema change will be assigned a `created` field representing the moment you queried for it, since these documents don't have the `created` field initialized.

To test your new changes, run your application using the following command:

```
$ node server
```

Then, use your favorite REST tool to issue a POST request or use cURL, and execute the following command:

```
$ curl -X POST -H "Content-Type: application/json" -d
'{"firstName":"First", "lastName":"Last","email":"user@example.com","user
name":"username","password":"password"}' localhost:3000/users
```

A new user document will be created with a default created field initialized at the moment of creation.

Using schema modifiers

Sometimes, you may want to perform a manipulation over schema fields before saving them or presenting them to the client. For this purpose, Mongoose uses a feature called modifiers. A modifier can either change the field's value before saving the document or represent it differently at query time.

Predefined modifiers

The simplest modifiers are the predefined ones included with Mongoose. For instance, string-type fields can have a trim modifier to remove whitespaces, an uppercase modifier to uppercase the field value, and so on. To understand how predefined modifiers work, let's make sure the username of your users is clear from a leading and trailing whitespace. To do so, all you have to do is change your app/models/user.server.model.js file to look like the following code snippet:

```
var mongoose = require('mongoose'),
    Schema = mongoose.Schema;

var UserSchema = new Schema({
  firstName: String,
  lastName: String,
  email: String,
  username: {
    type: String,
    trim: true
  },
  password: String,
  created: {
```

```
        type: Date,
        default: Date.now
    }
});
```

```
mongoose.model('User', UserSchema);
```

Notice the `trim` property added to the `username` field. This will make sure your username data will be kept trimmed.

Custom setter modifiers

Predefined modifiers are great, but you can also define your own custom setter modifiers to handle data manipulation before saving the document. To understand this better, let's add a new website field to your `User` model. The `website` field should begin with `'http://'` or `'https://'`, but instead of forcing your customer to add this in the UI, you can simply write a custom modifier that validates the existence of these prefixes and adds them when necessary. To add your custom modifier, you will need to create the new `website` field with a `set` property as follows:

```
var UserSchema = new Schema({
  ...
  website: {
    type: String,
    set: function(url) {
      if (!url) {
        return url;
      } else {
        if (url.indexOf('http://') !== 0    && url.indexOf('https://')
!== 0) {
          url = 'http://' + url;
        }

        return url;
      }
    }
  },
  ...
});
```

Now, every user created will have a properly formed website URL that is modified at creation time. But what if you already have a big collection of user documents? You can of course migrate your existing data, but when dealing with big datasets, it would have a serious performance impact, so you can simply use getter modifiers.

Custom getter modifiers

Getter modifiers are used to modify existing data before outputting the documents to next layer. For instance, in our previous example, a getter modifier would sometimes be better to change already existing user documents by modifying their `website` field at query time instead of going over your MongoDB collection and updating each document. To do so, all you have to do is change your `UserSchema` like the following code snippet:

```
var UserSchema = new Schema({
  ...
  website: {
    type: String,
    get: function(url) {
      if (!url) {
        return url;
      } else {
if (url.indexOf('http://') !== 0   && url.indexOf('https://') !== 0) {
          url = 'http://' + url;
        }

        return url;
      }
    }
  },
  ...
});

UserSchema.set('toJSON', { getters: true });
```

You simply changed the setter modifier to a getter modifier by changing the `set` property to `get`. But the important thing to notice here is how you configured your schema using `UserSchema.set()`. This will force Mongoose to include getters when converting the MongoDB document to a JSON representation and will allow the output of documents using `res.json()` to include the getter's behavior. If you didn't include this, you would have your document's JSON representation ignoring the getter modifiers.

 Modifiers are powerful and can save you a lot of time, but they should be used with caution to prevent unpredicted application behavior. It is recommended you visit `http://mongoosejs.com/docs/api.html` for more information.

Adding virtual attributes

Sometimes you may want to have dynamically calculated document properties, which are not really presented in the document. These properties are called virtual attributes and can be used to address several common requirements. For instance, let's say you want to add a new `fullName` field, which will represent the concatenation of the user's first and last names. To do so, you will have to use the `virtual()` schema method, so a modified `UserSchema` would include the following code snippet:

```
UserSchema.virtual('fullName').get(function() {
  return this.firstName + ' ' + this.lastName;
});

UserSchema.set('toJSON', { getters: true, virtuals: true });
```

In the preceding code example, you added a virtual attribute named `fullName` to your `UserSchema`, added a `getter` method to that virtual attribute, and then configured your schema to include virtual attributes when converting the MongoDB document to a JSON representation.

But virtual attributes can also have setters to help you save your documents as you prefer instead of just adding more field attributes. In this case, let's say you wanted to break an input's `fullName` field into your first and last name fields. To do so, a modified virtual declaration would look like the following code snippet:

```
UserSchema.virtual('fullName').get(function() {
  return this.firstName + ' ' + this.lastName;
}).set(function(fullName) {
  var splitName = fullName.split(' ');
  this.firstName = splitName[0] || '';
  this.lastName = splitName[1] || '';
});
```

Virtual attributes are a great feature of Mongoose, allowing you to modify document representation as they're being moved through your application's layers without getting persisted to MongoDB.

Optimizing queries using indexes

As we previously discussed, MongoDB supports various types of indexes to optimize query execution. Mongoose also supports the indexing functionality and even allows you to define secondary indexes.

The basic example of indexing is the `unique` index, which validates the uniqueness of a document field across a collection. In our example, it is common to keep usernames unique, so in order to tell that to MongoDB, you will need to modify your `UserSchema` definition to include the following code snippet:

```
var UserSchema = new Schema({
    ...
    username: {
        type: String,
        trim: true,
        unique: true
    },
    ...
});
```

This will tell MongoDB to create a unique index for the username field of the `users` collections. Mongoose also supports the creation of secondary indexes using the `index` property. So, if you know that your application will use a lot of queries involving the `email` field, you could optimize these queries by creating an e-mail secondary index as follows:

```
var UserSchema = new Schema({
    ...
    email: {
        type: String,
        index: true
    },
    ...
});
```

Indexing is a wonderful feature of MongoDB, but you should keep in mind that it might cause you some trouble. For example, if you define a `unique` index on a collection where data is already stored, you might encounter some errors while running your application until you fix the issues with your collection data. Another common issue is Mongoose's automatic creation of indexes when the application starts, a feature that could cause major performance issues when running in a production environment.

Defining custom model methods

Mongoose models are pretty packed with both static and instance predefined methods, some of which you already used before. However, Mongoose also lets you define your own custom methods to empower your models, giving you a modular tool to separate your application logic properly. Let's go over the proper way of defining these methods.

Defining custom static methods

Model static methods give you the liberty to perform model-level operations, such as adding extra `find` methods. For instance, let's say you want to search users by their username. You could of course define this method in your controller, but that wouldn't be the right place for it. What you're looking for is a static model method. To add a static method, you will need to declare it as a member of your schema's `statics` property. In our case, adding a `findOneByUsername()` method would look like the following code snippet:

```
UserSchema.statics.findOneByUsername = function (username,
  callback) {
  this.findOne({ username: new RegExp(username, 'i') }, callback);
};
```

This method is using the model's `findOne()` method to retrieve a user's document that has a certain username. Using the new `findOneByUsername()` method would be similar to using a standard static method by calling it directly from the `User` model as follows:

```
User.findOneByUsername('username', function(err, user){
  ...
});
```

You can of course come up with many other static methods; you'll probably need them when developing your application, so don't be afraid to add them.

Defining custom instance methods

Static methods are great, but what if you need methods that perform instance operations? Well, Mongoose offers support for those too, helping you slim down your code base and properly reuse your application code. To add an instance method, you will need to declare it as a member of your schema's `methods` property. Let's say you want to validate your user's password with an `authenticate()` method. Adding this method would then be similar to the following code snippet:

```
UserSchema.methods.authenticate = function(password) {
  return this.password === password;
};
```

This will allow you to call the `authenticate()` method from any `User` model instance as follows:

```
user.authenticate('password');
```

As you can see, defining custom model methods is a great way to keep your project properly organized while making reuse of common code. In the upcoming chapters, you'll discover how both the instance and static methods can be very useful.

Model validation

One of the major issues when dealing with data marshaling is validation. When users input information to your application, you'll often have to validate that information before passing it on to MongoDB. While you can validate your data at the logic layer of your application, it is more useful to do it at the model level. Luckily, Mongoose supports both simple predefined validators and more complex custom validators. Validators are defined at the field level of a document and are executed when the document is being saved. If a validation error occurs, the save operation is aborted and the error is passed to the callback.

Predefined validators

Mongoose supports different types of predefined validators, most of which are
type-specific. The basic validation of any application is of course the existence
of value. To validate field existence in Mongoose, you'll need to use the `required`
property in the field you want to validate. Let's say you want to verify the existence
of a `username` field before you save the user document. To do so, you'll need to
make the following changes to your `UserSchema`:

```
var UserSchema = new Schema({
  ...
  username: {
    type: String,
    trim: true,
    unique: true,
    required: true
  },
  ...
});
```

This will validate the existence of the `username` field when saving the document,
thus preventing the saving of any document that doesn't contain that field.

Besides the `required` validator, Mongoose also includes type-based predefined
validators, such as the `enum` and `match` validators for strings. For instance, to validate
your `email` field, you would need to change your `UserSchema` as follows:

```
var UserSchema = new Schema({
  ...
  email: {
    type: String,
    index: true,
    match: /.+\@.+\..+/
  },
  ...
});
```

The usage of a `match` validator here will make sure the `email` field value matches
the given regex expression, thus preventing the saving of any document where the
e-mail doesn't conform to the right pattern.

Another example is the `enum` validator, which can help you define a set of strings that are available for that field value. Let's say you add a `role` field. A possible validation would look like this:

```
var UserSchema = new Schema({
  ...
  role: {
    type: String,
    enum: ['Admin', 'Owner', 'User']
  },
  ...
});
```

The preceding condition will allow the insertion of only these three possible strings, and thus prevent you from saving the document.

> To learn more about predefined validators, it is recommended you to visit `http://mongoosejs.com/docs/validation.html` for more information.

Custom validators

Other than predefined validators, Mongoose also enables you to define your own custom validators. Defining a custom validator is done using the `validate` property. The `validate` property value should be an array consisting of a validation function and an error message. Let's say you want to validate the length of your user's password. To do so, you would have to make these changes in your `UserSchema`:

```
var UserSchema = new Schema({
  ...
  password: {
    type: String,
    validate: [
      function(password) {
        return password.length >= 6;
      },
      'Password should be longer'
    ]
  },
  ...
});
```

This validator will make sure your user's password is at least six characters long, or else it will prevent the saving of documents and pass the error message you defined to the callback.

Mongoose validation is a powerful feature that allows you to control your model and supply proper error handling, which you can use to help your users understand what went wrong. In the upcoming chapters, you'll see how you can use Mongoose validators to handle the user's input and prevent common data inconsistencies.

Using Mongoose middleware

Mongoose middleware are functions that can intercept the process of the `init`, `validate`, `save`, and `remove` instance methods. Middleware are executed at the instance level and have two types: `pre` middleware and `post` middleware.

Using pre middleware

`Pre` middleware gets executed before the operation happens. For instance, a `pre-save` middleware will get executed before the saving of the document. This functionality makes `pre` middleware perfect for more complex validations and default values assignment.

A `pre` middleware is defined using the `pre()` method of the schema object, so validating your model using a `pre` middleware will look like the following code snippet:

```
UserSchema.pre('save', function(next) {
  if (...) {
    next()
  } else {
    next(new Error('An Error Occured'));
  }
});
```

Using post middleware

A `post` middleware gets executed after the operation happens. For instance, a `post-save` middleware will get executed after saving the document. This functionality makes `post` middleware perfect to log your application logic.

A post middleware is defined using the post() method of the schema object, so logging your model's save() method using a post middleware will look something like the following code snippet:

```
UserSchema.post('save', function(next) {
  if(this.isNew) {
    console.log('A new user was created.');
  } else {
    console.log('A user updated is details.');
  }
});
```

Notice how you can use the model isNew property to understand whether a model instance was created or updated.

Mongoose middleware are great for performing various operations, including logging, validation, and performing various data consistency manipulations. But don't worry if you feel overwhelmed right now because later in this book, you'll understand them better.

 To learn more about middleware, it is recommended that you visit http://mongoosejs.com/docs/middleware.html.

Using Mongoose DBRef

Although MongoDB doesn't support joins, it does support the reference of a document to another document using a convention named DBRef. Mongoose includes support for DBRefs using the ObjectID schema type and the use of the ref property. Mongoose also supports the population of the parent document with the child document when querying the database.

To understand this better, let's say you create another schema for blog posts called PostSchema. Because a user authors a blog post, PostSchema will contain an author field that will be populated by a User model instance. So, a PostSchema will have to look like the following code snippet:

```
var PostSchema = new Schema({
  title: {
    type: String,
    required: true
  },
```

```
    content: {
      type: String,
      required: true
    },
    author: {
      type: Schema.ObjectId,
      ref: 'User'
    }
});
```

```
    mongoose.model('Post', PostSchema);
```

Notice the `ref` property telling Mongoose that the `author` field will use the `User` model to populate the value.

Using this new schema is a simple task. To create a new blog post, you will need to retrieve or create an instance of the `User` model, create an instance of the `Post` model, and then assign the `post author` property with the `user` instance. An example of this should be as follows:

```
    var user = new User();
    user.save();

    var post = new Post();
    post.author = user;
    post.save();
```

Mongoose will create a DBRef in the MongoDB post document and will later use it to retrieve the referenced document.

Since the DBRef is only an `ObjectID` reference to a real document, Mongoose will have to populate the `post` instance with the `user` instance. To do so, you'll have to tell Mongoose to populate the `post` object using the `populate()` method when retrieving the document. For instance, a `find()` method that populates the `author` property will look like the following code snippet:

```
    Post.find().populate('author').exec(function(err, posts) {
      ...
    });
```

Mongoose will then retrieve all the documents in the `posts` collection and populate their `author` attribute.

DBRefs are an awesome feature of MongoDB. Mongoose's support for this feature enables you to calmly rely on object references to keep your model organized. Later in this book, we'll use DBRef to support our application logic.

 To find out more about DBRefs, it is recommended that you visit `http://mongoosejs.com/docs/populate.html`.

Summary

In this chapter, you met the robust Mongoose model. You connected to your MongoDB instance and created your first Mongoose schema and model. You also learned how to validate your data and modify it using Schema modifiers and Mongoose middleware. You were introduced to virtual attributes and modifiers, and you learned to use them to change the representation of your documents. You also discovered the MongoDB DBRef feature and the way Mongoose utilizes that feature. In the next chapter, we'll go over the Passport authentication module, which will use your User model to address user authentication.

6
Managing User Authentication Using Passport

Passport is a robust Node.js authentication middleware that helps you to authenticate requests sent to your Express application. Passport uses strategies to utilize both local authentication and OAuth authentication providers, such as Facebook, Twitter, and Google. Using Passport strategies, you'll be able to seamlessly offer different authentication options to your users while maintaining a unified User model. In this chapter, you'll go through the following basic features of Passport:

- Understanding Passport strategies
- Integrating Passport into your users' MVC architecture
- Using Passport's local strategy to authenticate users
- Utilizing Passport OAuth strategies
- Offering authentication through social OAuth providers

Introducing Passport

Authentication is a vital part of most web applications. Handling user registration and sign-in is an important feature, which can sometimes present a development overhead. Express, with its lean approach, lacks this feature, so, as is usual with node, an external module is needed. Passport is a Node.js module that uses the middleware design pattern to authenticate requests. It allows developers to offer various authentication methods using a mechanism called strategies, which allows you to implement a complex authentication layer while keeping your code clean and simple. Just as with any other Node.js module, before you can start using it in your application, you will first need to install it. The examples in this chapter will continue directly from those in previous chapters. So for this chapter, copy the final example from *Chapter 5, Introduction to Mongoose*, and let's start from there.

Installing Passport

Passport uses different modules, each representing a different authentication strategy, but all of which depend on the base Passport module. To install the Passport base module in your application's modules folders, change your `package.json` file as follows:

```
{
   "name": "MEAN",
   "version": "0.0.6",
   "dependencies": {
      "express": "~4.8.8",
      "morgan": "~1.3.0",
      "compression": "~1.0.11",
      "body-parser": "~1.8.0",
      "method-override": "~2.2.0",
      "express-session": "~1.7.6",
      "ejs": "~1.0.0",
      "mongoose": "~3.8.15",
      "passport": "~0.2.1"
   }
}
```

Before you continue developing your application, make sure you install the new Passport dependency. To do so, go to your application's folder, and issue the following command in your command-line tool:

```
$ npm install
```

This will install the specified version of Passport in your `node_modules` folder. Once the installation process has successfully finished, you will need to configure your application to load the Passport module.

Configuring Passport

To configure Passport, you will need to set it up in a few steps. To create the Passport configuration file, go to the `config` folder and create a new file named `passport.js`. Leave it empty for now; we will return to it in a bit. Next, you'll need to require the file you just created, so change your `server.js` file, as follows:

```
process.env.NODE_ENV = process.env.NODE_ENV || 'development';

var mongoose = require('./config/mongoose'),
    express = require('./config/express'),
    passport = require('./config/passport');

var db = mongoose();
var app = express();
var passport = passport();

app.listen(3000);

module.exports = app;

console.log('Server running at http://localhost:3000/');
```

Next, you'll need to register the Passport middleware in your Express application. To do so, change your `config/express.js` file, as follows:

```
var config = require('./config'),
    express = require('express'),
    morgan = require('morgan'),
    compress = require('compression'),
    bodyParser = require('body-parser'),
    methodOverride = require('method-override'),
    session = require('express-session'),
    passport = require('passport');

module.exports = function() {
  var app = express();

  if (process.env.NODE_ENV === 'development') {
    app.use(morgan('dev'));
```

```
    } else if (process.env.NODE_ENV === 'production') {
      app.use(compress());
    }

    app.use(bodyParser.urlencoded({
      extended: true
    }));
    app.use(bodyParser.json());
    app.use(methodOverride());

    app.use(session({
      saveUninitialized: true,
      resave: true,
      secret: config.sessionSecret
    }));
    app.set('views', './app/views');
    app.set('view engine', 'ejs');

    app.use(passport.initialize());
    app.use(passport.session());

    require('../app/routes/index.server.routes.js')(app);
    require('../app/routes/users.server.routes.js')(app);

    app.use(express.static('./public'));

    return app;
  };
```

Let's go over the code you just added. First, you required the Passport module, and then you registered two middleware: the `passport.initialize()` middleware, which is responsible for bootstrapping the Passport module and the `passport.session()` middleware, which is using the Express session to keep track of your user's session.

Passport is now installed and configured, but to start using it, you will have to install at least one authentication strategy. We'll begin with the local strategy, which provides a simple username/password authentication layer; but first, let's discuss how Passport strategies work.

Understanding Passport strategies

To offer its various authentication options, Passport uses separate modules that implement different authentication strategies. Each module provides a different authentication method, such as username/password authentication and OAuth authentication. So, in order to offer Passport-supported authentication, you'll need to install and configure the strategies modules that you'd like to use. Let's begin with the local authentication strategy.

Using Passport's local strategy

Passport's local strategy is a Node.js module that allows you to implement a username/password authentication mechanism. You'll need to install it like any other module and configure it to use your `User` Mongoose model. Let's begin by installing the local strategy module.

Installing Passport's local strategy module

To install Passport's local strategy module, you'll need to change your `package.json` file, as follows:

```json
{
  "name": "MEAN",
  "version": "0.0.6",
  "dependencies": {
    "express": "~4.8.8",
    "morgan": "~1.3.0",
    "compression": "~1.0.11",
    "body-parser": "~1.8.0",
    "method-override": "~2.2.0",
    "express-session": "~1.7.6",
    "ejs": "~1.0.0",
    "mongoose": "~3.8.15",
    "passport": "~0.2.1",
    "passport-local": "~1.0.0"
  }
}
```

Then, go to your application's root folder, and issue the following command in your command-line tool:

```
$ npm install
```

This will install the specified version of the local strategy module in your node_ modules folder. When the installation process has successfully finished, you'll need to configure Passport to use the local strategy.

Configuring Passport's local strategy

Each authentication strategy you'll use is basically a node module that lets you define how that strategy will be used. In order to maintain a clear separation of logic, each strategy should be configured in its own separated file. In your config folder, create a new folder named strategies. Inside this new folder, create a file named local. js that contains the following code snippet:

```
var passport = require('passport'),
    LocalStrategy = require('passport-local').Strategy,
    User = require('mongoose').model('User');

module.exports = function() {
  passport.use(new LocalStrategy(function(username, password, done) {
    User.findOne({
      username: username
    }, function(err, user) {
      if (err) {
        return done(err);
      }

      if (!user) {
        return done(null, false, {
          message: 'Unknown user'
        });
      }
      if (!user.authenticate(password)) {
        return done(null, false, {
          message: 'Invalid password'
        });
      }

      return done(null, user);
    });
  }));
};
```

The preceding code begins by requiring the Passport module, the local strategy module's strategy object, and your User Mongoose model. Then, you register the strategy using the passport.use() method that uses an instance of the LocalStrategy object. Notice how the LocalStrategy constructor takes a callback function as an argument. It will later call this callback when trying to authenticate a user.

The callback function accepts three arguments—username, password, and a done callback—which will be called when the authentication process is over. Inside the callback function, you will use the User Mongoose model to find a user with that username and try to authenticate it. In the event of an error, you will pass the error object to the done callback. When the user is authenticated, you will call the done callback with the user Mongoose object.

Remember the empty config/passport.js file? Well, now that you have your local strategy ready, you can go back and use it to configure the local authentication. To do so, go back to your config/passport.js file and paste the following lines of code:

```
var passport = require('passport'),
    mongoose = require('mongoose');

module.exports = function() {
  var User = mongoose.model('User');

  passport.serializeUser(function(user, done) {
    done(null, user.id);
  });

  passport.deserializeUser(function(id, done) {
    User.findOne({
      _id: id
    }, '-password -salt', function(err, user) {
      done(err, user);
    });
  });

  require('./strategies/local.js')();
};
```

In the preceding code snippet, the `passport.serializeUser()` and `passport.deserializeUser()` methods are used to define how Passport will handle user serialization. When a user is authenticated, Passport will save its `_id` property to the session. Later on when the `user` object is needed, Passport will use the `_id` property to grab the `user` object from the database. Notice how we used the field options argument to make sure Mongoose doesn't fetch the user's `password` and `salt` properties. The second thing the preceding code does is including the local strategy configuration file. This way, your `server.js` file will load the Passport configuration file, which in turn will load its strategies configuration file. Next, you'll need to modify your `User` model to support Passport's authentication.

Adapting the User model

In the previous chapter, we started discussing the `User` model and created its basic structure. In order to use the `User` model in your MEAN application, you'll have to modify it to address a few authentication process requirements. These changes will include modifying `UserSchema`, adding a `pre` middleware, and adding some new instance methods. To do so, go to your `app/models/user.js` file, and change it as follows:

```
var mongoose = require('mongoose'),
    crypto = require('crypto'),
    Schema = mongoose.Schema;

var UserSchema = new Schema({
  firstName: String,
  lastName: String,
  email: {
    type: String,
    match: [/.+\@.+\..+/, "Please fill a valid e-mail address"]
  },
  username: {
    type: String,
    unique: true,
    required: 'Username is required',
    trim: true
  },
  password: {
    type: String,
    validate: [
    function(password) {
        return password && password.length > 6;
      }, 'Password should be longer'
    ]
```

```
    },
    salt: {
      type: String
    },
    provider: {
      type: String,
      required: 'Provider is required'
    },
    providerId: String,
    providerData: {},
    created: {
      type: Date,
      default: Date.now
    }
});

UserSchema.virtual('fullName').get(function() {
  return this.firstName + ' ' + this.lastName;
}).set(function(fullName) {
  var splitName = fullName.split(' ');
  this.firstName = splitName[0] || '';
  this.lastName = splitName[1] || '';
});

UserSchema.pre('save', function(next) {
  if (this.password) {
    this.salt = new
      Buffer(crypto.randomBytes(16).toString('base64'), 'base64');
    this.password = this.hashPassword(this.password);
  }

  next();
});

UserSchema.methods.hashPassword = function(password) {
  return crypto.pbkdf2Sync(password, this.salt, 10000,
    64).toString('base64');
};

UserSchema.methods.authenticate = function(password) {
  return this.password === this.hashPassword(password);
};
```

```
UserSchema.statics.findUniqueUsername = function(username, suffix,
  callback) {
  var _this = this;
  var possibleUsername = username + (suffix || '');

  _this.findOne({
    username: possibleUsername
  }, function(err, user) {
    if (!err) {
      if (!user) {
        callback(possibleUsername);
      } else {
        return _this.findUniqueUsername(username, (suffix || 0) +
          1, callback);
      }
    } else {
      callback(null);
    }
  });
};

UserSchema.set('toJSON', {
  getters: true,
  virtuals: true
});

mongoose.model('User', UserSchema);
```

Let's go over these changes. First, you added four fields to your UserSchema object:
a salt property, which you'll use to hash your password; a provider property,
which will indicate the strategy used to register the user; a providerId property,
which will indicate the user identifier for the authentication strategy; and a
providerData property, which you'll later use to store the user object retrieved
from OAuth providers.

Next, you created a pre-save middleware to handle the hashing of your users'
passwords. It is widely known that storing a clear text version of your users'
passwords is a very bad practice that can result in the leakage of your users'
passwords. To handle this issue, your pre-save middleware performs two
important steps: first, it creates an autogenerated pseudo-random hashing salt,
and then it replaces the current user password with a hashed password using the
hashPassword() instance method.

You also added two instance methods: a `hashPassword()` instance method, which is used to hash a password string by utilizing Node.js' `crypto` module, and an `authenticate()` instance method, which accepts a string argument, hashes it, and compares it to the current user's hashed password. Finally, you added the `findUniqueUsername()` static method, which is used to find an available unique username for new users. You'll use this method later in this chapter when you deal with OAuth authentication.

That completes the modifications in your `User` model, but there are a few other things to care of before you can test your application's authentication layer.

Creating the authentication views

Just as with any web application, you will need to have signup and sign-in pages in order to handle user authentication. We'll create those views using the EJS template engine, so in your `app/views` folder, create a new file named `signup.ejs`. In your newly created file, paste the following code snippet:

```
<!DOCTYPE html>
<html>
<head>
  <title>
    <%=title %>
  </title>
</head>
<body>
  <% for(var i in messages) { %>
    <div class="flash"><%= messages[i] %></div>
  <% } %>
  <form action="/signup" method="post">
    <div>
      <label>First Name:</label>
      <input type="text" name="firstName" />
    </div>
    <div>
      <label>Last Name:</label>
      <input type="text" name="lastName" />
    </div>
    <div>
      <label>Email:</label>
      <input type="text" name="email" />
    </div>
    <div>
```

```
      <label>Username:</label>
      <input type="text" name="username" />
    </div>
    <div>
      <label>Password:</label>
      <input type="password" name="password" />
    </div>
    <div>
      <input type="submit" value="Sign up" />
    </div>
  </form>
</body>
</html>
```

The signup.ejs view simply contains an HTML form, an EJS tag, which renders the title variable, and an EJS loop, which renders the messages list variable. Go back to your app/views folder, and create another file named signin.ejs. Inside this file, paste the following code snippet:

```
<!DOCTYPE html>
<html>
<head>
  <title>
    <%=title %>
  </title>
</head>
<body>
  <% for(var i in messages) { %>
    <div class="flash"><%= messages[i] %></div>
  <% } %>
  <form action="/signin" method="post">
    <div>
      <label>Username:</label>
      <input type="text" name="username" />
    </div>
    <div>
      <label>Password:</label>
      <input type="password" name="password" />
    </div>
    <div>
      <input type="submit" value="Sign In" />
    </div>
  </form>
</body>
</html>
```

As you can notice, the `signin.ejs` view is even simpler and also contains an HTML form, an EJS tag, which renders the `title` variable, and an EJS loop, which renders the `messages` list variable. Now that you have your model and views set, it's time to connect them using your `Users` controller.

Modifying the user controller

To alter the `Users` controller, go to your `app/controllers/users.server. controller.js` file, and change its content, as follows:

```
var User = require('mongoose').model('User'),
  passport = require('passport');

var getErrorMessage = function(err) {
  var message = '';

  if (err.code) {
    switch (err.code) {
      case 11000:
      case 11001:
        message = 'Username already exists';
        break;
      default:
        message = 'Something went wrong';
    }
  } else {
    for (var errName in err.errors) {
      if (err.errors[errName].message) message = err.errors[errName].
message;
    }
  }

  return message;
};

exports.renderSignin = function(req, res, next) {
  if (!req.user) {
    res.render('signin', {
      title: 'Sign-in Form',
      messages: req.flash('error') || req.flash('info')
    });
  } else {
    return res.redirect('/');
```

```
    }
  };
  exports.renderSignup = function(req, res, next) {
    if (!req.user) {
      res.render('signup', {
        title: 'Sign-up Form',
        messages: req.flash('error')
      });
    } else {
      return res.redirect('/');
    }
  };

  exports.signup = function(req, res, next) {
    if (!req.user) {
      var user = new User(req.body);
      var message = null;

      user.provider = 'local';

      user.save(function(err) {
        if (err) {
          var message = getErrorMessage(err);

          req.flash('error', message);
          return res.redirect('/signup');
        }
        req.login(user, function(err) {
          if (err) return next(err);
          return res.redirect('/');
        });
      });
    } else {
      return res.redirect('/');
    }
  };

  exports.signout = function(req, res) {
    req.logout();
    res.redirect('/');
  };
```

The `getErrorMessage()` method is a private method that returns a unified error message from a Mongoose error object. It is worth noticing that there are two possible errors here: a MongoDB indexing error handled using the error code and a Mongoose validation error handled using the `err.errors` object.

The next two controller methods are quite simple and will be used to render the sign-in and signup pages. The `signout()` method is also simple and uses the `req.logout()` method, which is provided by the Passport module to invalidate the authenticated session.

The `signup()` method uses your `User` model to create new users. As you can see, it first creates a `user` object from the HTTP request body. Then, try saving it to MongoDB. If an error occurs, the `signup()` method will use the `getErrorMessage()` method to provide the user with an appropriate error message. If the user creation was successful, the user session will be created using the `req.login()` method. The `req.login()` method is exposed by the Passport module and is used to establish a successful login session. After the login operation is completed, a `user` object will be signed to the `req.user` object.

 The `req.login()` will be called automatically while using the `passport.authenticate()` method, so a manual call for `req.login()` is primarily used when registering new users.

In the preceding code though, a module you're not yet familiar with is used. When an authentication process is failing, it is common to redirect the request back to the signup or sign-in pages. This is done here when an error occurs, but how can your user tell what exactly went wrong? The problem is that when redirecting to another page, you cannot pass variables to that page. The solution would be to use some sort of mechanism to pass temporary messages between requests. Fortunately, that mechanism already exists in the form of a node module named `Connect-Flash`.

Displaying flash error messages

The `Connect-Flash` module is a node module that allows you to store temporary messages in an area of the session object called `flash`. Messages stored on the `flash` object will be cleared once they are presented to the user. This architecture makes the `Connect-Flash` module perfect to transfer messages before redirecting the request to another page.

Installing the Connect-Flash module

To install the Connect-Flash module in your application's modules folders, you'll need to change your package.json file, as follows:

```
{
  "name": "MEAN",
  "version": "0.0.6",
  "dependencies": {
    "express": "~4.8.8",
    "morgan": "~1.3.0",
    "compression": "~1.0.11",
    "body-parser": "~1.8.0",
    "method-override": "~2.2.0",
    "express-session": "~1.7.6",
    "ejs": "~1.0.0",
    "connect-flash": "~0.1.1",
    "mongoose": "~3.8.15",
    "passport": "~0.2.1",
    "passport-local": "~1.0.0"
  }
}
```

As usual, before you can continue developing your application, you will need to install your new dependency. Go to your application's folder, and issue the following command in your command-line tool:

```
$ npm install
```

This will install the specified version of the Connect-Flash module in your node_modules folder. When the installation process is successfully finished, your next step would be to configure your Express application to use the Connect-Flash module.

Configuring Connect-Flash module

To configure your Express application to use the new Connect-Flash module, you'll have to require the new module in your Express configuration file and use the app.use() method to register it with your Express application. To do so, make the following changes in your config/express.js file:

```
var config = require('./config'),
    express = require('express'),
    morgan = require('morgan'),
    compress = require('compression'),
```

```
    bodyParser = require('body-parser'),
    methodOverride = require('method-override'),
    session = require('express-session'),
    flash = require('connect-flash'),
    passport = require('passport');

module.exports = function() {
  var app = express();

  if (process.env.NODE_ENV === 'development') {
    app.use(morgan('dev'));
  } else if (process.env.NODE_ENV === 'production') {
    app.use(compress());
  }

  app.use(bodyParser.urlencoded({
    extended: true
  }));
  app.use(bodyParser.json());
  app.use(methodOverride());

  app.use(session({
    saveUninitialized: true,
    resave: true,
    secret: config.sessionSecret
  }));

  app.set('views', './app/views');
  app.set('view engine', 'ejs');

  app.use(flash());
  app.use(passport.initialize());
  app.use(passport.session());

  require('../app/routes/index.server.routes.js')(app);
  require('../app/routes/users.server.routes.js')(app);

  app.use(express.static('./public'));

  return app;
};
```

This will tell your Express application to use Connect-Flash and create the new flash area in the application session.

Using Connect-Flash module

Once installed, the Connect-Flash module exposes the req.flash() method, which allows you to create and retrieve flash messages. To understand it better, let's observe the changes you've made to your Users controller. First, let's take a look at the renderSignup() and renderSignin() methods, which are responsible for rendering the sign-in and signup pages:

```
exports.renderSignin = function(req, res, next) {
  if (!req.user) {
    res.render('signin', {
      title: 'Sign-in Form',
      messages: req.flash('error') || req.flash('info')
    });
  } else {
    return res.redirect('/');
  }
};

exports.renderSignup = function(req, res, next) {
  if (!req.user) {
    res.render('signup', {
      title: 'Sign-up Form',
      messages: req.flash('error')
    });
  } else {
    return res.redirect('/');
  }
};
```

As you can see, the res.render() method is executed with the title and messages variables. The messages variable uses req.flash() to read the messages written to the flash. Now if you'll go over the signup() method, you'll notice the following line of code:

```
req.flash('error', message);
```

This is how error messages are written to the flash, again using the req.flash() method. After you learned how to use the Connect-Flash module, you might have noticed that we're lacking a signin() method. This is because Passport provides you with an authentication method, which you can use directly in your routing definition. To wrap up, let's proceed to the last part that needs to be modified: the Users routing definition file.

Wiring the user's routes

Once you have your model, controller, and views configured, all that is left to do is define the user's routes. To do so, make the following changes in your `app/routes/users.server.routes.js` file:

```
var users = require('../../app/controllers/users.server.controller'),
    passport = require('passport');

module.exports = function(app) {
  app.route('/signup')
      .get(users.renderSignup)
      .post(users.signup);

  app.route('/signin')
      .get(users.renderSignin)
      .post(passport.authenticate('local', {
        successRedirect: '/',
        failureRedirect: '/signin',
        failureFlash: true
      }));

  app.get('/signout', users.signout);
};
```

As you can notice, most of the routes definitions here are basically directing to methods from your user controller. The only different route definition is the one where you're handling any POST request made to the /signin path using the `passport.authenticate()` method.

When the `passport.authenticate()` method is executed, it will try to authenticate the user request using the strategy defined by its first argument. In this case, it will try to authenticate the request using the local strategy. The second parameter this method accepts is an `options` object, which contains three properties:

- `successRedirect`: This property tells Passport where to redirect the request once it successfully authenticated the user

- `failureRedirect`: This property tells Passport where to redirect the request once it failed to authenticate the user

- `failureFlash`: This property tells Passport whether or not to use flash messages

You've almost completed the basic authentication implementation. To test it out, make the following changes to the `app/controllers/index.server.controller.js` file:

```
exports.render = function(req, res) {
  res.render('index', {
    title: 'Hello World',
    userFullName: req.user ? req.user.fullName : ''
  });
};
```

This will pass the authenticated user's full name to your home page template. You will also have to make the following changes in your `app/views/index.ejs` file:

```
<!DOCTYPE html>
<html>
  <head>
      <title><%= title %></title>
  </head>
  <body>
    <% if ( userFullName ) { %>
      <h2>Hello <%=userFullName%> </h2>
      <a href="/signout">Sign out</a>
    <% } else { %>
      <a href="/signup">Signup</a>
      <a href="/signin">Signin</a>
    <% } %>
    <br>
      <img src="img/logo.png" alt="Logo">
  </body>
</html>
```

That's it! Everything is ready to test your new authentication layer. Go to your root application folder and use the node command-line tool to run your application:

```
$ node server
```

Test your application by visiting `http://localhost:3000/signin` and `http://localhost:3000/signup`. Try signing up, and then sign in and don't forget to go back to your home page to see how the user details are saved through the session.

Understanding Passport OAuth strategies

OAuth is an authentication protocol that allows users to register with your web application using an external provider, without the need to input their username and password. OAuth is mainly used by social platforms, such as Facebook, Twitter, and Google, to allow users to register with other websites using their social account.

 To learn more about how OAuth works, visit the OAuth protocol website at `http://oauth.net/`.

Setting up OAuth strategies

Passport support the basic OAuth strategy, which enables you to implement any OAuth-based authentication. However, it also supports a user authentication through major OAuth providers using wrapper strategies that help you avoid the need to implement a complex mechanism by yourself. In this section, we'll review the top OAuth providers and how to implement their Passport authentication strategy.

 Before you begin, you will have to contact the OAuth provider and create a developer application. This application will have both an OAuth client ID and an OAuth client secret, which will allow you to verify your application against the OAuth provider.

Handling OAuth user creation

The OAuth user creation should be a bit different than the local `signup()` method. Since users are signing up using their profile from other providers, the profile details are already present, which means you will need to validate them differently. To do so, go back to your `app/controllers/users.server.controller.js` file, and add the following module method:

```
exports.saveOAuthUserProfile = function(req, profile, done) {
  User.findOne({
    provider: profile.provider,
    providerId: profile.providerId
  }, function(err, user) {
    if (err) {
      return done(err);
    } else {
```

```
          if (!user) {
            var possibleUsername = profile.username ||
              ((profile.email) ? profile.email.split('@')[0] : '');

            User.findUniqueUsername(possibleUsername, null,
              function(availableUsername) {
              profile.username = availableUsername;

              user = new User(profile);

              user.save(function(err) {
                if (err) {
                  var message = _this.getErrorMessage(err);

                  req.flash('error', message);
                  return res.redirect('/signup');
                }

                return done(err, user);
              });
            });
          } else {
            return done(err, user);
          }
        }
      });
    };
```

This method accepts a user profile, and then looks for an existing user with these `providerId` and `provider` properties. If it finds the user, it calls the `done()` callback method with the user's MongoDB document. However, if it cannot find an existing user, it will find a unique username using the `User` model's `findUniqueUsername()` static method and save a new user instance. If an error occurs, the `saveOAuthUserProfile()` method will use the `req.flash()` and `getErrorMessage()` methods to report the error; otherwise, it will pass the user object to the `done()` callback method. Once you have figured out the `saveOAuthUserProfile()` method, it is time to implement the first OAuth authentication strategy.

Using Passport's Facebook strategy

Facebook is probably the world's largest OAuth provider. Many modern web applications offer their users the ability to register with the web application using their Facebook profile. Passport supports Facebook OAuth authentication using the `passport-facebook` module. Let's see how you can implement a Facebook-based authentication in a few simple steps.

Installing Passport's Facebook strategy

To install Passport's Facebook module in your application's modules folders, you'll need to change your `package.json` file as follows:

```
{
    "name": "MEAN",
    "version": "0.0.6",
    "dependencies": {
        "express": "~4.8.8",
        "morgan": "~1.3.0",
        "compression": "~1.0.11",
        "body-parser": "~1.8.0",
        "method-override": "~2.2.0",
        "express-session": "~1.7.6",
        "ejs": "~1.0.0",
        "connect-flash": "~0.1.1",
        "mongoose": "~3.8.15",
        "passport": "~0.2.1",
        "passport-local": "~1.0.0",
        "passport-facebook": "~1.0.3"
    }
}
```

Before you can continue developing your application, you will need to install the new Facebook strategy dependency. To do so, go to your application's root folder, and issue the following command in your command-line tool:

```
$ npm install
```

This will install the specified version of Passport's Facebook strategy in your `node_modules` folder. Once the installation process has successfully finished, you will need to configure the Facebook strategy.

Configuring Passport's Facebook strategy

Before you begin configuring your Facebook strategy, you will have to go to Facebook's developer home page at `https://developers.facebook.com/`, create a new Facebook application, and set the local host as the application domain. After configuring your Facebook application, you will get a Facebook application ID and secret. You'll need those to authenticate your users via Facebook, so let's save them in our environment configuration file. Go to the `config/env/development.js` file and change it as follows:

```
module.exports = {
  db: 'mongodb://localhost/mean-book',
  sessionSecret: 'developmentSessionSecret',
  facebook: {
    clientID: 'Application Id',
    clientSecret: 'Application Secret',
    callbackURL: 'http://localhost:3000/oauth/facebook/callback'
  }
};
```

Don't forget to replace `Application Id` and `Application Secret` with your Facebook application's ID and secret. The `callbackURL` property will be passed to the Facebook OAuth service, which will redirect to that URL after the authentication process is over.

Now, go to your `config/strategies` folder, and create a new file named `facebook.js` that contains the following code snippet:

```
var passport = require('passport'),
    url = require('url'),
    FacebookStrategy = require('passport-facebook').Strategy,
    config = require('../config'),
    users = require('../../app/controllers/users.server.controller');

module.exports = function() {
  passport.use(new FacebookStrategy({
    clientID: config.facebook.clientID,
    clientSecret: config.facebook.clientSecret,
    callbackURL: config.facebook.callbackURL,
    passReqToCallback: true
  },
  function(req, accessToken, refreshToken, profile, done) {
    var providerData = profile._json;
    providerData.accessToken = accessToken;
    providerData.refreshToken = refreshToken;
```

```
        var providerUserProfile = {
          firstName: profile.name.givenName,
          lastName: profile.name.familyName,
          fullName: profile.displayName,
          email: profile.emails[0].value,
          username: profile.username,
          provider: 'facebook',
          providerId: profile.id,
          providerData: providerData
        };

        users.saveOAuthUserProfile(req, providerUserProfile, done);
      }));
  };
```

Let's go over the preceding code snippet for a moment. You begin by requiring the Passport module, the Facebook `Strategy` object, your environmental configuration file, your `User` Mongoose model, and the `Users` controller. Then, you register the strategy using the `passport.use()` method and creating an instance of a `FacebookStrategy` object. The `FacebookStrategy` constructor takes two arguments: the Facebook application information and a callback function that it will call later when trying to authenticate a user.

Take a look at the callback function you defined. It accepts five arguments: the HTTP request object, an `accessToken` object to validate future requests, a `refreshToken` object to grab new access tokens, a profile object containing the user profile, and a `done` callback to be called when the authentication process is over.

Inside the callback function, you will create a new user object using the Facebook profile information and the controller's `saveOAuthUserProfile()` method, which you previously created, to authenticate the current user.

Remember the `config/passport.js` file? Well, now that you have your Facebook strategy configured, you can go back to it and load the strategy file. To do so, go back to the `config/passport.js` file and change it, as follows:

```
var passport = require('passport'),
    mongoose = require('mongoose');

module.exports = function() {
  var User = mongoose.model('User');
```

```
passport.serializeUser(function(user, done) {
  done(null, user.id);
});

passport.deserializeUser(function(id, done) {
  User.findOne({
    _id: id
  }, '-password -salt', function(err, user) {
    done(err, user);
  });
});

require('./strategies/local.js')();
require('./strategies/facebook.js')();
};
```

This will load your Facebook strategy configuration file. Now, all that is left to do is set the routes needed to authenticate users via Facebook and include a link to those routes in your sign-in and signup pages.

Wiring Passport's Facebook strategy routes

Passport OAuth strategies support the ability to authenticate users directly using the `passport.authenticate()` method. To do so, go to `app/routes/users.server.routes.js`, and append the following lines of code after the local strategy routes definition:

```
app.get('/oauth/facebook', passport.authenticate('facebook', {
  failureRedirect: '/signin'
}));
app.get('/oauth/facebook/callback', passport.authenticate('facebook',
{
  failureRedirect: '/signin',
  successRedirect: '/'
}));
```

The first route will use the `passport.authenticate()` method to start the user authentication process, while the second route will use the `passport.authenticate()` method to finish the authentication process once the user has linked their Facebook profile.

That's it! Everything is set up for your users to authenticate via Facebook. All you have to do now is go to your app/views/signup.ejs and app/views/signin.ejs files, and add the following line of code right before the closing BODY tag:

```
<a href="/oauth/facebook">Sign in with Facebook</a>
```

This will allow your users to click on the link and register with your application via their Facebook profile.

Using Passport's Twitter strategy

Another popular OAuth provider is Twitter, and a lot of web applications offer their users the ability to register with the web application using their Twitter profile. Passport supports the Twitter OAuth authentication method using the passport-twitter module. Let's see how you can implement a Twitter-based authentication in a few simple steps.

Installing Passport's Twitter strategy

To install Passport's Twitter strategy module in your application's modules folders, you'll need to change your package.json file, as follows:

```
{
  "name": "MEAN",
  "version": "0.0.6",
  "dependencies": {
    "express": "~4.8.8",
    "morgan": "~1.3.0",
    "compression": "~1.0.11",
    "body-parser": "~1.8.0",
    "method-override": "~2.2.0",
    "express-session": "~1.7.6",
    "ejs": "~1.0.0",
    "connect-flash": "~0.1.1",
    "mongoose": "~3.8.15",
    "passport": "~0.2.1",
    "passport-local": "~1.0.0",
    "passport-facebook": "~1.0.3",
    "passport-twitter": "~1.0.2"
  }
}
```

Before you continue developing your application, you will need to install the new Twitter strategy dependency. Go to your application's root folder, and issue the following command in your command-line tool:

```
$ npm install
```

This will install the specified version of Passport's Twitter strategy in your node_modules folder. Once the installation process has successfully finished, you will need to configure the Twitter strategy.

Configuring Passport's Twitter strategy

Before we begin configuring your Twitter strategy, you will have to go to the Twitter developers' home page at https://dev.twitter.com/ and create a new Twitter application. After configuring your Twitter application, you will get a Twitter application ID and secret. You'll need them to authenticate your users via Twitter, so let's add them in our environment configuration file. Go to the config/env/ development.js file, and change it as follows:

```
module.exports = {
  db: 'mongodb://localhost/mean-book',
  sessionSecret: 'developmentSessionSecret',
  facebook: {
    clientID: 'Application Id',
    clientSecret: 'Application Secret',
    callbackURL: 'http://localhost:3000/oauth/facebook/callback'
  },
  twitter: {
    clientID: 'Application Id',
    clientSecret: 'Application Secret',
    callbackURL: 'http://localhost:3000/oauth/twitter/callback'
  }
};
```

Don't forget to replace Application Id and Application Secret with your Twitter application's ID and secret. The callbackURL property will be passed to the Twitter OAuth service, which will redirect the user to that URL after the authentication process is over.

As stated earlier, in your project, each strategy should be configured in its own separated file, which will help you keep your project organized. Go to your config/ strategies folder, and create a new file named twitter.js containing the following lines of code:

```
var passport = require('passport'),
    url = require('url'),
    TwitterStrategy = require('passport-twitter').Strategy,
    config = require('../config'),
    users = require('../../app/controllers/users.server.controller');
```

```
module.exports = function() {
  passport.use(new TwitterStrategy({
    consumerKey: config.twitter.clientID,
    consumerSecret: config.twitter.clientSecret,
    callbackURL: config.twitter.callbackURL,
    passReqToCallback: true
  },
  function(req, token, tokenSecret, profile, done) {
    var providerData = profile._json;
    providerData.token = token;
    providerData.tokenSecret = tokenSecret;

    var providerUserProfile = {
      fullName: profile.displayName,
      username: profile.username,
      provider: 'twitter',
      providerId: profile.id,
      providerData: providerData
    };

    users.saveOAuthUserProfile(req, providerUserProfile, done);
  }));
};
```

You begin by requiring the Passport module, the Twitter `Strategy` object, your environmental configuration file, your `User` Mongoose model, and the `Users` controller. Then, you register the strategy using the `passport.use()` method, and create an instance of a `TwitterStrategy` object. The `TwitterStrategy` constructor takes two arguments: the Twitter application information and a callback function that it will call later when trying to authenticate a user.

Take a look at the callback function you defined. It accepts five arguments: the HTTP request object, a `token` object and a `tokenSecret` object to validate future requests, a profile object containing the user profile, and a `done` callback to be called when the authentication process is over.

Inside the callback function, you will create a new user object using the Twitter profile information and the controller's `saveOAuthUserProfile()` method, which you previously created, to authenticate the current user.

Now that you have your Twitter strategy configured, you can go back to the `config/passport.js` file and load the strategy file as follows:

```
var passport = require('passport'),
    mongoose = require('mongoose');

module.exports = function() {
  var User = mongoose.model('User');

  passport.serializeUser(function(user, done) {
    done(null, user.id);
  });

  passport.deserializeUser(function(id, done) {
    User.findOne({
      _id: id
    }, '-password -salt', function(err, user) {
      done(err, user);
    });
  });

  require('./strategies/local.js')();
  require('./strategies/facebook.js')();
  require('./strategies/twitter.js')();
};
```

This will load your Twitter strategy configuration file. Now all that is left to do is set the routes needed to authenticate users via Twitter and include a link to those routes in your sign-in and signup pages.

Wiring Passport's Twitter strategy routes

To add Passport's Twitter routes, go to your `app/routes/users.server.routes.js` file, and paste the following code after the Facebook strategy routes:

```
app.get('/oauth/twitter', passport.authenticate('twitter', {
  failureRedirect: '/signin'
}));

app.get('/oauth/twitter/callback', passport.authenticate('twitter', {
  failureRedirect: '/signin',
  successRedirect: '/'
}));
```

The first route will use the `passport.authenticate()` method to start the user authentication process, while the second route will use `passport.authenticate()` method to finish the authentication process once the user has used their Twitter profile to connect.

That's it! Everything is set up for your user's Twitter-based authentication. All you have to do is go to your `app/views/signup.ejs` and `app/views/signin.ejs` files and add the following line of code right before the closing BODY tag:

```
<a href="/oauth/twitter">Sign in with Twitter</a>
```

This will allow your users to click on the link and register with your application via their Twitter profile.

Using Passport's Google strategy

The last OAuth provider we'll implement is Google as a lot of web applications offer their users the ability to register with the web application using their Google profile. Passport supports the Google OAuth authentication method using the `passport-google-oauth` module. Let's see how you can implement a Google-based authentication in a few simple steps.

Installing Passport's Google strategy

To install Passport's Google strategy module in your application's modules folders, you'll need to change your `package.json` file, as follows:

```
{
  "name": "MEAN",
  "version": "0.0.6",
  "dependencies": {
    "express": "~4.8.8",
    "morgan": "~1.3.0",
    "compression": "~1.0.11",
    "body-parser": "~1.8.0",
    "method-override": "~2.2.0",
    "express-session": "~1.7.6",
    "ejs": "~1.0.0",
    "connect-flash": "~0.1.1",
    "mongoose": "~3.8.15",
    "passport": "~0.2.1",
    "passport-local": "~1.0.0",
    "passport-facebook": "~1.0.3",
```

```
      "passport-twitter": "~1.0.2",
      "passport-google-oauth": "~0.1.5"
   }
}
```

Before you can continue developing your application, you will need to install the new Google strategy dependency. Go to your application's root folder, and issue the following command in your command-line tool:

```
$ npm install
```

This will install the specified version of Passport's Google strategy in your `node_modules` folder. Once the installation process has successfully finished, you will need to configure the Google strategy.

Configuring Passport's Google strategy

Before we begin configuring your Google strategy, you will have to go to the Google developers' home page at `https://console.developers.google.com/`and create a new Google application. In your application's settings, set the JAVASCRIPT ORIGINS property to `http://localhost` and the REDIRECT URIS property to `http://localhost/oauth/google/callback`. After configuring your Google application, you will get a Google application ID and secret. You'll need them to authenticate your users via Google, so let's add them in our environment configuration file. Go to the `config/env/development.js` file, and change it as follows:

```
module.exports = {
  db: 'mongodb://localhost/mean-book',
  sessionSecret: 'developmentSessionSecret',
  facebook: {
    clientID: 'Application Id',
    clientSecret: 'Application Secret',
    callbackURL:
      'http://localhost:3000/oauth/facebook/callback'
  },
  twitter: {
    clientID: 'Application Id',
    clientSecret: 'Application Secret',
    callbackURL: 'http://localhost:3000/oauth/twitter/callback'
  },
  google: {
    clientID: 'Application Id',
    clientSecret: 'Application Secret',
    callbackURL: 'http://localhost:3000/oauth/google/callback'
  }
};
```

Don't forget to replace `Application Id` and `Application Secret` with your Google application's ID and secret. The `callbackURL` property will be passed to the Google OAuth service, which will redirect the user to that URL after the authentication process is over.

To implement the Google authentication strategy, go to your `config/strategies` folder, and create a new file named `google.js` containing the following lines of code:

```
var passport = require('passport'),
    url = require('url'),
    GoogleStrategy = require('passport-google-oauth').OAuth2Strategy,
    config = require('../config'),
    users = require('../../app/controllers/users.server.controller');

module.exports = function() {
  passport.use(new GoogleStrategy({
    clientID: config.google.clientID,
    clientSecret: config.google.clientSecret,
    callbackURL: config.google.callbackURL,
    passReqToCallback: true
  },
  function(req, accessToken, refreshToken, profile, done) {
    var providerData = profile._json;
    providerData.accessToken = accessToken;
    providerData.refreshToken = refreshToken;

    var providerUserProfile = {
      firstName: profile.name.givenName,
      lastName: profile.name.familyName,
      fullName: profile.displayName,
      email: profile.emails[0].value,
      username: profile.username,
      provider: 'google',
      providerId: profile.id,
      providerData: providerData
    };

    users.saveOAuthUserProfile(req, providerUserProfile, done);
  }));
};
```

Test your application by visiting `http://localhost:3000/signin` and `http://localhost:3000/signup`. Try signing up and signing in using the new OAuth methods. Don't forget to visit your home page to see how the user details are saved throughout the session.

 Passport has similar support for many additional OAuth providers. To learn more, it is recommended that you visit `http://passportjs.org/guide/providers/`.

Summary

In this chapter, you learned about the Passport authentication module. You discovered its strategies and how to handle their installation and configuration. You also learned how to properly register your users and how to authenticate their requests. You went through Passport's local strategy and learned how to authenticate users using a username and password and how Passport supports the different OAuth authentication providers. In the next chapter, you'll discover the last piece of the MEAN puzzle, when we introduce you to AngularJS.

7
Introduction to AngularJS

The last piece of the MEAN puzzle is, of course, AngularJS. Back in 2009, while building their JSON as platform service, developers Miško Hevery and Adam Abrons noticed that the common JavaScript libraries weren't enough. The nature of their rich web applications raised the need for a more structured framework that would reduce redundant work and keep the project code organized. Abandoning their original idea, they decided to focus on the development of their framework, naming it AngularJS and releasing it under an open source license. The idea was to bridge the gap between JavaScript and HTML and to help popularize single-page application development. In this chapter, we'll cover the following topics:

- Understanding the key concepts of AngularJS
- Introducing Bower's frontend dependencies manager
- Installing and configuring AngularJS
- Creating and organizing an AngularJS application
- Utilizing Angular's MVC architecture properly
- Utilizing AngularJS services and implementing the `Authentication` service

Introducing AngularJS

AngularJS is a frontend JavaScript framework designed to build single-page applications using the MVC architecture. The AngularJS approach is to extend the functionality of HTML using special attributes that bind JavaScript business logic with HTML elements. The AngularJS ability to extend HTML allows cleaner DOM manipulation through client-side templating and two-way data binding that seamlessly synchronizes between models and views. AngularJS also improves the application's code structure and testability using MVC and dependency injection. Although starting with AngularJS is easy, writing larger applications is a more complex task, which requires a broader understanding of the framework's key concepts.

Key concepts of AngularJS

With its two-way data binding, AngularJS makes it very easy to get started with your first application. However, when progressing into real-world application development, things can get more complicated. So, before we can continue with our MEAN application development, it would be best to clarify a few key concepts of AngularJS.

The core module of AngularJS

The core module of AngularJS is loaded with everything you need to bootstrap your application. It contains several objects and entities that enable the basic operation of an AngularJS application.

The angular global object

The `angular` global object contains a set of methods that you'll use to create and launch your application. It's also worth noticing that the `angular` object wraps a leaner subset of jQuery called **jqLite**, which enables Angular to perform basic DOM manipulation. Another key feature of the `angular` object is its static methods, which you'll use to create, manipulate, and edit the basic entities of your application including, the creation and retrieval of modules.

AngularJS modules

With AngularJS, everything is encapsulated in modules. Whether you choose to work with a single application module or break your application into various modules, your AngularJS application will rely on at least one module to operate.

Application modules

Every AngularJS application needs at least one module to bootstrap, and we'll refer to this module as the application module. AngularJS modules are created and retrieved using the `angular.module(name, [requires], [configFn])` method, which accepts three arguments:

- `name`: This is a string defining the module name
- `requires`: This is an array of strings defining other modules as dependencies
- `configFN`: This is a function that will run when the module is being registered

When calling the `angular.module()` method with a single argument, it will retrieve an existing module with that name; if it can't find one, it will throw an error. However, when calling the `angular.module()` method with multiple arguments, AngularJS will create a module with the given name, dependencies, and configuration function. Later in this chapter, you will use the `angular.module()` method with the name of your module and a list of dependencies to create your application module.

External modules

The AngularJS team has decided to support the continuous development of the framework by breaking Angular's functionality into external modules. These modules are being developed by the same team that creates the core framework and are being installed separately to provide extra functionality that is not required by the core framework to operate. Later in this chapter, you'll see an example of an external module, when we discuss the routing of an application.

Third-party modules

In the same way the AngularJS team supports its external modules, it also encourages outside vendors to create third-party modules, which extends the framework functionality and provides developers with an easier starting point. Later in this book, you will encounter third-party modules that will help you speed up your application development.

Two-way data binding

One of the most popular features of AngularJS is its two-way data binding mechanism. Two-way data binding enables AngularJS applications to always keep the model synchronized with the view and vice versa. This means that what the view renders is always the projection of the model. To understand this better, the AngularJS team provides the following diagram:

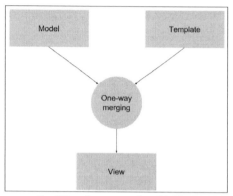

Traditional one-way data binding

As you can see from the preceding diagram, most templating systems bind the model with templates in one direction. So, every time the model changes, the developer has to make sure that these changes reflect in the view. A good example is our EJS template engine, which binds the application data and EJS template to produce an HTML page. Fortunately, AngularJS templates are different. Take a look at the following diagram:

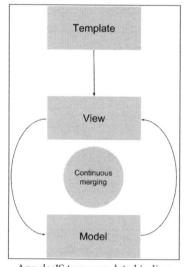

AngularJS two-way data binding

AngularJS uses the browser to compile HTML templates, which contain special directives and binding instructions that produce a live view. Any events that happen in the view automatically update the model, while any changes occurring in the model immediately get propagated to the view. This means the model is always the single source of data for the application state, which substantially improves the development process. Later in this chapter, you will learn about AngularJS scopes and how controllers and views use them in referring to the application model.

Dependency injection

A dependency injection is a software design pattern popularized by a software engineer named Martin Fowler. The main principle behind dependency injection is the inversion of control in a software development architecture. To understand this better, let's have a look at the following `notifier` example:

```
var Notifier = function() {
   this.userService = new UserService();
};

Notifier.prototype.notify = function() {
   var user = this.userService.getUser();

   if (user.role === 'admin') {
     alert('You are an admin!');
   } else {
     alert('Hello user!');
   }
};
```

Our `Notifier` class creates an instance of a `userService`, and when the `notify ()` method is called, it alerts a different message based on the user role. Now this can work pretty well, but what happens when you want to test your `Notifier` class? You will create a `Notifier` instance in your test, but won't be able to pass a mock `userService` object to test the different results of the `notify` method. Dependency injection solves this by moving the responsibility of creating the `userService` object to the creator of the `Notifier` instance, whether it is another object or a test. This creator is often referred to as the injector. A revised, injection-dependent version of this example will be as follows:

```
var Notifier = function(userService) {
   this.userService = userService;
};
```

```
Notifier.prototype.notify = function() {
  var user = this.userService.getUser();

  if (user.role === 'admin') {
    alert('You are an admin!');
  } else {
    alert('Hello user!');
  }
};
```

Now, whenever you create an instance of the `Notifier` class, the injector will be responsible for injecting a `userService` object into the constructor, making it possible to control the behavior of the `Notifier` instance outside of its constructor, a design often described as inversion of control.

Dependency injection in AngularJS

Now that you know how dependency injection works, let's review the implementation AngularJS uses. To understand this better, let's go over the following example of a module's `controller ()` method, which creates an AngularJS controller:

```
angular.module('someModule').controller('SomeController',
function($scope) {
  ...
});
```

In this example, the `controller` method accepts two arguments: the controller's name and the controller's constructor function. The controller's constructor function is being injected with an AngularJS object named `$scope`. AngularJS knows how to inject the right object here because its `injector` object can read the function argument's names. But developers often use a minifying service to obfuscate and minimize JavaScript files for production deployment needs. A minifying service will make our controller look as follows:

```
angular.module('someModule').controller('SomeController', function(a)
{ ... });
```

So, now the AngularJS injector won't be able to understand which object it should inject. To solve this, AngularJS provides better syntax to annotate dependencies. Instead of passing a function as a second argument, you can pass an annotated array of dependencies that won't change when minified and will let the injector know which dependencies this controller constructor is expecting.

An annotated version of our controller will be as follows:

```
angular.module('someModule').controller('SomeController', ['$scope',
function($scope) {


}]);
```

Now, even if you obfuscate your code, the list of dependencies will stay intact, so the controller can function properly.

 While we used the `controller()` method to explain this principle, it is also valid with any other AngularJS entity.

AngularJS directives

We previously stated that AngularJS extends HTML instead of building against it. The mechanism that allows this is called directives. AngularJS directives are markers, usually attributes or element names, which enable the AngularJS compiler to attach a specified behavior to a DOM element and its children elements. Basically, directives are the way AngularJS interacts with DOM elements and are what enables the basic operation of an AngularJS application. What makes this feature even more special is the ability to write your own custom directives that it imparts.

Core directives

AngularJS comes prebundled with necessary directives, which define the functionality of an Angular application. A directive is usually placed on an element as an attribute or defined as the element name. In this section, we'll review the most popular core directives, but you will encounter more of Angular's directives along the book examples.

The most basic directive is called `ng-app` and is placed on the DOM element (usually the page's `body` or `html` tag) you want Angular to use as the root application element. A `body` tag with the `ng-app` directive will be as follows:

```
<body ng-app></body>
```

We'll discuss the `ng-app` directive in greater detail in the next section, but for now, let's discuss other common core directives included in Angular's core:

- `ng-controller`: This tells the compiler which controller class to use to manage this element view
- `ng-model`: This is placed on input elements and binds the input value to a property on the model

- `ng-show`/`ng-hide`: This shows and hides an element according to a Boolean expression
- `ng-repeat`: This iterates over a collection and duplicates the element for each item

We'll explain how to use each of these directives throughout the book, but it is also important to remember that these are just a small portion of the vast selection of AngularJS core directives, and while we introduce more directives ahead, it would probably be best for you to explore them yourself using the AngularJS official documentation at `http://docs.angularjs.org/api/`.

Custom directives

We won't discuss custom directives in this book but it is worth mentioning that you can also write your own custom directives. Custom directives make it possible for you to obfuscate redundant code, keep your application cleaner and more readable, and improve the way you can test your application.

 Third-party vendors have created a lot of supplemental, open source directives, which can substantially expedite your development process.

Bootstrapping an AngularJS application

Bootstrapping an AngularJS application means that we tell Angular which DOM element is the root element of the application and when to initiate the Angular application. This could be done either automatically after the page assets are loaded or manually using JavaScript. Manual bootstrapping is usually useful when you'd like to control the bootstrap flow to make sure certain logic is being executed before the AngularJS application is started, while automatic bootstrap is useful in simpler scenarios.

Automatic bootstrap

To automatically bootstrap the AngularJS application, you will need to use the `ng-app` directive. Once the application JavaScript files are loaded, AngularJS will look for DOM elements marked with this directive and will bootstrap an individual application for each element. The `ng-app` directive can be placed as an attribute without a value or with the name of the module that you'd like to use as the main application module. It is important to remember that you should create this module using the `angular.module()` method, or AngularJS will throw an exception and won't bootstrap your application.

Manual bootstrap

To manually bootstrap an application, you will need to use the `angular.bootstrap(element, [modules], [config])` method, which accepts three arguments:

- `element`: This is the DOM element where you want to bootstrap your application
- `modules`: This is an array of strings defining the modules you want to attach to the application
- `config`: This an object defining configuration options for the application

Usually, we'll call this function in when the page is loaded using the jqLite document-ready event.

After going through this quick overview of the AngularJS key concepts, we can now continue with the implementation of an AngularJS application in our MEAN application. The examples in this chapter will continue directly from those in previous chapters, so for this chapter, copy the final example from *Chapter 6, Managing User Authentication Using Passport*, and let's start from there.

Installing AngularJS

Since AngularJS is a frontend framework, installing it requires the inclusion of Angular's JavaScript files in the main page of your application. This could be done in various ways, and the easiest one would be to download the files you need and store them in the `public` folder. Another approach is to use Angular's CDN and load the files directly from the CDN server. While these two approaches are simple and easy to understand, they both have a strong flaw. Loading a single third-party JavaScript file is readable and direct, but what happens when you start adding more vendor libraries to your project? More importantly, how can you manage your dependencies versions? In the same way, the Node.js ecosystem solved this issue by using npm. Frontend dependencies can be managed using a similar tool called Bower.

Meeting the Bower dependencies manager

Bower is a package manager tool, designed to download and maintain frontend, third-party libraries. Bower is a Node.js module, so to begin using it, you will have to install it globally using npm:

```
$ npm install -g bower
```

> Your OS user might not have the necessary permissions to install packages globally, so use a super user or `sudo`.

Once you have Bower installed, it's time to learn how to use it. Like `npm`, Bower uses a dedicated JSON file to indicate which packages and what versions to install. To manage your frontend packages, go to the root folder of your application and create a file named `bower.json` containing the following lines of code:

```
{
  name: MEAN,
  version: 0.0.7,
  dependencies: { }
}
```

As you're already experienced with the `package.json` file, this structure should already look familiar. Basically, you define your project metadata and describe its frontend packages using the `dependencies` property. You'll populate this field in a moment, but there is one more detail to notice regarding Bower's configuration.

> In order to use Bower, you will also need to install Git. Visit http://git-scm.com/ to download and install Git on your system. If you're using Windows, make sure you enabled Git on the command prompt or use the Git bash tool for all Bower-related commands.

Configuring the Bower dependencies manager

Bower installation process downloads the packages content and automatically place them under a `bower_components` default folder in the root application folder. Since these are frontend packages that should be served as static files, and considering that our MEAN application only serves static files placed under the `public` folder, you will have to change the default installation location for Bower packages. Configuring the Bower installation process is done using a dedicated configuration file called `.bowerrc`.

To install your frontend packages in a different location, go to the root folder of your application and create a file named `.bowerrc` that contains the following lines of code:

```
{
  directory: public/lib
}
```

From now on, when you run the Bower installation process, third-party packages will be placed under the public/lib folder.

 You can learn more about Bower's features by visiting the official documentation at http://bower.io.

Installing AngularJS using Bower

Once you have Bower installed and configured, it is time to use it and install the AngularJS framework. Go back to your bower.json file and change it as follows:

```
{
  name: MEAN,
  version: 0.0.7,
  dependencies: {
    angular: ~1.2
  }
}
```

This will have Bower installing the latest 1.2.x Version of AngularJS. To start the installation process, navigate to the application's folder in your command-line tool and run the following command:

```
$ bower install
```

This will fetch the AngularJS package files and place them under the public/lib/angular folder. Once you have AngularJS installed, it is time to add it to your project's main application page. Since AngularJS is a single-page framework, the entire application logic will take place in the same Express application page.

Configuring AngularJS

To start using AngularJS, you will need to include the framework JavaScript file in your main EJS view. In our case, we will use the app/views/index.ejs file as the main application page. Go to your app/views/index.ejs file and change it, as follows:

```
<!DOCTYPE html>
<html xmlns:ng="http://angularjs.org">
<head>
  <title><%= title %></title>
</head>
<body>
```

```
<% if (userFullName) { %>
  <h2>Hello <%=userFullName%> </h2>
  <a href="/signout">Sign out</a>
<% } else { %>
  <a href="/signup">Signup</a>
  <a href="/signin">Signin</a>
<% } %>


<script type="text/javascript" src="/lib/angular/angular.js"></script>
</body>
</html>
```

Now that you have AngularJS installed and included in the main application page, it is time to understand how to organize your AngularJS application's structure.

Structuring an AngularJS application

As you might remember from *Chapter 3, Building an Express Web Application*, your application's structure depends on the complexity of your application. We previously decided to use the horizontal approach for the entire MEAN application; however, as we stated before, MEAN applications can be constructed in various ways, and an AngularJS application structure is a different topic, which is often discussed by the community and the AngularJS development team. There are many doctrines for different purposes, some of which are a bit more complicated, while others offer a simpler approach. In this section, we'll introduce a recommended structure. Since AngularJS is a frontend framework, you'll use the public folder of our Express application as the root folder for the AngularJS application so that every file is available statically.

The AngularJS team offers several options to structure your application according to its complexity. A simple application will have a horizontal structure where entities are arranged in modules and folders according to their type, and a main application file is placed at the root folder of the application. An example application structure of that kind can be viewed in the following screenshot:

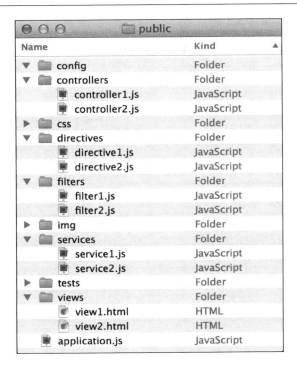

As you can notice, this is a very comfortable solution for small applications with a few entities. However, your application might be more complex with several different features and many more entities. This structure cannot handle an application of that sort since it obfuscates the behavior of each application file, will have a bloated folder with too many files, and will generally be very difficult to maintain. For this purpose, the AngularJS team offers a different approach to organizing your files in a vertical manner. A vertical structure positions every file according to its functional context, so different types of entities can be sorted together according to their role in a feature or section. This is similar to the vertical approach we introduced in *Chapter 3, Building an Express Web Application*. However, the difference is that only AngularJS sections or logical units will have a standalone module folder structure with a module file placed in the root module folder.

An example of an AngularJS application vertical structure can be seen in the following screenshot:

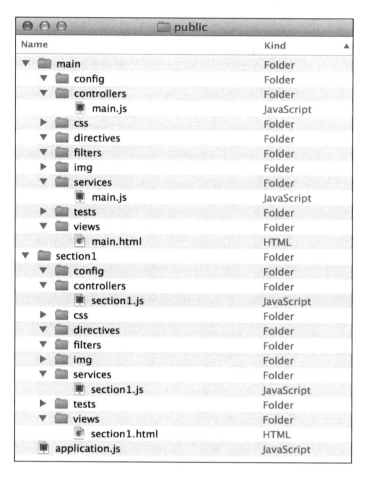

As you can notice, each module has its own folder structure with subfolders for different types of entities. This allows you to encapsulate each section, but there is still a minor problem with this structure. As you develop your AngularJS application, you will discover that you end up with many files having the same name since they serve different functionalities of the same section. This is a common issue, which can be very inconvenient when using your IDE or text editor. A better approach would be to use the naming convention that we introduced in *Chapter 3, Building an Express Web Application*. The following screenshot shows a clearer structure:

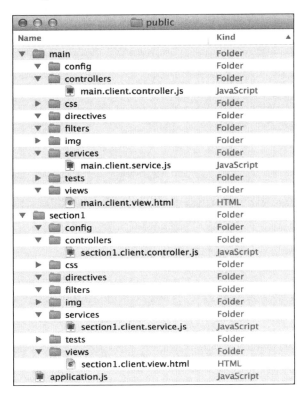

Each file is placed in a proper folder with a proper filename that usefully describes what sort of code it contains. Now that you know the basic best practices of naming and structuring your application, let's go back to the example project and start building your AngularJS application.

Bootstrapping your AngularJS application

To bootstrap your application and start using AngularJS, we will use the manual bootstrapping mechanism. This will allow you to better control the initialization process of your application. To do so, clear the contents of the public folder except for the Bower lib folder. Then, create a file named application.js inside the public folder, and paste the following code in it:

```
var mainApplicationModuleName = 'mean';

var mainApplicationModule = angular.module(mainApplicationModuleName
, []);

angular.element(document).ready(function() {
  angular.bootstrap(document, [mainApplicationModuleName]);
});
```

As you can notice, first you created a variable containing the main application's module name, which you then used to create a the main application module following the angular.module() method. Then, you used the angular object jqLite functionality to bind a function to the document-ready event. In that function, you used the angular.bootstrap() method to initiate a new AngularJS application using the main application module.

The next thing you need to do is include this JavaScript file in your index.ejs view. You should also throw in an Angular example code to validate that everything is working properly. Go to the app/views/index.ejs file and change it, as follows:

```
<!DOCTYPE html>
<html xmlns:ng="http://angularjs.org">
<head>
  <title><%= title %></title>
</head>
<body>
  <% if (userFullName) { %>
    <h2>Hello <%=userFullName%> </h2>
    <a href="/signout">Sign out</a>
  <% } else { %>
    <a href="/signup">Signup</a>
    <a href="/signin">Signin</a>
  <% } %>
```

```
<section>
  <input type="text" id="text1" ng-model="name">
  <input type="text" id="text2" ng-model="name">
</section>

<script type="text/javascript" src="/lib/angular/angular.js"></script>

<script type="text/javascript" src="/application.js"></script>
</body>
</html>
```

Here, you included the new application JavaScript file and added two text boxes that used the `ng-model` directive to illustrate Angular's data binding. Once you've made these changes, everything is ready to test your AngularJS application. In your command-line tool, navigate to the MEAN application's root folder, and run your application with the help of the following command:

```
$ node server
```

When your application is running, use your browser and open your application URL at `http://localhost:3000`. You should see two textboxes next to each other. Try typing in one of the text boxes, and you should see Angular's two-way data binding in action. In the next section, you'll learn how to use AngularJS MVC entities.

AngularJS MVC entities

AngularJS is an opinioned framework that allows you to use the MVC design pattern to create rich and maintainable web applications. In this section, you'll learn about views, controllers, and how the data model is implemented using the scope object. To begin with implementing the MVC pattern, create a module folder named `example` in your `public` folder. In the `example` folder, create two subfolders named `controllers` and `views`. Now that you have your example module structured, create a file named `example.client.module.js` inside the `public/example` folder. In this file, you're going to create a new AngularJS module using the `angular.module()` method. In the `public/example/example.client.module.js` file, paste the following code:

```
angular.module('example', []);
```

This will create an AngularJS module, but you still need to include the module file in your application page and the module as a dependency of your main application module. Let's begin by removing the two-textboxes code examples and adding a new SCRIPT tag that loads your module file. To do so, change your app/views/index. ejs file as follows:

```
<!DOCTYPE html>
<html xmlns:ng="http://angularjs.org">
<head>
  <title><%= title %></title>
</head>
<body>
  <% if (userFullName) { %>
    <h2>Hello <%=userFullName%> </h2>
    <a href="/signout">Sign out</a>
  <% } else { %>
    <a href="/signup">Signup</a>
    <a href="/signin">Signin</a>
  <% } %>

  <script type="text/javascript" src="/lib/angular/angular.js"></
script>

  <script type="text/javascript" src="/example/example.client.module.
js"></script>

  <script type="text/javascript" src="/application.js"></script>
</body>
</html>
```

Now add the example module as a dependency of the main application module by going to your public/application.js file and changing it, as follows:

```
var mainApplicationModuleName = 'mean';

var mainApplicationModule = angular.module(mainApplicationModuleName,
['example']);

angular.element(document).ready(function() {
  angular.bootstrap(document, [mainApplicationModuleName]);
});
```

Once you're done, test your changes by running your MEAN application and verifying that there are no JavaScript errors. You shouldn't witness any changes in your application since we haven't utilized the new example module yet. When you're sure your new module is properly defined, move on to the next section to learn how to use AngularJS views.

AngularJS views

AngularJS views are HTML templates rendered by the AngularJS compiler to produce a manipulated DOM on your page. To start with your first view, create a new `example.client.view.html` file inside your `public/example/views` folder, and paste the following lines of code:

```
<section>
  <input type=text id=text1 ng-model=name>
  <input type=text id=text2 ng-model=name>
</section>
```

To use this template as a view, you'll have to go back to your `app/views/index.ejs` file and change it again, as follows:

```
<!DOCTYPE html>
<html xmlns:ng="http://angularjs.org">
<head>
  <title><%= title %></title>
</head>
<body>
  <% if (userFullName) { %>
    <h2>Hello <%=userFullName%> </h2>
    <a href="/signout">Sign out</a>
  <% } else { %>
    <a href="/signup">Signup</a>
    <a href="/signin">Signin</a>
  <% } %>

  <section ng-include="'example/views/example.client.view.html'"></section>

  <script type="text/javascript" src="/lib/angular/angular.js"></script>

  <script type="text/javascript" src="/example/example.client.module.js"></script>

  <script type="text/javascript" src="/application.js"></script>
</body>
</html>
```

In the preceding code snippet, you used the new `ng-include` directive, which loads a template from a specified path, compiles it into a view, and then places the rendered result inside the directive DOM element. To test your view, use your command-line tool, and navigate to the MEAN application's root folder. Then run your application by typing the following command:

```
$ node server
```

Once your application is running, use your browser, and open the application URL at `http://localhost:3000`. You should see the two-textboxes example again; try typing in one of the textboxes, and see how the data binding works the same way inside views. Views are great, but what makes them even better are controllers.

AngularJS controllers and scopes

Controllers are basically constructor functions, which AngularJS uses to create a new instance of a controller object. Their purpose is to augment data model reference objects called scopes. Therefore, the AngularJS team rightfully defines a scope as the glue between the view and the controller. Using a scope object, the controller can manipulate the model, which automatically propagates these changes to the view and vice versa.

Controller instances are usually created when you use the `ng-controller` directive. The AngularJS compiler uses the controller name from the directive to instantiate a new controller instance, while utilizing dependency injection to pass the scope object to that controller instance. The controller is then used either to set up the scope initial state or to extend its functionality.

Since DOM elements are arranged in a hierarchical structure, scopes mimic that hierarchy. This means that each scope has a parent scope up until the parentless object called the root scope. This is important, because aside from referencing their own model, scopes can also inherit the model of their parent scopes. So if a model property cannot be found in a current scope object, Angular will look for this property in the parent scope, and so on, until it finds the property or reaches the root scope.

To understand this better, let's use a controller to set an initial model state for our view. Inside your `public/example/controllers` folder, create a new file called `example.client.controller.js` containing the following code snippet:

```
angular.module('example').controller('ExampleController', ['$scope',
    function($scope) {
        $scope.name = 'MEAN Application';
    }
]);
```

Let's review this for a moment. First, you used the `angular.module()` method
to retrieve your example module. Then, you used the AngularJS module's
`controller()` method to create a new `ExampleController` constructor function. In
your constructor function, you applied the dependency injection to inject the `$scope`
object. Finally, you used the `$scope` object to define a `name` property, which will later
be used by your view. To use this controller, you'll need to include its JavaScript file
in the main application's page and add the `ng-controller` directive to your view.
Start by changing your `app/views/index.ejs` as follows:

```
<!DOCTYPE html>
<html xmlns:ng="http://angularjs.org">
<head>
  <title><%= title %></title>
</head>
<body>
  <% if (userFullName) { %>
    <h2>Hello <%=userFullName%> </h2>
    <a href="/signout">Sign out</a>
  <% } else { %>
    <a href="/signup">Signup</a>
    <a href="/signin">Signin</a>
  <% } %>

  <section ng-include="'example/views/example.client.view.html'"></section>

  <script type="text/javascript" src="/lib/angular/angular.js"></script>

  <script type="text/javascript" src="/example/example.client.module.js"></script>
  <script type="text/javascript" src="/example/controllers/example.client.controller.js"></script>

  <script type="text/javascript" src="/application.js"></script>
</body>
</html>
```

Now change your `public/example/views/example.client.view.html` file
as follows:

```
<section ng-controller=ExampleController>
  <input type=text id=text1 ng-model=name>
  <input type=text id=text2 ng-model=name>
</section>
```

That's it! To test your new controller, use your command-line tool, and navigate to the MEAN application's root folder. Then run your application as follows:

```
$ node server
```

Once your application is running, use your browser and open your application URL at `http://localhost:3000`. You should see the two-textboxes example again but with an initial value already set up.

While views, controllers, and scopes are a great way to build your application, AngularJS has much more to offer. In the next section, you'll drop the `ng-include` directive and learn how to use the `ngRoute` module to manage your application routing.

AngularJS routing

An AngularJS MVC implementation would not be complete if it didn't offer some way of controlling the application URL routing. While you could leverage the `ng-include` directive to offer some routing features, it would be a mess to use it with multiple views. For that purpose, the AngularJS team developed the `ngRoute` module that allows you to define URL paths and their corresponding templates, which will be rendered whenever the user navigates to those paths.

Since AngularJS is a single-page framework, `ngRoute` will manage the routing entirely in the browser. This means that instead of fetching web pages from the server, AngularJS will load the defined template, compile it, and place the result inside a specific DOM element. The server will only serve the template as a static file but won't respond to the URL changing. This change will also turn our Express server into a more API-oriented backend. Let's begin by installing the `ngRoute` module using Bower.

> The ngRoute module has two URL modes: a legacy mode using the URL hash part to support older browsers and an HTML5 mode using the history API supported by newer browsers. In this book, we'll use the legacy mode to offer broader browser compatibility.

Installing the ngRoute module

Installing the `ngRoute` module is easy; simply go to your `bower.json` file and change it as follows:

```
{
  name: MEAN,
  version: 0.0.7,
  dependencies: {
    angular: ~1.2,
    angular-route: ~1.2
  }
}
```

Now use your command-line tool to navigate to the MEAN application root folder, and install the new `ngRoute` module:

```
$ bower update
```

When bower finishes installing the new dependency, you would see a new folder named `angular-route` in your `public/lib` folder. Next, you will need to include the module file in your application main page, so edit your `app/views/index.ejs` file as follows:

```
<!DOCTYPE html>
<html xmlns:ng="http://angularjs.org">
<head>
  <title><%= title %></title>
</head>
<body>
  <% if (userFullName) { %>
    <h2>Hello <%=userFullName%> </h2>
    <a href="/signout">Sign out</a>
  <% } else { %>
    <a href="/signup">Signup</a>
    <a href="/signin">Signin</a>
  <% } %>

  <section ng-include="'example/views/example.client.view.html'"></section>

  <script type="text/javascript" src="/lib/angular/angular.js"></script>
  <script type="text/javascript" src="/lib/angular-route/angular-route.js"></script>
```

```
    <script type="text/javascript" src="/example/example.client.module.
js"></script>
    <script type="text/javascript" src="/example/controllers/example.
client.controller.js"></script>

    <script type="text/javascript" src="/application.js"></script>
  </body>
  </html>
```

Finally, you will need to add the ngRoute module as a dependency for your main application's module, so change your public/application.js file as follows:

```
var mainApplicationModuleName = 'mean';

var mainApplicationModule = angular.module(mainApplicationModuleName,
  ['ngRoute', 'example']);

angular.element(document).ready(function() {
  angular.bootstrap(document, [mainApplicationModuleName]);
});
```

When you're done with these changes, the ngRoute module will be set up and ready to be configured and used.

Configuring the URL scheme

The ngRoute module's default behavior is to use the URL hash part for routing. Since it is usually used for in-page linking, when the hash part changes, the browser will not make a request to the server. This enables AngularJS to support older browsers while maintaining a decent routing scheme. So, a common AngularJS route would be similar to this one: http://localhost:3000/#/example.

However, single-page applications have one major problem. They are not indexable by search engine crawlers and can suffer from poor SEO. To solve this issue, the major search engine makers offer developers a way to mark their application as a single-page application. That way, the search engine crawlers know your application is using AJAX to render new paths and can wait for the result before it leaves your page. To mark your application routes as single-page application routes, you will need to use a routing scheme called Hashbangs. Hashbangs are implemented by adding an exclamation mark right after the hash sign, so an example URL would be http://localhost:3000/#!/example.

Luckily, AngularJS supports `Hashbangs` configuration using a module configuration block and the `$locationProvider` service of AngularJS. To configure your application routing, go to the `public/application.js` file and make the following changes:

```
var mainApplicationModuleName = 'mean';

var mainApplicationModule = angular.module(mainApplicationModuleName,
['ngRoute', 'example']);

mainApplicationModule.config(['$locationProvider',
  function($locationProvider) {
    $locationProvider.hashPrefix('!');
  }
]);

angular.element(document).ready(function() {
  angular.bootstrap(document, [mainApplicationModuleName]);
});
```

Once you're done configuring the application's URL scheme, it's time to use the `ngRoute` module and configure your first route.

AngularJS application routes

The `ngRoute` module packs several key entities to manage your routes. We'll begin with the `$routeProvider` object, which provides several methods to define your AngularJS application routing behavior. To use the `$routeProvider` object, you will need to create a module configuration block, inject the `$routeProvider` object, and use it to define your routes. Begin by creating a new folder named `config` inside the `public/example` folder. In your new folder, create a file named `example.client.routes.js` containing the following lines of code:

```
angular.module('example').config(['$routeProvider',
  function($routeProvider) {
    $routeProvider.
    when('/', {
      templateUrl: 'example/views/example.client.view.html'
    }).
    otherwise({
      redirectTo: '/'
    });
  }
]);
```

Let's review the preceding code snippet for a moment. You used the `angular.module()` method to grab the example module and executed the `config()` method to create a new configuration block. Then, you applied DI to inject the `$routeProvider` object to your configuration function, and the `$routeProvider.when()` method to define a new route. The first argument of the `$routeProvider.when()` method is the route's URL, and the second one is an options object, where you defined your template's URL. Finally, you used the `$routeProvider.otherwise()` method to define the behavior of the router when the user navigates to an undefined URL. In this case, you simply redirected the user request to the route you defined before.

Another entity that is packed in the `ngRoute` module is the `ng-view` directive. The `ng-view` directive tells the AngularJS router which DOM element to use to render the routing views. When the user navigates to a specified URL, AngularJS will render the template inside the DOM element marked with this directive. So, to finalize your routing configuration, you will need to include the new JavaScript file in your main application page and add an element with the `ng-view` directive. To do so, change your `app/views/index.ejs` file as follows:

```
<!DOCTYPE html>
<html xmlns:ng="http://angularjs.org">
<head>
  <title><%= title %></title>
</head>
<body>
  <% if (userFullName) { %>
    <h2>Hello <%=userFullName%> </h2>
    <a href="/signout">Sign out</a>
  <% } else { %>
    <a href="/signup">Signup</a>
    <a href="/signin">Signin</a>
  <% } %>

  <section ng-view></section>

  <script type="text/javascript" src="/lib/angular/angular.js"></script>
  <script type="text/javascript" src="/lib/angular-route/angular-route.js"></script>

  <script type="text/javascript" src="/example/example.client.module.js"></script>
  <script type="text/javascript" src="/example/controllers/example.client.controller.js"></script>
```

```
<script type="text/javascript" src="/example/config/example.client.
routes.js"></script>

<script type="text/javascript" src="/application.js"></script>
</body>
</html>
```

Once you're done, everything will be set up to test your routing configuration. Use your command-line tool, and navigate to the MEAN application's root folder. Then, run your application with the help of the following command:

```
$ node server
```

Once your application is running, use your browser and navigate to `http://localhost:3000`. You will notice that the AngularJS router redirects your request to `http://localhost:3000/#!/`. This means your routing configuration works and you should see the two-textboxes example again.

 To learn more about the `ngRoute` module, it is recommended that you visit its official documentation at `http://docs.angularjs.org/api/ngRoute`.

AngularJS services

AngularJS services are singleton entities that are usually used to share information between different entities of the same AngularJS application. Services can be used to fetch data from your server, share cached data, and inject global objects into other AngularJS components. Since there is a single instance of each service, it is also possible to use two-way data binding between different unrelated entities of your AngularJS application. There are two kinds of services: AngularJS prebundled services and custom services. Let's begin by reviewing the former.

AngularJS prebundled services

AngularJS comes prebundled with many services to abstract common development tasks. Commonly used services include:

- `$http`: This is an AngularJS service used to handle AJAX requests
- `$resource`: This is an AngularJS service used to handle RESTful APIs
- `$location`: This is an AngularJS service used to handle URL manipulations
- `$q`: This is an AngularJS service used to handle promises

- $rootScope: This is an AngularJS service that returns the root scope object
- $window: This is an AngularJS service that returns the browser window object

There are many other services as well as extra module services that the AngularJS team constantly maintains, but one of the most powerful features of AngularJS is the ability to define your own custom services.

 You can learn more about AngularJS built-in services by visiting the official documentation at http://docs.angularjs.org/api/.

Creating AngularJS services

Whether to wrap global objects for better testability or for the purpose of sharing your code, creating custom services is a vital part of AngularJS application development. Creating services can be done using one of three module methods: provider(), service(),and factory(). Each of these methods allows you to define a service name and service function that serve different purposes:

- provider(): This is the most verbose method, which provides the most comprehensive way to define a service.
- service(): This is used to instantiate a new singleton object from the service function. You should use it when you're defining a service as a prototype.
- factory(): This is used to provide the value returning from the invoked service function. You should use it when you want to share objects and data across your application.

In your daily development, you'll probably use either the factory() or service() methods since the provider() is usually overkill. An example service created using the factory() method will be as follows:

```
angular.module('example').factory('ExampleService', [
  function() {
    return true;
  }
]);
```

An example service created using the service() method will be as follows:

```
angular.module('example').service('ExampleService', [
  function() {
    this.someValue = true;
```

```
      this.firstMethod = function() {

      }
      this.secondMethod = function() {

      }
    }
  ]);
```

You'll feel more comfortable using each method when you get further ahead with developing your MEAN application.

 You can learn more about creating AngularJS custom services by looking at the official documentation at http://docs.angularjs.org/guide/providers.

Using AngularJS services

Using AngularJS services is very easy since they can be injected into AngularJS components. Your example controller will be able to use ExampleService when you inject it, as follows:

```
angular.module('example').controller('ExampleController', ['$scope',
'ExampleService',
  function($scope, ExampleService) {
    $scope.name = 'MEAN Application';
  }
]);
```

This will make ExampleService available to the controller, which can use it to share information or consume shared information. Let's see how you can use the services to solve one of the main pitfalls when developing a MEAN application.

Managing AngularJS authentication

Managing an AngularJS authentication is one of the most discussed issues of the AngularJS community. The problem is that while the server holds the information about the authenticated user, the AngularJS application is not aware of that information. One solution is to use the $http service and ask the server about the authentication status; however, this solution is flawed since all the AngularJS components will have to wait for the response to return causing inconsistencies and development overhead. A better solution would be to make the Express application render the user object directly in the EJS view and then use an AngularJS service to wrap that object.

Rendering the user object

To render the authenticated user object, you'll have to make several changes.
Let's begin by changing the `app/controllers/index.server.controller.js`
file, as follows:

```javascript
exports.render = function(req, res) {
  res.render('index', {
    title: 'Hello World',
    user: JSON.stringify(req.user)
  });
};
```

Next, go to your `app/views/index.ejs` file and make the following changes:

```html
<!DOCTYPE html>
<html xmlns:ng="http://angularjs.org">
<head>
  <title><%= title %></title>
</head>
<body>
  <% if (user) { %>
    <a href="/signout">Sign out</a>
  <% } else { %>
    <a href="/signup">Signup</a>
    <a href="/signin">Signin</a>
  <% } %>

  <section ng-view></section>

  <script type="text/javascript">
    window.user = <%- user || 'null' %>;
  </script>

  <script type="text/javascript" src="/lib/angular/angular.js"></script>
  <script type="text/javascript" src="/lib/angular-route/angular-route.js"></script>

  <script type="text/javascript" src="/example/example.client.module.js"></script>
  <script type="text/javascript" src="/example/controllers/example.client.controller.js"></script>
  <script type="text/javascript" src="/example/config/example.client.routes.js"></script>
```

```
<script type="text/javascript" src="/application.js"></script>
</body>
</html>
```

This will render the user object as a JSON representation right in your main view application. When the AngularJS application bootstraps, the authentication state will already be available. If the user is authenticated, the `user` object will become available; otherwise, the `user` object will be NULL. Let's see how you can use AngularJS services to share the user information.

Adding the Authentication service

Before you can create your `Authentication` service, it would be best to create a specific module that will hold all user-related logic. We'll call this module the `users` module. In your `public` folder, create a new folder named `users`. In this folder, create a folder named `services` and a file named `users.client.module.js`. In the `users.client.module.js` file, create your `angular` module, as follows:

```
angular.module('users', []);
```

Now create your service file named `authentication.client.service.js` inside your `public/users/services` folder. In your new service file, paste the following code snippet:

```
angular.module('users').factory('Authentication', [
  function() {
    this.user = window.user;

    return {
      user: this.user
    };
  }
]);
```

Notice how we referenced the `window.user` object from the AngularJS service. The last thing you should do is include the module and service files in your main application page. Go to `app/views/index.ejs` and add your new JavaScript files, as follows:

```
<!DOCTYPE html>
<html xmlns:ng="http://angularjs.org">
<head>
  <title><%= title %></title>
</head>
<body>
```

```html
<% if (user) { %>
  <a href="/signout">Sign out</a>
<% } else { %>
  <a href="/signup">Signup</a>
  <a href="/signin">Signin</a>
<% } %>

<section ng-view></section>

<script type="text/javascript">
  window.user = <%- user || 'null' %>;
</script>

<script type="text/javascript" src="/lib/angular/angular.js"></script>
<script type="text/javascript" src="/lib/angular-route/angular-route.js"></script>

<script type="text/javascript" src="/example/example.client.module.js"></script>
<script type="text/javascript" src="/example/controllers/example.client.controller.js"></script>
<script type="text/javascript" src="/example/config/example.client.routes.js"></script>

<script type="text/javascript" src="/users/users.client.module.js"></script>
<script type="text/javascript" src="/users/services/authentication.client.service.js"></script>

<script type="text/javascript" src="/application.js"></script>
</body>
</html>
```

Next, you will need to include your new user module as the main application module dependency. Another important change would be to solve Facebook's redirect bug that adds a hash part to the application's URL after the OAuth authentication round-trip. To do so, modify your public/application.js file as follows:

```javascript
var mainApplicationModuleName = 'mean';

var mainApplicationModule = angular.module(mainApplicationModuleName,
['ngRoute', 'users', 'example']);
```

```
mainApplicationModule.config(['$locationProvider',
    function($locationProvider) {
        $locationProvider.hashPrefix('!');
    }
]);


if (window.location.hash === '#_=_') window.location.hash = '#!';


angular.element(document).ready(function() {
    angular.bootstrap(document, [mainApplicationModuleName]);
});
```

That's it! Your new user module should now be available as well as its
`Authentication` service. The final step will be to use the `Authentication` service
inside another AngularJS component.

Using the Authentication service

The difficult part is behind you since all you have left to do is inject the
`Authentication` service to your desired AngularJS entity, and you'll be able to use
the `user` object. Let's use the `Authentication` service inside our example controller.
Open your `public/example/controllers/example.client.controller.js` file
and make the following changes:

```
angular.module('example').controller('ExampleController', ['$scope',
'Authentication',
    function($scope, Authentication) {
        $scope.name = Authentication.user ? Authentication.user.fullName :
'MEAN Application';
    }
]);
```

In the preceding code snippet, you injected the `Authentication` service to the
controller and used it to reference the model name field to the user `fullName` field.
To test your `Authentication` service, use your command-line tool and navigate to
the MEAN application's root folder. Then run your application:

`$ node server`

Once your application is running, use your browser and navigate to `http://
localhost:3000/#!/`. Try to sign in, and you should see the user's full name
in the two-textboxes example.

Summary

In this chapter, you learned about the basic principles of AngularJS. You went through Angular's key concepts and learned how they fit in the architecture of the AngularJS application. You also learned how to use Bower to install AngularJS and how to structure and bootstrap your application. You discovered AngularJS MVC entities and how they work together. You also used the ngRoute module to configure your application routing scheme. Near the end of this chapter, you learned about AngularJS services and how to use them to manage users' authentication. In the next chapter, you'll connect everything you learned so far to create your first MEAN CRUD module.

8
Creating a MEAN CRUD Module

In the previous chapters, you learned how to set up each framework and how to connect them all together. In this chapter, you're going to implement the basic operational building blocks of a MEAN application, the CRUD module. CRUD modules consist of a base entity with the basic functionality of creating, reading, updating, and deleting entity instances. In a MEAN application, your CRUD module is built from the server-side Express components and an AngularJS client module. In this chapter, we'll cover the following topics:

- Setting up the Mongoose model
- Creating the Express controller
- Wiring the Express routes
- Creating and organizing the AngularJS module
- Introduction to the AngularJS ngResource module
- Implementing the AngularJS module MVC

Introducing CRUD modules

CRUD modules are the basic building block of a MEAN application. Each CRUD module consists of a two MVC structure supporting the module Express and AngularJS functionality. The Express part is built upon a Mongoose model, an Express controller, and an Express routes file. The AngularJS module is a bit more complex and contains a set of views, and an AngularJS controller, service, and routing configuration. In this chapter, you'll learn how to combine these components together to build an example `Article` CRUD module. The examples in this chapter will continue directly from those in previous chapters, so copy the final example from *Chapter 7, Introduction to AngularJS*, and let's start from there.

Setting up the Express components

Let's begin with the Express part of the module. First, you'll create a Mongoose model that will be used to save and validate your articles. Then, you'll move on to the Express controller that will deal with the business logic of your module. Finally, you'll wire the Express routes to produce a RESTful API for your controller methods. We'll begin with the Mongoose model.

Creating the Mongoose model

The Mongoose model will consist of four simple properties that will represent our `Article` entity. Let's begin by creating the Mongoose model file in the `app/models` folder, create a new file named `article.server.model.js` that contains the following code snippet:

```
var mongoose = require('mongoose'),
    Schema = mongoose.Schema;

var ArticleSchema = new Schema({
  created: {
    type: Date,
    default: Date.now
  },
  title: {
    type: String,
    default: '',
    trim: true,
    required: 'Title cannot be blank'
  },
  content: {
```

```
      type: String,
      default: '',
      trim: true
    },
    creator: {
      type: Schema.ObjectId,
      ref: 'User'
    }
});
```

```
mongoose.model('Article', ArticleSchema);
```

You should be familiar with this code snippet, so let's quickly go over this model. First, you included your model dependencies and then you used the Mongoose `Schema` object to create a new `ArticleSchema`. The `ArticleSchema` defines four model fields:

- `created`: This is a date field that represents the time at which the article was created
- `title`: This is a string field that represents the article title; notice how you used the required validation to make sure all articles have a title
- `content`: This is a string field that represents the article content
- `creator`: This is a reference object that represents the user who created the article

In the end, you registered the `Article` Mongoose model to allow you to use it in the `Articles` Express controller. Next, you'll need to make sure your application is loading the model file, so go back to the `config/mongoose.js` file and change it as follows:

```
var config = require('./config'),
    mongoose = require('mongoose');

module.exports = function() {
  var db = mongoose.connect(config.db);

  require('../app/models/user.server.model');
  require('../app/models/article.server.model');

  return db;
};
```

This will load your new model file and make sure your application can use your `Article` model. Once you have your model configured, you'll be able to create your `Articles` controller.

Setting up the Express controller

The Express controller is responsible for managing articles related functionality on the server side. It is built to offer the basic CRUD operations to manipulate the MongoDB article documents. To begin writing the Express controller, go to your app/controllers folder and create a new file named articles.server. controller.js. In your newly created file, add the following dependencies:

```
var mongoose = require('mongoose'),
    Article = mongoose.model('Article');
```

In the preceding lines of code, you basically just included your Article mongoose model. Now, before you begin creating the CRUD methods, it is recommended that you create an error handling method for validation and other server errors.

The error handling method of the Express controller

In order to handle Mongoose errors, it is preferable to write a simple error handling method that will take care of extracting a simple error message from the Mongoose error object and provide it to your controller methods. Go back to your app/ controllers/articles.server.controller.js file and append the following lines of code:

```
var getErrorMessage = function(err) {
  if (err.errors) {
    for (var errName in err.errors) {
      if (err.errors[errName].message) return err.errors[errName].
        message;
    }
  } else {
    return 'Unknown server error';
  }
};
```

The getErrorMessage() method gets the Mongoose error object passed as an argument then iterates over the errors collection and extract the first message. This is done because you don't want to overwhelm your users with multiple error messages at once. Now that you have error handling set up, it is time to write your first controller method.

The create() method of the Express controller

The `create()` method of the Express controller will provide the basic functions to create a new article document. It will use the HTTP request body as the JSON base object for the document and will use the model `save()` method to save it to MongoDB. To implement the `create()` method, append the following lines of code in your `app/controllers/articles.server.controller.js` file:

```
exports.create = function(req, res) {
    var article = new Article(req.body);
    article.creator = req.user;

    article.save(function(err) {
        if (err) {
            return res.status(400).send({
                message: getErrorMessage(err)
            });
        } else {
            res.json(article);
        }
    });
};
```

Let's go over the `create()` method code. First, you created a new `Article` model instance using the HTTP request body. Next, you added the authenticated Passport user as the article `creator()`. Finally, you used the Mongoose instance `save()` method to save the article document. In the `save()` callback function, it is worth noticing how you either return an error response and an appropriate HTTP error code or the new `article` object as a JSON response. Once you're done with the `create()` method, you will move on to implement the read operation. The read operation consists of two methods, one that retrieves a list of articles and a second method that retrieves a particular article. Let's begin with the method that lists a collection of articles.

The list() method of the Express controller

The `list()` method of the Express controller will provide the basic operations to retrieve a list of existing articles. It will use the model's `find()` method to retrieve all the documents in the articles collection then output a JSON representation of this list. To implement the `list()` method, append the following lines of code in your `app/controllers/articles.server.controller.js` file:

```
exports.list = function(req, res) {
    Article.find().sort('-created').populate('creator', 'firstName
        lastName fullName').exec(function(err, articles) {
        if (err) {
```

```
            return res.status(400).send({
                message: getErrorMessage(err)
            });
        } else {
            res.json(articles);
        }
    });
};
```

In this controller method, notice how you used the `find()` function of Mongoose to get the collection of article documents, and while we could add a MongoDB query of some sort, for now we'll retrieve all the documents in the collection. Next, you'll notice how the articles collection is sorted using the created property. Then, you can see how the `populate()` method of Mongoose was used to add some user fields to the `creator` property of the `articles` objects. In this case, you populated the `firstName`, `lastName`, and `fullName` properties of the `creator` user object.

The rest of the CRUD operations involve a manipulation of a single existing article document. You could of course implement the retrieval of the article document in each method by itself, basically repeating this logic. However, the Express router has a neat feature for handling route parameters, so before you'll implement the rest of your Express CRUD functionality, you'll first learn how to leverage the route parameter middleware to save some time and code redundancy.

The read() middleware of the Express controller

The `read()` method of the Express controller will provide the basic operations to read an existing article document from the database. Since you're writing a sort of a RESTful API, the common usage of this method will be handled by passing the article's ID field as a route parameter. This means that your requests to the server will contain an `articleId` parameter in their paths.

Fortunately, the Express router provides the `app.param()` method for handling route parameters. This method allows you to attach a middleware for all requests containing the `articleId` route parameter. The middleware itself will then use the `articleId` provided to find the proper MongoDB document and add the retrieved `article` object to the request object. This will allow all the controller methods that manipulate an existing article to obtain the `article` object from the Express request object. To make this clearer, let's implement the route parameter middleware. Go to your `app/controllers/articles.server.controller.js` file and append the following lines of code:

```
exports.articleByID = function(req, res, next, id) {
    Article.findById(id).populate('creator', 'firstName lastName
        fullName').exec(function(err, article) {
```

```
      if (err) return next(err);
      if (!article) return next(new Error('Failed to load article '
        + id));

      req.article = article;
      next();
    });
  };
```

As you can see, the middleware function signature contains all the Express middleware arguments and an `id` argument. It then uses the `id` argument to find an article and reference it using the `req.article` property. Notice how the `populate()` method of the Mongoose model was used to add some user fields to the `creator` property of the `article` object. In this case, you populated the `firstName`, `lastName`, and `fullName` properties of the `creator` user object.

When you connect your Express routes, you'll see how to add the `articleByID()` middleware to different routes, but for now let's add the `read()` method of the Express controller, which will return an `article` object. To add the `read()` method, append the following lines of code to your `app/controllers/articles.server. controller.js` file:

```
  exports.read = function(req, res) {
    res.json(req.article);
  };
```

Quite simple, isn't it? That's because you already took care of obtaining the `article` object in the `articleByID()` middleware, so now all you have to do is just output the `article` object as a JSON representation. We'll connect the middleware and routes in next sections but before we'll do that, let's finish implementing the Express controller CRUD functionality.

The update() method of the Express controller

The `update()` method of the Express controller will provide the basic operations to update an existing article document. It will use the existing `article` object as the base object, and then update the `title` and `content` fields using the HTTP request body. It will also use the model `save()` method to save the changes to the database. To implement the `update()` method, go to your `app/controllers/articles. server.controller.js` file and append the following lines of code:

```
  exports.update = function(req, res) {
    var article = req.article;

    article.title = req.body.title;
```

```
      article.content = req.body.content;

      article.save(function(err) {
        if (err) {
          return res.status(400).send({
            message: getErrorMessage(err)
          });
        } else {
          res.json(article);
        }
      });
};
```

As you can see, the `update()` method also makes the assumption that you already obtained the `article` object in the `articleByID()` middleware. So, all you have to do is just update the `title` and `content` fields, save the article, and then output the updated `article` object as a JSON representation. In case of an error, it will output the appropriate error message using the `getErrorMessage()` method you wrote before and an HTTP error code. The last CRUD operation left to implement is the `delete()` method; so let's see how you can add a simple `delete()` method to your Express controller.

The delete() method of the Express controller

The `delete()` method of the Express controller will provide the basic operations to delete an existing article document. It will use the model `remove()` method to delete the existing article from the database. To implement the `delete()` method, go to your `app/controllers/articles.server.controller.js` file and append the following lines of code:

```
exports.delete = function(req, res) {
  var article = req.article;

  article.remove(function(err) {
    if (err) {
      return res.status(400).send({
        message: getErrorMessage(err)
      });
    } else {
      res.json(article);
    }
  });
};
```

Again, you can see how the delete() method also makes use of the already obtained article object by the articleByID() middleware. So, all you have to do is just invoke the Mongoose model's remove() method and then output the deleted article object as a JSON representation. In case of an error, it will instead output the appropriate error message using the getErrorMessage() method you wrote before and an HTTP error code.

Congratulations! You just finished implementing your Express controller's CRUD functionality. Before you continue to wire the Express routes that will invoke these methods, let's take some time to implement two authorization middleware.

Implementing an authentication middleware

While building your Express controller, you probably noticed that most methods require your user to be authenticated. For instance, the create() method won't be operational if the req.user object is not assigned. While you can check this assignment inside your methods, this will enforce you to implement the same validation code over and over. Instead you can just use the Express middleware chaining to block unauthorized requests from executing your controller methods. The first middleware you should implement will check whether a user is authenticated at all. Since it is an authentication-related method, it would be best to implement it in the Express users controller, so go to the app/controllers/users.server.controller.js file and append the following lines of code:

```
exports.requiresLogin = function(req, res, next) {
  if (!req.isAuthenticated()) {
    return res.status(401).send({
      message: 'User is not logged in'
    });
  }

  next();
};
```

The requiresLogin() middleware uses the Passport initiated req.isAuthenticated() method to check whether a user is currently authenticated. If it finds out the user is indeed signed in, it will call the next middleware in the chain; otherwise it will respond with an authentication error and an HTTP error code. This middleware is great, but if you want to check whether a specific user is authorized to perform a certain action, you will need to implement an article specific authorization middleware.

Implementing an authorization middleware

In your CRUD module, there are two methods that edit an existing article document. Usually, the `update()` and `delete()` methods should be restricted so that only the user who created the article will be able to use them. This means you need to authorize any request made to these methods to validate whether the current article is being edited by its creator. To do so, you will need to add an authorization middleware to your `Articles` controller, so go to the `app/controllers/articles.server.controller.js` file and append the following lines of code:

```
exports.hasAuthorization = function(req, res, next) {
    if (req.article.creator.id !== req.user.id) {
        return res.status(403).send({
            message: 'User is not authorized'
        });
    }
    next();
};
```

The `hasAuthorization()` middleware is using the `req.article` and `req.user` objects to verify that the current user is the creator of the current article. This middleware also assumes that it gets executed only for requests containing the `articleId` route parameter. Now that you have all your methods and middleware in place, it is time to wire the routes that enable their execution.

Wiring the Express routes

Before we begin wiring the Express routes, let's do a quick overview of the RESTful API architectural design. The RESTful API provides a coherent service structure that represents a set of actions you can perform on an application resource. This means the API uses a predefined route structure along with the HTTP method name to provide context for HTTP requests. Though the RESTful architecture can be applied in different ways, a RESTful API usually complies with a few simple rules:

* A base URI per resource, in our case `http://localhost:3000/articles`
* A data structure, usually JSON, passed in the request body
* Usage of standard HTTP methods (for example, GET, POST, PUT, and DELETE)

Using these three rules, you'll be able to properly route HTTP requests to use the right controller method. So, your articles API will consist of five routes:

- GET http://localhost:3000/articles: This will return a list of articles
- POST http://localhost:3000/articles : This will create and return a new article
- GET http://localhost:3000/articles/:articleId: This will return a single existing article
- PUT http://localhost:3000/articles/:articleId: This will update and return a single existing article
- DELETE http://localhost:3000/articles/:articleId: This will delete and return a single article

As you probably noticed, these routes already have corresponding controller methods. You even have the articleId route parameter middleware already implemented, so all that is left to do is implement the Express routes. To do so, go to the app/routes folder and create a new file named articles.server.routes.js. In your newly created file, paste the following code snippet:

```
var users = require('../../app/controllers/users.server.controller'),
    articles = require('../../app/controllers/articles.server.
controller');

module.exports = function(app) {
  app.route('/api/articles')
      .get(articles.list)
      .post(users.requiresLogin, articles.create);

  app.route('/api/articles/:articleId')
      .get(articles.read)
      .put(users.requiresLogin, articles.hasAuthorization, articles.
update)
      .delete(users.requiresLogin, articles.hasAuthorization, articles.
delete);

  app.param('articleId', articles.articleByID);
};
```

[205]

In the preceding code snippet, you did several things. First, you required the `users` and `articles` controllers, and then you used the Express `app.route()` method to define the base routes for your CRUD operations. You used the Express routing methods to wire each controller method to a specific HTTP method. You can also notice how the POST method uses the `users.requiresLogin()` middleware since a user need to log in before they can create a new article. The same way the PUT and DELETE methods use both the `users.requiresLogin()` and `articles.hasAuthorization()` middleware, since users can only edit and delete the articles they created. Finally, you used the `app.param()` method to make sure every route that has the `articleId` parameter will first call the `articles.articleByID()` middleware. Next, you'll need to do is configure your Express application to load your new `Article` model and routes file.

Configuring the Express application

In order to use your new Express assets, you have to configure your Express application to load your route file. To do so, go back to your `config/express.js` file and change it as follows:

```
var config = require('./config'),
    express = require('express'),
    morgan = require('morgan'),
    compress = require('compression'),
    bodyParser = require('body-parser'),
    methodOverride = require('method-override'),
    session = require('express-session'),
    flash = require('connect-flash'),
    passport = require('passport');

module.exports = function() {
  var app = express();

  if (process.env.NODE_ENV === 'development') {
    app.use(morgan('dev'));
  } else if (process.env.NODE_ENV === 'production') {
    app.use(compress());
  }

  app.use(bodyParser.urlencoded({
    extended: true
  }));
  app.use(bodyParser.json());
  app.use(methodOverride());
```

```
app.use(session({
  saveUninitialized: true,
  resave: true,
  secret: config.sessionSecret
}));

app.set('views', './app/views');
app.set('view engine', 'ejs');

app.use(flash());
app.use(passport.initialize());
app.use(passport.session());

require('../app/routes/index.server.routes.js')(app);
require('../app/routes/users.server.routes.js')(app);
require('../app/routes/articles.server.routes.js')(app);

app.use(express.static('./public'));

return app;
};
```

This is it, your articles RESTful API is ready! Next, you'll learn how simple it is to use the ngResource module to let your AngularJS entities communicate with it.

Introducing the ngResource module

In *Chapter 7, Introduction to AngularJS*, we mentioned the $http service as means of communication between the AngularJS application and your backend API. While the $http service provides the developer with a low-level interface for the HTTP request, the AngularJS team figured out they could better help developers when it comes to RESTful APIs. Since the REST architecture is well structured, much of the client code dealing with AJAX requests could be obfuscated using a higher-level interface. For this purpose, the team created the ngResource module, which provides the developer with an easy way to communicate with a RESTful data source. It does so by presenting a factory, which creates an ngResource object that can handle the basic routes of a RESTful resource. We'll explain how it works in next sections but ngResource is an external module, so first you'll need to install it using Bower.

Installing the ngResource module

Installing the ngResource module is easy, simply go to your bower.json file and change it as follows:

```
{
  "name": "MEAN",
  "version": "0.0.8",
  "dependencies": {
    "angular": "~1.2",
    "angular-route": "~1.2",
    "angular-resource": "~1.2"
  }
}
```

Now, use your command-line tool to navigate to the MEAN application's root folder and install the new ngResource module:

```
$ bower update
```

When Bower finishes installing the new dependency, you will see a new folder named angular-resource in your public/lib folder. Next, you will need to include the module file in your application's main page, so edit your app/views/index.ejs file as follows:

```
<!DOCTYPE html>
<html xmlns:ng="http://angularjs.org">
<head>
  <title><%= title %></title>
</head>
<body>
  <% if (user) { %>
    <a href="/signout">Sign out</a>
  <% } else { %>
    <a href="/signup">Signup</a>
    <a href="/signin">Signin</a>
  <% } %>
  <section ng-view></section>

  <script type="text/javascript">
    window.user = <%- user || 'null' %>;
  </script>

  <script type="text/javascript" src="/lib/angular/angular.js"></script>
  <script type="text/javascript" src="/lib/angular-route/angular-route.js"></script>
```

```
<script type="text/javascript" src="/lib/angular-resource/angular-
resource.js"></script>


   <script type="text/javascript" src="/example/example.client.module.
js"></script>
   <script type="text/javascript" src="/example/controllers/example.
client.controller.js"></script>
   <script type="text/javascript" src="/example/config/example.client.
routes.js"></script>


   <script type="text/javascript" src="/users/users.client.module.
js"></script>
   <script type="text/javascript" src="/users/services/authentication.
client.service.js"></script>


   <script type="text/javascript" src="/application.js"></script>
</body>
</html>
```

Finally, you will need to add the ngResource module as a dependency for your main application module, so change your public/application.js file as follows:

```
var mainApplicationModuleName = 'mean';

var mainApplicationModule = angular.module(mainApplicationModuleName,
['ngResource', 'ngRoute', 'users', 'example']);

mainApplicationModule.config(['$locationProvider',
  function($locationProvider) {
    $locationProvider.hashPrefix('!');
  }
]);

if (window.location.hash === '#_=_') window.location.hash = '#!';

angular.element(document).ready(function() {
  angular.bootstrap(document, [mainApplicationModuleName]);
});
```

When you're done with these changes, the ngResource module will be set up and ready to use.

Using the $resource service

The ngResource module provides the developer with a new factory that can be injected to AngularJS entities. The $resource factory uses a base URL and a set of configuration options to allow the developer easy communication with RESTful endpoints. To use the ngResource module, you have to call the $resource factory method, which will return a $resource object. The $resource factory method accepts four arguments:

- Url: This is a parameterized base URL with parameters prefixed by a colon such as /users/:userId
- ParamDefaults: These are the default values for the URL parameters, which can include hardcoded values or a string prefixed with @ so the parameter value is extracted from the data object
- Actions: These are objects representing custom methods you can use to extend the default set of resource actions
- Options: These are objects representing custom options to extend the default behavior of $resourceProvider

The returned ngResource object will have several methods to handle the default RESTful resource routes, and it can optionally be extended by custom methods. The default resource methods are as follows:

- get(): This method uses a GET HTTP method and expects a JSON object response
- save(): This method uses a POST HTTP method and expects a JSON object response
- query(): This method uses a GET HTTP method and expects a JSON array response
- remove(): This method uses a DELETE HTTP method and expects a JSON object response
- delete(): This method uses a DELETE HTTP method and expects a JSON object response

Calling each of these methods will use the $http service and invoke an HTTP request with the specified HTTP method, URL, and parameters. The $resource instance method will then return an empty reference object that will be populated once the data is returned from the server. You can also pass a callback function that will get called once the reference object is populated. A basic usage of the $resource factory method would be as follows:

```
var Users = $resource('/users/:userId', {
  userId: '@id'
```

```
});

var user = Users.get({
  userId: 123
}, function() {
  user.abc = true;
  user.$save();
});
```

Notice how you can also use the $resource methods from the populated reference object. This is because the $resource methods returns a $resource instance populated with the data fields. In the next section, you'll learn how to use the $resource factory to communicate with your Express API.

Implementing the AngularJS MVC module

The second part of your CRUD module is the AngularJS MVC module. This module will contain an AngularJS service that will communicate with the Express API using the $resource factory, an AngularJS controller that will contain the client-side module logic, and a set of views that provide your users with an interface to perform CRUD operations. Before you begin creating your AngularJS entities, let's first create the module initial structure. Go to your application's public folder and create a new folder named articles. In this new folder, create the module initialization file named articles.client.module.js and paste the following line of code:

```
angular.module('articles', []);
```

This will handle module initialization for you, but you will also need to add your new module as a dependency of your main application module. To do so, change your public/application.js file as follows:

```
var mainApplicationModuleName = 'mean';

var mainApplicationModule = angular.module(mainApplicationModuleName,
  ['ngResource', 'ngRoute', 'users', 'example', 'articles']);

mainApplicationModule.config(['$locationProvider',
  function($locationProvider) {
    $locationProvider.hashPrefix('!');
  }
]);

if (window.location.hash === '#_=_') window.location.hash = '#!';
```

```
angular.element(document).ready(function() {
  angular.bootstrap(document, [mainApplicationModuleName]);
});
```

This will take care of loading your new module, so you can move on to create your module entities. We'll begin with the module service.

Creating the AngularJS module service

In order for your CRUD module to easily communicate with the API endpoints, it is recommended that you use a single AngularJS service that will utilize the $resource factory method. To do so, go to your public/articles folder and create a new folder named services. In this folder, create a new file named articles.client.service.js and add the following lines of code:

```
angular.module('articles').factory('Articles', ['$resource',
function($resource) {
  return $resource('api/articles/:articleId', {
    articleId: '@_id'
  }, {
    update: {
      method: 'PUT'
    }
  });
}]);
```

Notice how the service uses the $resource factory with three arguments: the base URL for the resource endpoints, a routing parameter assignment using the article's document _id field, and an actions argument extending the resource methods with an update() method that uses the PUT HTTP method. This simple service provides you with everything you need to communicate with your server endpoints, as you will witness in the next section.

Setting up the AngularJS module controller

As you already know, most of the module logic is usually implemented in an AngularJS controller. In this case, the controller should be able to provide you with all the methods needed to perform CRUD operations. You'll begin by creating the controller file. To do so, go to your public/articles folder and create a new folder named controllers. In this folder, create a new file named articles.client. controller.js with the following code snippet:

```
angular.module('articles').controller('ArticlesController', ['$scope',
'$routeParams', '$location', 'Authentication', 'Articles',
```

```
    function($scope, $routeParams, $location, Authentication, Articles)
  {
      $scope.authentication = Authentication;
  }
]);
```

Notice how your new `ArticlesController` is using four injected services:

- `$routeParams`: This is provided with the `ngRoute` module and holds references to route parameters of the AngularJS routes you'll define next
- `$location`: This allows you to control the navigation of your application
- `Authentication`: You created this service in the previous chapter and it provides you with the authenticated user information
- `Articles`: You created this service in the previous section and it provides you with a set of methods to communicate with RESTful endpoints

Another thing that you should notice is how your controller binds the `Authentication` service to the `$scope` object so that views will be able to use it as well. Once you have the controller defined, it will be easy to implement the controller CRUD methods.

The create() method of the AngularJS controller

The `create()` method of our AngularJS controller will provide the basic operations for creating a new article. To do so, it will use the `title` and `content` form fields from the view that called the method, and it will use the `Articles` service to communicate with the corresponding RESTful endpoint and save the new article document. To implement the `create()` method, go to your `public/articles/controllers/articles.client.controller.js` file and append the following lines of code inside your controller's constructor function:

```
$scope.create = function() {
  var article = new Articles({
    title: this.title,
    content: this.content
  });

  article.$save(function(response) {
    $location.path('articles/' + response._id);
  }, function(errorResponse) {
    $scope.error = errorResponse.data.message;
  });
};
```

Let's go over the `create()` method functionality. First, you used the title and content form fields, and then the `Articles` resource service to create a new article resource. Then, you used the article resource `$save()` method to send the new `article` object to the corresponding RESTful endpoint, along with two callbacks. The first callback will be executed when the server responds with a success (200) status code, marking a successful HTTP request. It will then use the `$location` service to navigate to the route that will present the created article. The second callback will be executed when the server responds with an error status code, marking a failed HTTP request. The callback will then assign the error message to the `$scope` object, so the view will be able to present it to the user.

The find() and findOne() methods of the AngularJS controller

Your controller will contain two read methods. The first will take care of retrieving a single article and the second will retrieve a collection of articles. Both methods will use the `Articles` service to communicate with the corresponding RESTful endpoints. To implement these methods, go to your `public/articles/controllers/articles.client.controller.js` file and append the following lines code inside your controller's constructor function:

```
$scope.find = function() {
  $scope.articles = Articles.query();
};

$scope.findOne = function() {
  $scope.article = Articles.get({
    articleId: $routeParams.articleId
  });
};
```

In the preceding code, you defined two methods: the `find()` method that will retrieve a list of articles and a `findOne()` method that will retrieve a single article based on the `articleId` route parameter, which the function obtains directly from the URL. The `find()` method uses the resource `query()` method because it expects a collection, while the `findOne()` method is using the resource `get()` method to retrieve a single document. Notice how both methods are assigning the result to the `$scope` variable so that views could use it to present the data.

The update() method of the AngularJS controller

The update() method of the AngularJS controller will provide the basic operations for updating an existing article. To do so, it will use the $scope.article variable, then update it using the view inputs, and the Articles service to communicate with the corresponding RESTful endpoint and save the updated document. To implement the update() method, go to your public/articles/controllers/articles. client.controller.js file and append the following lines of code inside your controller's constructor function:

```
$scope.update = function() {
  $scope.article.$update(function() {
    $location.path('articles/' + $scope.article._id);
  }, function(errorResponse) {
    $scope.error = errorResponse.data.message;
  });
};
```

In the update() method, you used the resource article's $update() method to send the updated article object to the corresponding RESTful endpoint, along with two callbacks. The first callback will be executed when the server responds with a success (200) status code, marking a successful HTTP request. It will then use the $location service to navigate to the route that will present the updated article. The second callback will be executed when the server responds with an error status code, marking a failed HTTP request. The callback will then assign the error message to the $scope object so that the view will be able to present it to the user.

The delete() method of the AngularJS controller

The delete() method of the AngularJS controller will provide the basic operations for deleting an existing article. Since the user might delete an article from the list view as well as the read view, the method will either use the $scope.article or $scope.articles variables. This means that it should also address the issue of removing the deleted article from the $scope.articles collection if necessary. The Articles service will be used again to communicate with the corresponding RESTful endpoint and delete the article document. To implement the delete() method, go to your public/articles/controllers/articles.client. controller.js file and append the following lines of code inside your controller's constructor function:

```
$scope.delete = function(article) {
  if (article) {
    article.$remove(function() {
      for (var i in $scope.articles) {
        if ($scope.articles[i] === article) {
```

```
        $scope.articles.splice(i, 1);
      }
    }
  });
  } else {
    $scope.article.$remove(function() {
      $location.path('articles');
    });
  }
};
```

The `delete()` method will first figure out whether the user is deleting an article from a list or directly from the `article` view. It will then use the article's `$remove()` method to call the corresponding RESTful endpoint. If the user deleted the article from a list view, it will then remove the deleted object from the articles collection; otherwise, it will delete the article then redirect the user back to the list view.

Once you finish setting up your controller, the next step is to implement the AngularJS views that will invoke the controller methods, and then connect them to the AngularJS routing mechanism.

Implementing the AngularJS module views

The next component of your CRUD module is the module views. Each view will take care of providing the user with an interface to execute the CRUD methods you created in the previous section. Before you begin creating the views, you will first need to create the views folder. Go to the `public/articles` folder, create a new folder named `views`, and then follow the instructions given in the next section to create your first view.

The create-article view

The `create-article` view will provide your user with an interface to create a new article. It will contain an HTML form and will use your controller's `create` method to save the new article. To create your view, go to the `public/articles/views` folder and create a new file named `create-article.client.view.html`. In your new file, paste the following code snippet:

```
<section data-ng-controller="ArticlesController">
<h1>New Article</h1>
  <form data-ng-submit="create()" novalidate>
    <div>
      <label for="title">Title</label>
```

```
      <div>
        <input type="text" data-ng-model="title" id="title"
placeholder="Title" required>
      </div>
    </div>
    <div>
      <label for="content">Content</label>
      <div>
        <textarea data-ng-model="content" id="content" cols="30"
rows="10" placeholder="Content"></textarea>
      </div>
    </div>
    <div>
      <input type="submit">
    </div>
    <div data-ng-show="error">
      <strong data-ng-bind="error"></strong>
    </div>
  </form>
</section>
```

The create-article view contains a simple form with two text input fields and a submit button. The text fields use the ng-model directive to bind the user input to the controller scope, and as you specified in the ng-controller directive, this controller will be your ArticlesController. It is also important to notice the ng-submit directive you placed on the form element. This directive tells AngularJS to call a specific controller method when the form is submitted; in this case, the form submission will execute your controller's create() method. The last thing you should notice is the error message at the end of the form that will be shown in case of a creation error.

The view-article view

The view-article view will provide your user with an interface to view an existing article. It will contain a set of HTML elements and will use your controller's findOne() method to get an existing article. Your view will also contain a set of buttons only visible to the article creator that will allow the creator to delete the article or navigate to the update-article view. To create the view, go to the public/articles/views folder and create a new file named view-article.client.view.html. In your new file, paste the following code snippet:

```
<section data-ng-controller="ArticlesController" data-ng-
init="findOne()">
  <h1 data-ng-bind="article.title"></h1>
```

```
<div data-ng-show="authentication.user._id == article.creator._id">
  <a href="/#!/articles/{{article._id}}/edit">edit</a>
  <a href="#" data-ng-click="delete();">delete</a>
</div>
<small>
  <em>Posted on</em>
  <em data-ng-bind="article.created | date:'mediumDate'"></em>
  <em>by</em>
  <em data-ng-bind="article.creator.fullName"></em>
</small>
<p data-ng-bind="article.content"></p>
</section>
```

The `view-article` view contains a simple set of HTML elements presenting the article information using the `ng-bind` directive. Similar to what you did in the `create-article` view, you used the `ng-controller` directive to tell the view to use the `ArticlesController`. However, since you need to load the article information, your view uses the `ng-init` directive to call the controller's `findOne()` method when the view is loaded. It is also important to notice how you used the `ng-show` directive to present the article edit and delete links only to the creator of the article. The first link will direct the user to the `update-article` view, while the second one will call the `delete()` method of your controller.

The edit-article view

The `edit-article` view will provide your user with an interface to update an existing article. It will contain an HTML form and will use your controller's `update()` method to save the updated article. To create this view go to the `public/articles/views` folder and create a new file named `edit-article.client.view.html`. In your new file, paste the following code snippet:

```
<section data-ng-controller="ArticlesController" data-ng-
init="findOne()">
  <h1>Edit Article</h1>
  <form data-ng-submit="update()" novalidate>
    <div>
      <label for="title">Title</label>
      <div>
        <input type="text" data-ng-model="article.title" id="title"
placeholder="Title" required>
      </div>
    </div>
    <div>
      <label for="content">Content</label>
```

```
    <div>
      <textarea data-ng-model="article.content" id="content"
cols="30" rows="10" placeholder="Content"></textarea>
      </div>
    </div>
    <div>
      <input type="submit" value="Update">
    </div>
    <div data-ng-show="error">
      <strong data-ng-bind="error"></strong>
    </div>
  </form>
</section>
```

The `edit-article` view contains a simple form with two text input fields and a submit button. In the `edit-article` view, the text fields use the `ng-model` directive to bind the user input to the controller's `scope.article` object. Since you need to load the article information before editing it, your view uses the `ng-init` directive to call the controller's `findOne()` method when the view is loaded. It is also important to notice the `ng-submit` directive you placed on the `form` element. This time, the directive tells AngularJS that the form submission should execute your controller's `update()` method. The last thing you should notice is the error message in the end of the form that will be shown in the case of an editing error.

The list-articles view

The `list-articles` view will provide your user with an interface to view the list of existing articles. It will contain a set of HTML elements and will use your controller's `find()` method to get the collection of articles. Your view will also use the `ng-repeat` directive to render a list of HTML elements, each representing a single article. If there aren't any existing articles, the view will offer the user to navigate to the `create-article` view. To create your view, go to the `public/articles/views` folder and create a new file named `list-articles.client.view.html`. In your new file, paste the following code snippet:

```
<section data-ng-controller="ArticlesController" data-ng-
init="find()">
  <h1>Articles</h1>
  <ul>
    <li data-ng-repeat="article in articles">
      <a data-ng-href="#!/articles/{{article._id}}" data-ng-
bind="article.title"></a>
      <br>
```

```
      <small data-ng-bind="article.created | date:'medium'"></small>
      <small>/</small>
      <small data-ng-bind="article.creator.fullName"></small>
      <p data-ng-bind="article.content"></p>
   </li>
  </ul>
  <div data-ng-hide="!articles || articles.length">
     No articles yet, why don't you <a href="/#!/articles/
create">create one</a>?
  </div>
</section>
```

The `list-articles` view contains a simple set of repeating HTML elements that represent the list of articles. It uses the `ng-repeat` directive to duplicate the list item for every article in the collection and displays each article's information using the `ng-bind` directive. In the same way as in other views, you used the `ng-controller` directive to connect the view to your `ArticlesController`. However, since you need to load the articles list, your view also uses the `ng-init` directive to call the controller's `find` method when the view is loaded. It is also important to notice how you used the `ng-hide` directive to ask the user to create a new article in case there are no existing articles.

By implementing your AngularJS views, you came very close to finishing your first CRUD module. All that is left to do is wire the module's routes.

Wiring the AngularJS module routes

To complete your CRUD module, you will need to connect your views to your AngularJS application routing mechanism. This means that you'll need to have a route specified for each view you created. To do so, go to the `public/articles` folder and create a new `config` folder. In your `config` folder, create a new file named `articles.client.routes.js` that contains the following code:

```
angular.module('articles').config(['$routeProvider',
   function($routeProvider) {
      $routeProvider.
      when('/articles', {
         templateUrl: 'articles/views/list-articles.client.view.html'
      }).
      when('/articles/create', {
         templateUrl: 'articles/views/create-article.client.view.html'
      }).
      when('/articles/:articleId', {
```

```
            templateUrl: 'articles/views/view-article.client.view.html'
        }).
        when('/articles/:articleId/edit', {
            templateUrl: 'articles/views/edit-article.client.view.html'
        });
    }
]);
```

As you can see, each view will be assigned with its own route. The last two views, which handle an existing article, will also include the `articleId` route parameters in their URL definition. This will enable your controller to extract the `articleId` parameter using the `$routeParams` service. Having your routes defined is the last thing you will have to configure in your CRUD module. All that is left to do is include your module files in the main application page and provide the user with some links to your CRUD module views.

Finalizing your module implementation

To complete your module implementation, you have to include the module JavaScript files in your main application page and change the example view from the previous chapter to properly show the links to your new module routes. Let's begin by changing your main application page; go to your `app/views/index.ejs` file and modify it as follows:

```
<!DOCTYPE html>
<html xmlns:ng="http://angularjs.org">
<head>
  <title><%= title %></title>
</head>
<body>
  <section ng-view></section>

  <script type="text/javascript">
    window.user = <%- user || 'null' %>;
  </script>

  <script type="text/javascript" src="/lib/angular/angular.js"></script>
  <script type="text/javascript" src="/lib/angular-route/angular-route.js"></script>
  <script type="text/javascript" src="/lib/angular-resource/angular-resource.js"></script>
```

```
  <script type="text/javascript" src="/articles/articles.client.
module.js"></script>
  <script type="text/javascript" src="/articles/controllers/articles.
client.controller.js"></script>
  <script type="text/javascript" src="/articles/services/articles.
client.service.js"></script>
  <script type="text/javascript" src="/articles/config/articles.
client.routes.js"></script>

  <script type="text/javascript" src="/example/example.client.module.
js"></script>
  <script type="text/javascript" src="/example/controllers/example.
client.controller.js"></script>
  <script type="text/javascript" src="/example/config/example.client.
routes.js"></script>

  <script type="text/javascript" src="/users/users.client.module.
js"></script>
  <script type="text/javascript" src="/users/services/authentication.
client.service.js"></script>

  <!--Bootstrap AngularJS Application-->
  <script type="text/javascript" src="/application.js"></script>
</body>
</html>
```

As you can probably see, the authentication links were also removed from the main page. However, don't worry; we'll add them in our home view of the example module. To do so, go to the public/example/views/example.client.view.html file and change it as follows:

```
<section ng-controller="ExampleController">
  <div data-ng-show="!authentication.user">
    <a href="/signup">Signup</a>
    <a href="/signin">Signin</a>
  </div>
  <div data-ng-show="authentication.user">
    <h1>Hello <span data-ng-bind="authentication.user.fullName"></
span></h1>
    <a href="/signout">Signout</a>
    <ul>
      <li><a href="/#!/articles">List Articles</a></li>
      <li><a href="/#!/articles/create">Create Article</a></li>
    </ul>
  </div>
</section>
```

Notice how the example view now shows the authentication links when the user is not authenticated and your articles module links once the user is signed in. To make this work, you will also need to make a slight change in your `ExampleController`. Go to the `public/example/controllers/example.client.controller.js` file and change the way you use your `Authentication` service:

```
angular.module('example').controller('ExampleController', ['$scope',
'Authentication',
    function($scope, Authentication) {
        $scope.authentication = Authentication;
    }
]);
```

This change will allow your example view to fully use the `Authentication` service. This is it! Everything is ready for you to test your new CRUD module. Use your command-line tool and navigate to the MEAN application's root folder. Then run your application:

```
$ node server
```

Once your application is running, use your browser and navigate to `http://localhost:3000/#!/`. You will see the sign up and sign in links; try signing in and watch how the home view changes. Then, try navigating to the `http://localhost:3000/#!/articles` URL and see how the `list-articles` view suggests that you create a new article. Continue to create a new article and try to edit and delete it using the views you previously created. Your CRUD module should be fully operational.

Summary

In this chapter, you learned how to build your first CRUD module. You started by defining the Mongoose model and Express controller and learned how implement each CRUD method. You also authorized your controller methods using Express middleware. Then, you defined a RESTful API for your module methods. You discovered the `ngRersource` module and learned how to use to the `$resource` factory to communicate with your API. Then, you created your AngularJS entities and implemented the AngularJS CRUD functionality. After connecting the four parts of a MEAN application and creating your first CRUD module, in the next chapter you'll use Socket.io to add real-time connectivity between your server and client applications.

9
Adding Real-time Functionality Using Socket.io

In previous chapters, you learned how to build your MEAN application and how to create CRUD modules. These chapters covered the basic functionalities of a web application; however, more and more applications require real-time communication between the server and browser. In this chapter, you'll learn how to connect your Express and AngularJS applications in real time using the Socket.io module. Socket.io enables Node.js developers to support real-time communication using `WebSockets` in modern browsers and legacy fallback protocols in older browsers. In this chapter, we'll cover the following topics:

- Setting up the Socket.io module
- Configuring the Express application
- Setting up the Socket.io/Passport session
- Wiring Socket.io routes
- Using the Socket.io client object
- Building a simple chat room

Introducing WebSockets

Modern web applications such as Facebook, Twitter, or Gmail are incorporating real-time capabilities, which enable the application to continuously present the user with recently updated information. Unlike traditional applications, in real-time applications the common roles of browser and server can be reversed since the server needs to update the browser with new data, regardless of the browser request state. This means that unlike the common HTTP behavior, the server won't wait for the browser's requests. Instead, it will send new data to the browser whenever this data becomes available.

This reverse approach is often called *Comet*, a term coined by a web developer named Alex Russel back in 2006 (the term was a word play on the AJAX term; both Comet and AJAX are common household cleaners in the US). In the past, there were several ways to implement a Comet functionality using the HTTP protocol.

The first and easiest way is XHR polling. In XHR polling, the browser makes periodic requests to the server. The server then returns an empty response unless it has new data to send back. Upon a new event, the server will return the new event data to the next polling request. While this works quite well for most browsers, this method has two problems. The most obvious one is that using this method generates a large number of requests that hit the server with no particular reason, since a lot of requests are returning empty. The second problem is that the update time depends on the request period. This means that new data will only get pushed to the browser on the next request, causing delays in updating the client state. To solve these issues, a better approach was introduced: XHR long polling.

In XHR long polling, the browser makes an XHR request to the server, but a response is not sent back unless the server has a new data. Upon an event, the server responds with the event data and the browser makes a new long polling request. This cycle enables a better management of requests, since there is only a single request per session. Furthermore, the server can update the browser immediately with new information, without having to wait for the browser's next request. Because of its stability and usability, XHR long polling has become the standard approach for real-time applications and was implemented in various ways, including Forever iFrame, multipart XHR, JSONP long polling using script tags (for cross-domain, real-time support), and the common long-living XHR.

However, all these approaches were actually hacks using the HTTP and XHR protocols in a way they were not meant to be used. With the rapid development of modern browsers and the increased adoption of the new HTML5 specifications, a new protocol emerged for implementing real-time communication: the full duplex WebSockets.

In browsers that support the `WebSockets` protocol, the initial connection between the server and browser is made over HTTP and is called an HTTP handshake. Once the initial connection is made, the browser and server open a single ongoing communication channel over a TCP socket. Once the socket connection is established, it enables bidirectional communication between the browser and server. This enables both parties to send and retrieve messages over a single communication channel. This also helps to lower server load, decrease message latency, and unify PUSH communication using a standalone connection.

However, `WebSockets` still suffer from two major problems. First and foremost is browser compatibility. The `WebSockets` specification is fairly new, so older browsers don't support it, and though most modern browsers now implement the protocol, a large group of users are still using these older browsers. The second problem is HTTP proxies, firewalls, and hosting providers. Since `WebSockets` use a different communication protocol than HTTP, a lot of these intermediaries don't support it yet and block any socket communication. As it has always been with the Web, developers are left with a fragmentation problem, which can only be solved using an abstraction library that optimizes usability by switching between protocols according to the available resources. Fortunately, a popular library called Socket.io was already developed for this purpose, and it is freely available for the Node.js developer community.

Introducing Socket.io

Created in 2010 by JavaScript developer, Guillermo Rauch, Socket.io aimed to abstract Node.js' real-time application development. Since then, it has evolved dramatically, released in nine major versions before being broken in its latest version into two different modules: Engine.io and Socket.io.

Previous versions of Socket.io were criticized for being unstable, since they first tried to establish the most advanced connection mechanisms and then fallback to more primitive protocols. This caused serious issues with using Socket.io in production environments and posed a threat to the adoption of Socket.io as a real-time library. To solve this, the Socket.io team redesigned it and wrapped the core functionality in a base module called Engine.io.

The idea behind Engine.io was to create a more stable real-time module, which first opens a long-polling XHR communication and then tries to upgrade the connection to a `WebSockets` channel. The new version of Socket.io uses the Engine.io module and provides the developer with various features such as events, rooms, and automatic connection recovery, which you would otherwise implement by yourself. In this chapter's examples, we will use the new Socket.io 1.0, which is the first version to use the Engine.io module.

Older versions of Socket.io prior to Version 1.0 are not using the new Engine.io module and therefore are much less stable in production environments.

When you include the Socket.io module, it provides you with two objects: a socket server object that is responsible for the server functionality and a socket client object that handles the browser's functionality. We'll begin by examining the server object.

The Socket.io server object

The Socket.io server object is where it all begins. You start by requiring the Socket. io module, and then use it to create a new Socket.io server instance that will interact with socket clients. The server object supports both a standalone implementation and the ability to use it in conjunction with the Express framework. The server instance then exposes a set of methods that allow you to manage the Socket.io server operations. Once the server object is initialized, it will also be responsible for serving the socket client JavaScript file for the browser.

A simple implementation of the standalone Socket.io server will look as follows:

```
var io = require('socket.io')();
io.on('connection', function(socket){ /* ... */ });
io.listen(3000);
```

This will open a Socket.io over the 3000 port and serve the socket client file at the URL http://localhost:3000/socket.io/socket.io.js. Implementing the Socket.io server in conjunction with an Express application will be a bit different:

```
var app = require('express')();
var server = require('http').Server(app);
var io = require('socket.io')(server);
io.on('connection', function(socket){ /* ... */ });
server.listen(3000);
```

This time, you first use the http module of Node.js to create a server and wrap the Express application. The server object is then passed to the Socket.io module and serves both the Express application and the Socket.io server. Once the server is running, it will be available for socket clients to connect. A client trying to establish a connection with the Socket.io server will start by initiating the handshaking process.

Socket.io handshaking

When a client wants to connect the Socket.io server, it will first send a handshake HTTP request. The server will then analyze the request to gather the necessary information for ongoing communication. It will then look for configuration middleware that is registered with the server and execute it before firing the connection event. When the client is successfully connected to the server, the connection event listener is executed, exposing a new socket instance.

Once the handshaking process is over, the client is connected to the server and all communication with it is handled through the socket instance object. For example, handling a client's disconnection event will be as follows:

```
var app = require('express')();
var server = require('http').Server(app);
var io = require('socket.io')(server);
io.on('connection', function(socket){
  socket.on('disconnect', function() {
    console.log('user has disconnected');
  });
});
server.listen(3000);
```

Notice how the `socket.on()` method adds an event handler to the disconnection event. Although the disconnection event is a predefined event, this approach works the same for custom events as well, as you will see in the following sections.

While the handshake mechanism is fully automatic, Socket.io does provide you with a way to intercept the handshake process using a configuration middleware.

The Socket.io configuration middleware

Although the Socket.io configuration middleware existed in previous versions, in the new version it is even simpler and allows you to manipulate socket communication before the handshake actually occurs. To create a configuration middleware, you will need to use the server's `use()` method, which is very similar to the Express application's `use()` method:

```
var app = require('express')();
var server = require('http').Server(app);
var io = require('socket.io')(server);

io.use(function(socket, next) {
  /* ... */
```

```
    next(null, true);
});

io.on('connection', function(socket){
  socket.on('disconnect', function() {
    console.log('user has disconnected');
  });
});


server.listen(3000);
```

As you can see, the `io.use()` method callback accepts two arguments: the `socket` object and a `next` callback. The `socket` object is the same socket object that will be used for the connection and it holds some connection properties. One important property is the `socket.request` property, which represents the handshake HTTP request. In the following sections, you will use the handshake request to incorporate the Passport session with the Socket.io connection.

The `next` argument is a callback method that accepts two arguments: an error object and Boolean value. The `next` callback tells Socket.io whether or not to proceed with the handshake process, so if you pass an error object or a false value to the `next` method, Socket.io will not initiate the socket connection. Now that you have a basic understanding of how handshaking works, it is time to discuss the Socket.io client object.

The Socket.io client object

The Socket.io client object is responsible for the implementation of the browser socket communication with the Socket.io server. You start by including the Socket.io client JavaScript file, which is served by the Socket.io server. The Socket.io JavaScript file exposes an `io()` method that connects to the Socket.io server and creates the client `socket` object. A simple implementation of the socket client will be as follows:

```
<script src="/socket.io/socket.io.js"></script>

<script>
  var socket = io();
  socket.on('connect', function() {
      /* ... */
  });
</script>
```

Notice the default URL for the Socket.io client object. Although this can be altered, you can usually leave it like this and just include the file from the default Socket.io path. Another thing you should notice is that the `io()` method will automatically try to connect to the default base path when executed with no arguments; however, you can also pass a different server URL as an argument.

As you can see, the socket client is much easier to implement, so we can move on to discuss how Socket.io handles real-time communication using events.

Socket.io events

To handle the communication between the client and the server, Socket.io uses a structure that mimics the `WebSockets` protocol and fires events messages across the server and client objects. There are two types of events: system events, which indicate the socket connection status, and custom events, which you'll use to implement your business logic.

The system events on the socket server are as follows:

- `io.on('connection', ...)`: This is emitted when a new socket is connected
- `socket.on('message', ...)`: This is emitted when a message is sent using the `socket.send()` method
- `socket.on('disconnect', ...)`: This is emitted when the socket is disconnected

The system events on the client are as follows:

- `socket.io.on('open', ...)`: This is emitted when the socket client opens a connection with the server
- `socket.io.on('connect', ...)`: This is emitted when the socket client is connected to the server
- `socket.io.on('connect_timeout', ...)`: This is emitted when the socket client connection with the server is timed out
- `socket.io.on('connect_error', ...)`: This is emitted when the socket client fails to connect with the server
- `socket.io.on('reconnect_attempt', ...)`: This is emitted when the socket client tries to reconnect with the server
- `socket.io.on('reconnect', ...)`: This is emitted when the socket client is reconnected to the server

- `socket.io.on('reconnect_error', ...)`: This is emitted when the socket client fails to reconnect with the server
- `socket.io.on('reconnect_failed', ...)`: This is emitted when the socket client fails to reconnect with the server
- `socket.io.on('close', ...)`: This is emitted when the socket client closes the connection with the server

Handling events

While system events are helping us with connection management, the real magic of Socket.io relies on using custom events. In order to do so, Socket.io exposes two methods, both on the client and server objects. The first method is the `on()` method, which binds event handlers with events and the second method is the `emit()` method, which is used to fire events between the server and client objects.

An implementation of the `on()` method on the socket server is very simple:

```
var app = require('express')();
var server = require('http').Server(app);
var io = require('socket.io')(server);

io.on('connection', function(socket){
    socket.on('customEvent', function(customEventData) {
        /* ... */
    });
});

server.listen(3000);
```

In the preceding code, you bound an event listener to the `customEvent` event. The event handler is being called when the socket client object emits the `customEvent` event. Notice how the event handler accepts the `customEventData` argument that is passed to the event handler from the socket client object.

An implementation of the `on()` method on the socket client is also straightforward:

```
<script src="/socket.io/socket.io.js"></script>

<script>
    var socket = io();
    socket.on('customEvent', function(customEventData) {
        /* ... */
    });
</script>
```

This time the event handler is being called when the socket server emits the customEvent event that sends customEventData to the socket client event handler.

Once you set your event handlers, you can use the emit() method to send events from the socket server to the socket client and vice versa.

Emitting events

On the socket server, the emit() method is used to send events to a single socket client or a group of connected socket clients. The emit() method can be called from the connected socket object, which will send the event to a single socket client, as follows:

```
io.on('connection', function(socket) {
    socket.emit('customEvent', customEventData);
});
```

The emit() method can also be called from the io object, which will send the event to all connected socket clients, as follows:

```
io.on('connection', function(socket) {
    io.emit('customEvent', customEventData);
});
```

Another option is to send the event to all connected socket clients except from the sender using the broadcast property, as shown in the following lines of code:

```
io.on('connection', function(socket) {
    socket.broadcast.emit('customEvent', customEventData);
});
```

On the socket client, things are much simpler. Since the socket client is only connected to the socket server, the emit() method will only send the event to the socket server:

```
var socket = io();
socket.emit('customEvent', customEventData);
```

Although these methods allow you to switch between personal and global events, they still lack the ability to send events to a group of connected socket clients. Socket. io offers two options to group sockets together: namespaces and rooms.

Socket.io namespaces

In order to easily control socket management, Socket.io allow developers to split socket connections according to their purpose using namespaces. So instead of creating different socket servers for different connections, you can just use the same server to create different connection endpoints. This means that socket communication can be divided into groups, which will then be handled separately.

Socket.io server namespaces

To create a socket server namespace, you will need to use the socket server `of()` method that returns a socket namespace. Once you retain the socket namespace, you can just use it the same way you use the socket server object:

```
var app = require('express')();
var server = require('http').Server(app);
var io = require('socket.io')(server);

io.of('/someNamespace').on('connection', function(socket){
  socket.on('customEvent', function(customEventData) {
    /* ... */
  });
});

io.of('/someOtherNamespace').on('connection', function(socket){
  socket.on('customEvent', function(customEventData) {
    /* ... */
  });
});


server.listen(3000);
```

In fact, when you use the `io` object, Socket.io actually uses a default empty namespace as follows:

```
io.on('connection', function(socket){
/* ... */
});
```

The preceding lines of code are actually equivalent to this:

```
io.of('').on('connection', function(socket){
/* ... */
});
```

Socket.io client namespaces

On the socket client, the implementation is a little different:

```
<script src="/socket.io/socket.io.js"></script>

<script>
  var someSocket = io('/someNamespace');
  someSocket.on('customEvent', function(customEventData) {
    /* ... */
  });

  var someOtherSocket = io('/someOtherNamespace');
  someOtherSocket.on('customEvent', function(customEventData) {
    /* ... */
  });
</script>
```

As you can see, you can use multiple namespaces on the same application without much effort. However, once sockets are connected to different namespaces, you will not be able to send an event to all these namespaces at once. This means that namespaces are not very good for a more dynamic grouping logic. For this purpose, Socket.io offers a different feature called rooms.

Socket.io rooms

Socket.io rooms allow you to partition connected sockets into different groups in a dynamic way. Connected sockets can join and leave rooms, and Socket.io provides you with a clean interface to manage rooms and emit events to the subset of sockets in a room. The rooms functionality is handled solely on the socket server but can easily be exposed to the socket client.

Joining and leaving rooms

Joining a room is handled using the socket join() method, while leaving a room is handled using the leave() method. So, a simple subscription mechanism can be implemented as follows:

```
io.on('connection', function(socket) {
    socket.on('join', function(roomData) {
        socket.join(roomData.roomName);
    })
```

```
socket.on('leave', function(roomData) {
    socket.leave(roomData.roomName);
})
});
```

Notice that the `join()` and `leave()` methods both take the room name as the first argument.

Emitting events to rooms

To emit events to all the sockets in a room, you will need to use the `in()` method. So, emitting an event to all socket clients who joined a room is quite simple and can be achieved with the help of the following code snippets:

```
io.on('connection', function(socket){
    io.in('someRoom').emit('customEvent', customEventData);
});
```

Another option is to send the event to all connected socket clients in a room except the sender by using the `broadcast` property and the `to()` method:

```
io.on('connection', function(socket){
    socket.broadcast.to('someRoom').emit('customEvent',
customEventData);
});
```

This pretty much covers the simple yet powerful room functionality of Socket.io. In the next section, you will learn how implement Socket.io in your MEAN application, and more importantly, how to use the Passport session to identify users in the Socket.io session. The examples in this chapter will continue directly from those in previous chapters, so copy the final example from *Chapter 8, Creating a MEAN CRUD Module*, and let's start from there.

 While we covered most of Socket.io features, you can learn more about Socket.io by visiting the official project page at `https://socket.io`.

Installing Socket.io

Before you can use the Socket.io module, you will need to install it using npm. To do so, change your package.json file as follows:

```
{
    "name": "MEAN",
    "version": "0.0.9",
    "dependencies": {
        "express": "~4.8.8",
        "morgan": "~1.3.0",
        "compression": "~1.0.11",
        "body-parser": "~1.8.0",
        "method-override": "~2.2.0",
        "express-session": "~1.7.6",
        "ejs": "~1.0.0",
        "connect-flash": "~0.1.1",
        "mongoose": "~3.8.15",
        "passport": "~0.2.1",
        "passport-local": "~1.0.0",
        "passport-facebook": "~1.0.3",
        "passport-twitter": "~1.0.2",
        "passport-google-oauth": "~0.1.5",
        "socket.io": "~1.1.0"
    }
}
```

To install the Socket.io module, go to your application's root folder and issue the following command in your command-line tool:

```
$ npm install
```

As usual, this will install the specified version of Socket.io in your node_modules folder. When the installation process is successfully over, your will need be to configure your Express application to work in conjunction with the Socket.io module and start your socket server.

Configuring the Socket.io server

After you've installed the Socket.io module, you will need to start the socket server in conjunction with the Express application. For this, you will have to make the following changes in your `config/express.js` file:

```js
var config = require('./config'),
  http = require('http'),
  socketio = require('socket.io'),
  express = require('express'),
  morgan = require('morgan'),
  compress = require('compression'),
  bodyParser = require('body-parser'),
  methodOverride = require('method-override'),
  session = require('express-session'),
  flash = require('connect-flash'),
  passport = require('passport');

module.exports = function() {
  var app = express();
  var server = http.createServer(app);
  var io = socketio.listen(server);

  if (process.env.NODE_ENV === 'development') {
    app.use(morgan('dev'));
  } else if (process.env.NODE_ENV === 'production') {
    app.use(compress());
  }

  app.use(bodyParser.urlencoded({
    extended: true
  }));
  app.use(bodyParser.json());
  app.use(methodOverride());

  app.use(session({
    saveUninitialized: true,
    resave: true,
    secret: config.sessionSecret
  }));

  app.set('views', './app/views');
  app.set('view engine', 'ejs');
```

```
app.use(flash());
app.use(passport.initialize());
app.use(passport.session());

require('../app/routes/index.server.routes.js')(app);
require('../app/routes/users.server.routes.js')(app);
require('../app/routes/articles.server.routes.js')(app);

app.use(express.static('./public'));

return server;
};
```

Let's go over the changes you made to your Express configuration. After including the new dependencies, you used the `http` core module to create a `server` object that wraps your Express `app` object. You then used the `socket.io` module and its `listen()` method to attach the Socket.io server with your `server` object. Finally, you returned the new `server` object instead of the Express application object. When the server starts, it will run your Socket.io server along with your Express application.

While you can already start using Socket.io, there is still one major problem with this implementation. Since Socket.io is a standalone module, requests that are sent to it are detached from the Express application. This means that the Express session information is not available in a socket connection. This raises a serious obstacle when dealing with your Passport authentication in the socket layer of your application. To solve this issue, you will need to configure a persistent session storage, which will allow you to share your session information between the Express application and Socket.io handshake requests.

Configuring the Socket.io session

To configure your Socket.io session to work in conjunction with your Express sessions, you have to find a way to share session information between Socket.io and Express. Since the Express session information is currently being stored in memory, Socket.io will not be able to access it properly. So, a better solution would be to store the session information in your MongoDB. Fortunately, there is node module named `connect-mongo` that allows you to store session information in a MongoDB instance almost seamlessly. To retrieve the Express session information, you will need some way to parse the signed session cookie information. For this purpose, you'll also install the `cookie-parser` module, which is used to parse the cookie header and populate the HTTP request object with cookies-related properties.

Installing the connect-mongo and cookie-parser modules

Before you can use the `connect-mongo` and `cookie-parser` modules, you will need to install it using npm. To do so, change your `package.json` file as follows:

```json
{
    "name": "MEAN",
    "version": "0.0.9",
    "dependencies": {
        "express": "~4.8.8",
        "morgan": "~1.3.0",
        "compression": "~1.0.11",
        "body-parser": "~1.8.0",
        "method-override": "~2.2.0",
        "express-session": "~1.7.6",
        "ejs": "~1.0.0",
        "connect-flash": "~0.1.1",
        "mongoose": "~3.8.15",
        "passport": "~0.2.1",
        "passport-local": "~1.0.0",
        "passport-facebook": "~1.0.3",
        "passport-twitter": "~1.0.2",
        "passport-google-oauth": "~0.1.5",
        "socket.io": "~1.1.0",
        "connect-mongo": "~0.4.1",
        "cookie-parser": "~1.3.3"
    }
}
```

To install the new modules, go to your application's root folder and issue the following command in your command-line tool:

```
$ npm install
```

As usual, this will install the specified versions of the `connect-mongo` and `cookie-parser` modules in your `node_modules` folder. When the installation process is successfully over, your next step will be to configure your Express application to use `connect-mongo` as session storage.

Configuring the connect-mongo module

To configure your Express application to store session information using the
connect-mongo module, you will have to make a few changes. First, you will need to
change your config/express.js file as follows:

```
var config = require('./config'),
  http = require('http'),
  socketio = require('socket.io'),
  express = require('express'),
  morgan = require('morgan'),
  compress = require('compression'),
  bodyParser = require('body-parser'),
  methodOverride = require('method-override'),
  session = require('express-session'),
  MongoStore = require('connect-mongo')(session),
  flash = require('connect-flash'),
  passport = require('passport');

module.exports = function(db) {
  var app = express();
  var server = http.createServer(app);
  var io = socketio.listen(server);

  if (process.env.NODE_ENV === 'development') {
    app.use(morgan('dev'));
  } else if (process.env.NODE_ENV === 'production') {
    app.use(compress());
  }

  app.use(bodyParser.urlencoded({
    extended: true
  }));
  app.use(bodyParser.json());
  app.use(methodOverride());

  var mongoStore = new MongoStore({
    db: db.connection.db
  });

  app.use(session({
    saveUninitialized: true,
    resave: true,
```

```
    secret: config.sessionSecret,
    store: mongoStore
}));

app.set('views', './app/views');
app.set('view engine', 'ejs');

app.use(flash());
app.use(passport.initialize());
app.use(passport.session());

require('../app/routes/index.server.routes.js')(app);
require('../app/routes/users.server.routes.js')(app);
require('../app/routes/articles.server.routes.js')(app);

app.use(express.static('./public'));

return server;
};
```

In the preceding code snippet, you configured a few things. First, you loaded the `connect-mongo` module, and then passed the Express session module to it. Then, you created a new `connect-mongo` instance and passed it your Mongoose connection object. Finally, you used the Express session store option to let the Express session module know where to store the session information.

As you can see, your Express configuration method requires a `db` argument. This argument is the Mongoose connection object, which will be passed to the Express configuration method from the `server.js` file when it requires the `express.js` file. So, go to your `server.js` file and change it as follows:

```
process.env.NODE_ENV = process.env.NODE_ENV || 'development';

var mongoose = require('./config/mongoose'),
    express = require('./config/express'),
    passport = require('./config/passport');

var db = mongoose();
var app = express(db);
var passport = passport();
app.listen(3000);

module.exports = app;

console.log('Server running at http://localhost:3000/');
```

Once the Mongoose connection is created, the `server.js` file will call the `express.js` module method and pass the Mongoose database property to it. In this way, Express will persistently store the session information in your MongoDB database so that it will be available for the Socket.io session. Next, you will need to configure your Socket.io handshake middleware to use the `connect-mongo` module and retrieve the Express session information.

Configuring the Socket.io session

To configure the Socket.io session, you'll need to use the Socket.io configuration middleware and retrieve your session user. Begin by creating a new file named `socketio.js` in your `config` folder to store all your Socket.io-related configurations. In your new file, add the following lines of code:

```
var config = require('./config'),
  cookieParser = require('cookie-parser'),
  passport = require('passport');

module.exports = function(server, io, mongoStore) {
  io.use(function(socket, next) {
    cookieParser(config.sessionSecret)(socket.request, {},
function(err) {
      var sessionId = socket.request.signedCookies['connect.sid'];

      mongoStore.get(sessionId, function(err, session) {
        socket.request.session = session;

        passport.initialize()(socket.request, {}, function() {
          passport.session()(socket.request, {}, function() {
            if (socket.request.user) {
              next(null, true);
            } else {
              next(new Error('User is not authenticated'), false);
            }
          })
        });
      });
    });
  });

  io.on('connection', function(socket) {
/* ... */
  });
};
```

You now have your server handlers implemented, but how will you configure the socket server to include these handlers? To do so, you will need to go back to your `config/socketio.js` file and slightly modify it:

```
var config = require('./config'),
  cookieParser = require('cookie-parser'),
  passport = require('passport');

module.exports = function(server, io, mongoStore) {
  io.use(function(socket, next) {
    cookieParser(config.sessionSecret)(socket.request, {},
function(err) {
      var sessionId = socket.request.signedCookies['connect.sid'];

      mongoStore.get(sessionId, function(err, session) {
        socket.request.session = session;

        passport.initialize()(socket.request, {}, function() {
          passport.session()(socket.request, {}, function() {
            if (socket.request.user) {
              next(null, true);
            } else {
              next(new Error('User is not authenticated'), false);
            }
          })
        });
      });
    });
  });

  io.on('connection', function(socket) {
    require('../app/controllers/chat.server.controller')(io, socket);
  });
};
```

Notice how the socket server `connection` event is used to load the chat controller. This will allow you to bind your event handlers directly with the connected socket.

Congratulations, you've successfully completed your server implementation! Next, you'll see how easy it is to implement the AngularJS chat functionality. Let's begin with the AngularJS service.

Creating the Socket service

The provided Socket.io client method is used to open a connection with the socket server and return a client instance that will be used to communicate with the server. Since it is not recommended to use global JavaScript objects, you can leverage the services singleton architecture and wrap your socket client.

Let's begin by creating the `public/chat` module folder. Then, create the `public/chat/chat.client.module.js` initialization file with the following line of code:

```
angular.module('chat', []);
```

Now, proceed to create a `public/chat/services` folder for your socket service. In the `public/chat/services` folder, create a new file named `socket.client.service.js` that contains the following code snippet:

```
angular.module('chat').service('Socket', ['Authentication',
'$location', '$timeout',
    function(Authentication, $location, $timeout) {
        if (Authentication.user) {
            this.socket = io();
        } else {
            $location.path('/');
        }

        this.on = function(eventName, callback) {
            if (this.socket) {
                this.socket.on(eventName, function(data) {
                    $timeout(function() {
                        callback(data);
                    });
                });
            }
        };

        this.emit = function(eventName, data) {
            if (this.socket) {
                this.socket.emit(eventName, data);
            }
        };

        this.removeListener = function(eventName) {
            if (this.socket) {
```

```
        this.socket.removeListener(eventName);
      }
    };
  }
]);
```

Let's review this code for a moment. After injecting the services, you checked whether the user is authenticated using the `Authentication` service. If the user is not authenticated, you redirected the request back to the home page using the `$location` service. Since AngularJS services are lazily loaded, the Socket service will only load when requested. This will prevent unauthenticated users from using the Socket service. If the user is authenticated, the service socket property is set by calling the `io()` method of Socket.io.

Next, you wrapped the socket `emit()`, `on()`, and `removeListenter()` methods with compatible service methods. It is worth checking the service `on()` method. In this method, you used a common AngularJS trick that involves the `$timeout` service. The problem we need to solve here is that AngularJS data binding only works for methods that are executed inside the framework. This means that unless you notify the AngularJS compiler about third-party events, it will not know about changes they cause in the data model. In our case, the socket client is a third-party library that we integrate in a service, so any events coming from the socket client might not initiate a binding process. To solve this problem, you can use the `$apply` and `$digest` methods; however, this often causes an error, since a digest cycle might already be in progress. A cleaner solution is to use `$timeout` trick. The `$timeout` service is a wrapper around the `window.setTimeout()` method, so calling it without the `timeout` argument will basically take care of the binding issue without any impact on user experience

Once you have the Socket service ready, all you have to do is implement the chat controller and chat view. Let's begin by defining the chat controller.

Creating the chat controller

The chat controller is where you implement your AngularJS chat functionality. To implement your chat controller, you'll first need to create a `public/chat/controllers` folder. In this folder, create a new file named `chat.client.controller.js` that contains the following code snippet:

```
angular.module('chat').controller('ChatController', ['$scope',
'Socket',
  function($scope, Socket) {
    $scope.messages = [];
```

```
    Socket.on('chatMessage', function(message) {
      $scope.messages.push(message);
    });

    $scope.sendMessage = function() {
      var message = {
        text: this.messageText,
      };

      Socket.emit('chatMessage', message);

      this.messageText = '';
    }

    $scope.$on('$destroy', function() {
      Socket.removeListener('chatMessage');
    })

  }
]);
```

In the controller, you first created a messages array and then implemented the
chatMessage event listener that will add retrieved messages to this array. Next,
you created a sendMessage() method that will send new messages by emitting the
chatMessage event to the socket server. Finally, you used the in-built $destroy
event to remove the chatMessage event listener from the socket client. The $destory
event will be emitted when the controller instance is deconstructed. This is important
because the event handler will still get executed unless you remove it.

Creating the chat view

The chat view will be constructed from a simple form and a list of chat messages.
To implement your chat view, you'll first need to create a public/chat/views
folder. In this folder, create a new file named chat.client.view.html that contains
the following code snippet:

```html
<section data-ng-controller="ChatController">
  <div data-ng-repeat="message in messages" data-ng-switch="message.
type">
    <strong data-ng-switch-when='status'>
      <span data-ng-bind="message.created | date:'mediumTime'"></span>
      <span data-ng-bind="message.username"></span>
      <span>is</span>
      <span data-ng-bind="message.text"></span>
```

```
    </strong>
    <span data-ng-switch-default>
      <span data-ng-bind="message.created | date:'mediumTime'"></span>
      <span data-ng-bind="message.username"></span>
      <span>:</span>
      <span data-ng-bind="message.text"></span>
    </span>
  </div>
  <form ng-submit="sendMessage();">
    <input type="text" data-ng-model="messageText">
    <input type="submit">
  </form>
</section>
```

In this view, you used the ng-repeat directive to render the messages list and the ng-switch directive to distinguish between status messages and regular messages. You also used the AngularJS date filter to properly present the message time. Finally, you finished the view with a simple form that uses the ng-submit directive to invoke the sendMessage() method. Next, you will need to add a chat route to present this view.

Adding chat routes

To present the view, you will need to add a new route for it. To do so, first create the public/chat/config folder. In this folder, create a new file named chat.client. routes.js that contains the following code snippet:

```
angular.module('chat').config(['$routeProvider',
  function($routeProvider) {
    $routeProvider.
    when('/chat', {
      templateUrl: 'chat/views/chat.client.view.html'
    });
  }
]);
```

This should already be a familiar pattern, so let's proceed to finalize the chat implementation.

Finalizing the chat implementation

To finalize your chat implementation, you will need to make a few changes in your main application page and include the Socket.io client file and your new chat files. Go to the `app/views/index.ejs` file and make the following changes:

```
<!DOCTYPE html>
<html xmlns:ng="http://angularjs.org">
  <head>
    <title><%= title %></title>
  </head>
  <body>
    <section ng-view></section>

    <script type="text/javascript">
      window.user = <%- user || 'null' %>;
    </script>

    <script type="text/javascript" src="/socket.io/socket.io.js"></script>
    <script type="text/javascript" src="/lib/angular/angular.js"></script>
    <script type="text/javascript" src="/lib/angular-route/angular-route.js"></script>
    <script type="text/javascript" src="/lib/angular-resource/angular-resource.js"></script>

    <script type="text/javascript" src="/articles/articles.client.module.js"></script>
    <script type="text/javascript" src="/articles/controllers/articles.client.controller.js"></script>
    <script type="text/javascript" src="/articles/services/articles.client.service.js"></script>
    <script type="text/javascript" src="/articles/config/articles.client.routes.js"></script>

    <script type="text/javascript" src="/example/example.client.module.js"></script>
    <script type="text/javascript" src="/example/controllers/example.client.controller.js"></script>
    <script type="text/javascript" src="/example/config/example.client.routes.js"></script>
```

```html
<script type="text/javascript" src="/users/users.client.module.
js"></script>
<script type="text/javascript" src="/users/services/
authentication.client.service.js"></script>

<script type="text/javascript" src="/chat/chat.client.module.
js"></script>
<script type="text/javascript" src="/chat/services/socket.client.
service.js"></script>
<script type="text/javascript" src="/chat/controllers/chat.client.
controller.js"></script>
<script type="text/javascript" src="/chat/config/chat.client.
routes.js"></script>

<script type="text/javascript" src="/application.js"></script>
</body>
</html>
```

Notice how we first added the Socket.io file. It's always a good practice to include third-party libraries before your application files. Now, you'll need to change the `public/application.js` file to include your new `chat` module:

```javascript
var mainApplicationModuleName = 'mean';

var mainApplicationModule = angular.module(mainApplicationModuleName,
['ngResource', 'ngRoute', 'users', 'example', 'articles', 'chat']);

mainApplicationModule.config(['$locationProvider',
  function($locationProvider) {
    $locationProvider.hashPrefix('!');
  }
]);

if (window.location.hash === '#_=_') window.location.hash = '#!';

angular.element(document).ready(function() {
  angular.bootstrap(document, [mainApplicationModuleName]);
});
```

To finish up your chat implementation, change your `public/example/views/example.client.view.html` file and add a new chat link:

```html
<section ng-controller="ExampleController">
  <div data-ng-show="!authentication.user">
    <a href="/signup">Signup</a>
```

```
        <a href="/signin">Signin</a>
    </div>
    <div data-ng-show="authentication.user">
        <h1>Hello <span data-ng-bind="authentication.user.fullName"></
span></h1>
        <a href="/signout">Signout</a>
        <ul>
            <li><a href="/#!/chat">Chat</a></li>
            <li><a href="/#!/articles">List Articles</a></li>
            <li><a href="/#!/articles/create">Create Article</a></li>
        </ul>
    </div>
</section>
```

Once you are finished with these changes, your new chat example should be ready to use. Use your command-line tool and navigate to the MEAN application's root folder. Then, run your application by typing the following command:

```
$ node server
```

Once your application is running, open two different browsers and sign up with two different users. Then, navigate to `http://localhost:3000/#!/chat` and try sending chat messages between your two clients. You'll be able to see how chat messages are being updated in real time. Your MEAN application now supports real-time communication.

Summary

In this chapter, you learned how the Socket.io module works. You went over the key features of Socket.io and learned how the server and client communicate. You configured your Socket.io server and learned how to integrate it with your Express application. You also used the Socket.io handshake configuration to integrate the Passport session. In the end, you built a fully functional chat example and learned how to wrap the Socket.io client with an AngularJS service. In the next chapter, you'll learn how to write and run tests to cover your application code.

10
Testing MEAN Applications

In previous chapters, you learned to build your real-time MEAN application. You went through Express and AngularJS basics and learned to connect all the parts together. However, when your application becomes bigger and more complex, you'll soon find out that it's very difficult to manually verify your code. You will then need to start testing your application automatically. Fortunately, testing a web application, which was once a complicated task, has become much easier with the help of new tools and suitable testing frameworks. In this chapter, you'll learn to cover your MEAN application code using modern test frameworks and popular tools. We'll cover the following topics:

- Introducing JavaScript TDD and BDD
- Setting up your testing environment
- Installing and configuring the Mocha test framework
- Writing Express model and controller tests
- Installing and configuring the Karma test runner
- Using Jasmine to unit test your AngularJS entities
- Writing and running **end-to-end** (**E2E**) AngularJS tests

Introducing JavaScript testing

As you already know, in the past couple of years, JavaScript has evolved dramatically. It was once a simple scripting language made for small web applications, but now it's the backbone for complex architectures, both in the server and the browser. However, this evolution has put developers in a situation where they need to manually manage a large code base that remained uncovered in terms of automated testing. While our fellow Java, .NET, or Ruby developers have been safely writing and running their tests, JavaScript developers remained in an uncharted territory, with the burden of figuring out how to properly test their applications. Lately, this void has been filled with the formation of new tools and testing frameworks written by the talented JavaScript community members. In this chapter, we'll cover some of these popular tools, but keep in mind that this field is very new and is constantly changing, so you'll also have to keep an eye out for newly emerging solutions.

In this chapter, we'll discuss two major types of tests: unit tests and E2E tests. Unit tests are written to validate the functionality of isolated units of code. This means a developer should aspire to write each unit test to cover the smallest testable part of the application. For example, a developer might write unit tests to validate that an ORM method works properly and gives the right validation errors as an output. However, quite often a developer will choose to write unit tests that verify bigger code units, mostly because these units perform an isolated operation together. If a developer wants to test a process that includes many of the software components combined, he will write an E2E test. E2E tests are written to validate cross-application functionality. These tests often force the developer to use more than one tool and cover different parts of the application in the same test, including UI, server, and database components. An example would be an E2E test that validates the signup process. Identifying the right tests is one of the crucial steps in writing a proper test suite for your application. However, setting appropriate conventions for the development team can make this process much easier.

Before we begin discussing JavaScript-specific tools, let's first look at a quick overview of the TDD paradigm and how it affects our daily development cycles.

TDD, BDD, and unit testing

Test-driven development (TDD) is a software development paradigm developed by software engineer and agile methodology advocate Kent Beck. In TDD, the developer starts by writing a (initially failing) test, which defines the requirements expected from an isolated unit of code. The developer is then required to implement the minimum amount of code that passes the test. When the test is successfully passed, the developers clean up the code and verify that all the tests are passing. The following diagram describes TDD cycles in a visual manner:

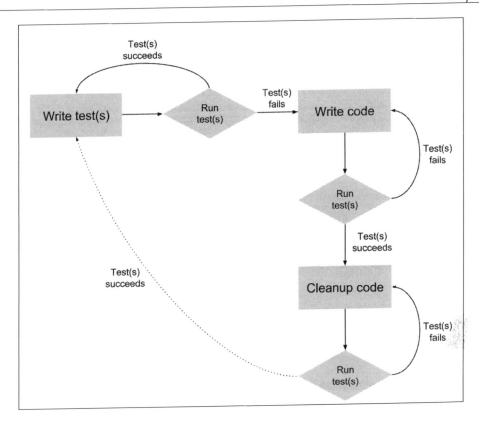

It is important to remember that although TDD has become a popular approach in modern software development, it is very difficult to implement in its purest form. To ease this process and improve team communication, a new approach was developed on top of TDD, called BDD, or behavior-driven development. The BDD paradigm is a subset of TDD, created by Dan North, which helps developers identify the scope of their unit tests and express their test process in a behavioral terminology. Basically TDD provides the wireframe for writing tests, and BDD provides the vocabulary to shape the way tests are written. Usually a BDD test framework provides the developer with a set of self-explanatory methods to describe the test process.

Although BDD provides us with a mechanism for writing tests, running these tests in a JavaScript environment is still a complicated task. Your application will probably run on different browsers and even different versions of the same browser. So, running the tests you wrote on a single browser will not provide you with proper coverage. To solve this issue, the JavaScript community has developed a various set of tools for writing, evaluating, and properly running your tests.

Test frameworks

Although you can start writing your tests using your own library, you'll soon find out that it is not very scalable and requires you to build a complex infrastructure. Fortunately, a respectable effort has been put into solving this issue, which resulted in several popular test frameworks that allow you to write your tests in a structured and common way. These test frameworks usually provide a set of methods to encapsulate tests. It is also very common for a test framework to provide some sort of API that enables you to run tests and integrate the results with other tools in your development cycle.

Assertion libraries

Though test frameworks provide the developer with a way to create and organize tests, they often lack the ability to actually test a Boolean expression that represents the test result. For instance, the Mocha test framework, which we'll introduce in the next section, doesn't provide the developer with an assertion tool. For this purpose, the community has developed several assertion libraries, which allows you to examine a certain predicate. The developer uses assertion expressions to indicate a predicate that should be true in the test context. When running the test, the assertion is evaluated, and if it turns out to be false, the test will fail.

Test runners

Test runners are utilities that enable the developer to easily run and evaluate tests. A test runner usually uses a defined testing framework along with a set of preconfigured properties to evaluate test results in different contexts. For instance, a test runner can be configured to run tests with different environment variables or run the same test on different testing platforms (usually browsers). We will present two different test runners in the AngularJS test section.

Now that we overviewed a set of terms associated with testing, we can finally explain how to test the different parts of your MEAN application. Although your code is written entirely in JavaScript, it does run on different platforms with different scenarios. In order to mitigate the testing process, we divided it into two different sections: testing Express components and testing AngularJS components. Let's begin with testing your Express application components.

Testing your Express application

In the Express part of your MEAN application, your business logic is mostly encapsulated inside controllers; however, you also have Mongoose models that obfuscate many tasks, including data manipulation and validations. So, to properly cover your Express application code, you will need to write tests that cover both models and controllers. In order to do so, you will use Mocha as your test framework, the Should.js assertion library for your models, and the SuperTest HTTP assertion library for your controllers. You will also need to create a new test environment configuration file that will provide you with special configuration options for testing purposes, for example, a dedicated MongoDB connection string. By the end of this section, you will learn to use the Mocha command-line tool to run and evaluate your test results. We'll begin with presenting the Mocha test framework.

Introducing Mocha

Mocha is a versatile test framework developed by Express creator TJ Holowaychuk. It supports both BDD and TDD unit tests, uses Node.js to run the tests, and allows the developer to run both synchronous and asynchronous tests. Since Mocha is minimal by structure, it doesn't include a built-in assertion library; instead, it supports the integration of popular assertion frameworks. It comes packed with a set of different reporters to present the test results and includes many features, such as pending tests, excluding tests, and skipping tests. The main interaction with Mocha is done using the command-line tool provided, which lets you configure the way tests are executed and reported.

The BDD interface for Mocha tests includes several descriptive methods, which enable the developer to easily describe the test scenario. These methods are as follows:

- `describe(description, callback)`: This is the basic method that wraps each test suite with a description. The callback function is used to define test specifications or subsuites.
- `it(description, callback)`: This is the basic method that wraps each test specification with a description. The callback function is used to define the actual test logic.
- `before(callback)`: This is a hook function that is executed once before all the tests in a test suite.
- `beforeEach(callback)`: This is a hook function that is executed before each test specification in a test suite.

- `after(callback)`: This is a hook function that is executed once after all the tests in a test suite are executed.
- `afterEach(callback)`: This is a hook function that is executed after each test specification in a test-suite is executed.

Using these basic methods will allow you to define unit tests by utilizing the BDD paradigm. However, any test cannot be concluded without including an assertion expression that determines the developer's expectations from the covered code. To support assertions, you will need to use an assertion library.

You can learn more about Mocha's features by visiting the official documentation at `http://visionmedia.github.io/mocha/`.

Introducing Should.js

The Should.js library, also developed by TJ Holowaychuk, aims to help developers write readable and expressive assertion expressions. Using Should.js, you'll be able to keep your test code better organized and produce useful error messages. The Should.js library extends `Object.prototype` with a non-enumerable getter that allows you to express how that object should behave. One of Should.js' powerful features is that every assertion returns a wrapped object, so assertions can be chained. This means that you can write readable expressions that pretty much describe the assertions associated with the tested object. For example, a chained assertion expression would be as follows:

```
user.should.be.an.Object.and.have.property('name', 'tj');
```

Notice how each helper property returns a Should.js object, which can be chained using another helper property (be, an, have, and so on) or tested using assertion properties and methods (`Object`, `property()`). You can learn more about Should.js features by visiting the official documentation at `https://github.com/shouldjs/should.js`.

While Should.js does an excellent job in testing objects, it will not help you with testing your HTTP endpoints. To do so, you will need to use a different kind of assertion library. This is where the minimal modularity of Mocha comes in handy.

Introducing SuperTest

SuperTest is another assertion library developed by TJ Holowaychuk, which differs from other assertion libraries by providing developers with an abstraction layer that makes HTTP assertions. This means that instead of testing objects, it will help you to create assertion expressions that test HTTP endpoints. In your case, it will help you to test your controller endpoints, thus covering the code that's exposed to the browser. To do so, it will make use of the Express application object and test the responses returned from your Express endpoints. An example SuperTest assertion expression is as follows:

```
request(app).get('/user')
  .set('Accept', 'application/json')
  .expect('Content-Type', /json/)
  .expect(200, done);
```

Notice how each method can be chained to another assertion expression. This will allow you to make several assertions on the same response using the `expect()` method. You can learn more about SuperTest's features by visiting the official documentation at `https://github.com/visionmedia/supertest`.

In the next section, you will learn how to leverage Mocha, Should.js, and SuperTest to test both your models and your controllers. Let's begin by installing these dependencies and properly configuring the test environment. The examples in this chapter will continue directly from those in previous chapters, so copy the final example from *Chapter 9, Adding Real-time Functionality Using Socket.io*, and let's take it from there.

Installing Mocha

Mocha is basically a Node.js module that provides command-line capabilities to run tests. The easiest way to use Mocha is to first install it as a global node module using npm. To do so, just issue the following command in your command-line tool:

```
$ npm install -g mocha
```

As usual, this will install the latest version of Mocha in your global `node_modules` folder. When the installation process is successfully finished, you'll be able to use the Mocha utility from your command line. Next, you'll need to install the Should.js and SuperTest assertion libraries in your project.

You may experience some trouble installing global modules. This is usually a permission issue, so use `sudo` or super user when running the global install command.

Installing the Should.js and SuperTest modules

Before you can start writing your tests, you will need to install both Should.js and SuperTest using npm. To do so, change your project's package.json file as follows:

```
{
    "name": "MEAN",
    "version": "0.0.10",
    "dependencies": {
        "express": "~4.8.8",
        "morgan": "~1.3.0",
        "compression": "~1.0.11",
        "body-parser": "~1.8.0",
        "method-override": "~2.2.0",
        "express-session": "~1.7.6",
        "ejs": "~1.0.0",
        "connect-flash": "~0.1.1",
        "mongoose": "~3.8.15",
        "passport": "~0.2.1",
        "passport-local": "~1.0.0",
        "passport-facebook": "~1.0.3",
        "passport-twitter": "~1.0.2",
        "passport-google-oauth": "~0.1.5",
        "socket.io": "~1.1.0",
        "connect-mongo": "~0.4.1",
        "cookie-parser": "~1.3.3"
    },
    "devDependencies": {
        "should": "~4.0.4",
        "supertest": "~0.13.0"
    }
}
```

As you can notice, we used a new property in the package.json file called devDependencies. This npm feature will allow us to configure development-oriented dependencies separately from other application dependencies. It means that when we deploy our application to a production environment, you'll get faster installation time and decreased project size. However, when you run the install command in other environments, these packages will be installed just like any other dependency.

To install your new dependencies, go to your application's root folder and issue the following command in your command-line tool:

```
$ npm install
```

This will install the specified versions of Should.js and SuperTest in your project's node_modules folder. When the installation process is successfully finished, you will be able to use these modules in your tests. Next, you'll need to prepare your project for testing by creating a new environment configuration file and setting up your test environment.

Configuring your test environment

Since you're going to run tests that include database manipulation, it would be safer to use a different configuration file to run tests. Fortunately, your project is already configured to use different configuration files according to the NODE_ENV variable. While the application automatically uses the config/env/development.js file, when running in a test environment, we will make sure to set the NODE_ENV variable to test. All you need to do is create a new configuration file named test.js in the config/env folder. In this new file, paste the following code snippet:

```
module.exports = {
  db: 'mongodb://localhost/mean-book-test',
  sessionSecret: 'Your Application Session Secret',
  viewEngine: 'ejs',
  facebook: {
    clientID: 'APP_ID',
    clientSecret: 'APP_SECRET',
    callbackURL: 'http://localhost:3000/oauth/facebook/callback'
  },
  twitter: {
    clientID: 'APP_ID',
    clientSecret: 'APP_SECRET',
    callbackURL: 'http://localhost:3000/oauth/twitter/callback'
  },
  google: {
    clientID: 'APP_ID',
    clientSecret: 'APP_SECRET',
    callbackURL: 'http://localhost:3000/oauth/google/callback'
  }
};
```

As you can notice, we changed the db property to use a different MongoDB database. Other properties remain the same, but you can change them later to test different configurations of your application.

You'll now need to create a new folder for your test files. To do so, go to your app folder and create a new folder named tests. Once you're done setting up your environment, you can continue to the next section and write your first tests.

Writing your first Mocha test

Before you begin writing your tests, you will first need to identify and break your Express application's components into testable units. Since most of your application logic is already divided into models and controllers, the obvious way to go about this would be to test each model and controller individually. The next step would be to break this component into logical units of code and test each unit separately. For instance, take each method in your controller and write a set of tests for each method. You can also decide to test a couple of your controller's methods together when each method doesn't perform any significant operation by itself. Another example would be to take your Mongoose model and test each model method.

In BDD, every test begins by describing the test's purpose in a natural language. This is done using the `describe()` method, which lets you define the test scenario's description and functionality. Describe blocks can be nested, which enables you to further elaborate on each test. Once you have your test's descriptive structure ready, you will be able to define a test specification using the `it()` method. Each `it()` block will be regarded as a single unit test by the test framework. Each test will also include a single assertion expression or multiple assertion expressions. The assertion expressions will basically function as Boolean test indicators for your test assumptions. When an assertion expression fails, it will usually provide the test framework with a traceable error object.

While this pretty much explains most of the tests you'll encounter, you'll also be able to use supportive methods that execute certain functionality in context with your tests. These supportive methods can be configured to run before or after a set of tests, and even before or after each test is executed.

In the following examples, you'll learn to easily use each method to test the articles module that you created in *Chapter 8, Creating a MEAN CRUD Module*. For the sake of simplicity, we will only implement a basic test suite for each component. This test suite could and should be largely expanded to ultimately provide decent code coverage.

 Although TDD clearly states that tests should be written before you start coding features, the structure of this book forces us to write tests that examine an already existing code. If you wish to implement real TDD in your development process, you should be aware that development cycles should begin by first writing the appropriate tests.

Testing the Express model

In the model's test example, we'll write two tests that verify the model save method. To begin testing your `Article` Mongoose model, you will need to create a new file named `article.server.model.tests.js` in your `app/tests` folder. In your new file, paste the following lines of code:

```
var app = require('../../server.js'),
    should = require('should'),
    mongoose = require('mongoose'),
    User = mongoose.model('User'),
    Article = mongoose.model('Article');

var user, article;

describe('Article Model Unit Tests:', function() {
  beforeEach(function(done) {
    user = new User({
      firstName: 'Full',
      lastName: 'Name',
      displayName: 'Full Name',
      email: 'test@test.com',
      username: 'username',
      password: 'password'
    });

    user.save(function() {
      article = new Article({
        title: 'Article Title',
        content: 'Article Content',
        user: user
      });

      done();
    });
  });

  describe('Testing the save method', function() {
    it('Should be able to save without problems', function() {
```

```
        article.save(function(err) {
          should.not.exist(err);
        });
      });

      it('Should not be able to save an article without a title',
    function() {
          article.title = '';

          article.save(function(err) {
            should.exist(err);
          });
        });
      });

    afterEach(function(done) {
      Article.remove(function() {
        User.remove(function() {
          done();
        });
      });
    });
  });
```

Let's start breaking down the test code. First, you required your module dependencies and defined your global variables. Then, you began your test using a describe() method, which informs the test tool this test is going to examine the Article model. Inside the describe block, we began by creating new user and article objects using the beforeEach() method. The beforeEach() method is used to define a block of code that runs before each test is executed. You can also replace it with the before() method, which will only get executed once, before all the tests are executed. Notice how the beforeEach() method informs the test framework that it can continue with the tests execution by calling the done() callback. This will allow the database operations to be completed before actually executing the tests.

Next, you created a new describe block indicating that you were about to test the model save method. In this block, you created two tests using the it() method. The first test used the article object to save a new article. Then, you used the Should.js assertion library to validate that no error occurred. The second test checked the Article model validation by assigning an invalid value to the title property. This time, the Should.js assertion library was used to validate that an error actually occured when trying to save an invalid article object.

You finished your tests by cleaning up the `Article` and `User` collections using the `afterEach()` method. Like with the `beforeEach()` method, this code will run after each test is executed, and can also be replaced with an `after()` method. The `done()` method is also used here in the same manner.

Congratulations, you created your first unit test! As we stated earlier, you can continue expanding this test suite to cover more of the model code, which you probably will when dealing with more complicated objects. Next, we'll see how you can write more advanced unit tests when covering your controller's code.

Testing the Express controller

In the controller test example, we'll write two tests to check the controller's methods that retrieve articles. When setting out to write these tests, we have two options: either test the controller's methods directly or use the defined controller's Express routes in the tests. Although it is preferable to test each unit separately, we would choose to go with the second option since our routes' definition is quite simple, so we can benefit from writing more inclusive tests. To begin testing your articles controller, you will need to create a new file named `articles.server.controller.tests.js` in your `app/tests` folder. In your new file, paste the following code snippet:

```
var app = require('../../server'),
    request = require('supertest'),
    should = require('should'),
    mongoose = require('mongoose'),
    User = mongoose.model('User'),
    Article = mongoose.model('Article');

var user, article;

describe('Articles Controller Unit Tests:', function() {
  beforeEach(function(done) {
    user = new User({
      firstName: 'Full',
      lastName: 'Name',
      displayName: 'Full Name',
      email: 'test@test.com',
      username: 'username',
      password: 'password'
    });

    user.save(function() {
      article = new Article({
```

```
          title: 'Article Title',
          content: 'Article Content',
          user: user
        });

      article.save(function(err) {
        done();
      });
    });
  });

  describe('Testing the GET methods', function() {
    it('Should be able to get the list of articles', function(done){
      request(app).get('/api/articles/')
        .set('Accept', 'application/json')
        .expect('Content-Type', /json/)
        .expect(200)
        .end(function(err, res) {
          res.body.should.be.an.Array.and.have.lengthOf(1);
          res.body[0].should.have.property('title', article.title);
          res.body[0].should.have.property('content', article.
content);

          done();
        });
    });

    it('Should be able to get the specific article', function(done) {
      request(app).get('/api/articles/' + article.id)
        .set('Accept', 'application/json')
        .expect('Content-Type', /json/)
        .expect(200)
        .end(function(err, res) {
          res.body.should.be.an.Object.and.have.property('title',
article.title);
          res.body.should.have.property('content', article.content);

          done();
        });
    });
  });

  afterEach(function(done) {
```

```
        Article.remove().exec();
        User.remove().exec();
        done();
    });
});
```

Just as with your model test, first you required your module dependencies and defined your global variables. Then, you started your test using a `describe()` method, which informs the test tool this test is going to examine the `Articles` controller. Inside the `describe` block, we began by creating new `user` and `article` objects using the `beforeEach()` method. This time, we saved the article before initiating the tests, and then continued with test execution by calling the `done()` callback.

Next, you created a new `describe` block indicating that you were about to test the controllers' GET methods. In this block, you created two tests using the `it()` method. The first test uses the SuperTest assertion library to issue an HTTP GET request at the endpoint that returns the list of articles. It then examines the HTTP response variables, including the content-type header and the HTTP response code. When it verifies the response is returned properly, it uses three Should.js assertion expressions to test the response body. The response body should be an array of articles that includes a single article that should be similar to the article you created in the `beforeEach()` method.

The second test uses the SuperTest assertion library to issue an HTTP GET request at the endpoint that returns a single article. It then examines the HTTP response variables including the `content-type` header and the HTTP response code. Once it verifies that the response is returned properly, it uses three Should.js assertion expressions to test the response body. The response body should be a single `article` object and should be similar to the article you created in the `beforeEach()` method.

Just as before, you finished your tests by cleaning up the `Article` and `User` collections using the `afterEach()` method. Once you're done setting up the testing environment and creating your tests, all you have left to do is run them using Mocha's command-line tool.

Running your Mocha test

To run your Mocha test, you need to use Mocha's command-line utility that you previously installed. To do so, use your command-line tool and navigate to your project's base folder. Then, issue the following command:

```
$ NODE_ENV=test mocha --reporter spec app/tests
```

Windows users should first execute the following command:

```
> set NODE_ENV=test
```

Then run Mocha using the following command:

```
> mocha --reporter spec app/tests
```

The preceding command will do a few things. First, it will set the NODE_ENV variable to test, forcing your MEAN application to use the test environment configuration file. Then, it will execute the Mocha command-line utility, with the --reporter flag, telling Mocha to use the spec reporter and the path to your tests folder. The test results should be reported in your command-line tool and will be similar to the following screenshot:

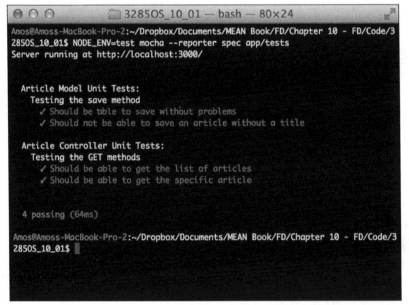

Mocha's test results

This concludes the test coverage of your Express application. You can use these methods to expand your test suite and dramatically improve application development. It is recommended that you set your test conventions from the beginning of your development process; otherwise, writing tests can become an overwhelming experience. Next, you'll learn to test your AngularJS components and write E2E tests.

Testing your AngularJS application

For years, testing frontend code was a complex task. Running tests across different browsers and platforms was complicated, and since most of the application code was unstructured, test tools mainly focused on UI E2E tests. However, the shift towards MVC frameworks allowed the community to create better test utilities, improving the way developers write both unit and E2E tests. In fact, the AngularJS team is so focused on testing that every feature developed by the team is designed with testability in mind.

Furthermore, platform fragmentation also created a new layer of tools called test runners, which allow developers to easily run their tests in different contexts and platforms. In this section, we'll focus on tools and frameworks associated with AngularJS applications, explaining how to best use them to write and run both unit and E2E tests. We'll start with the test framework that will serve us in both cases, the Jasmine test framework.

 Although we can use Mocha or any other test framework, using Jasmine is currently the easiest and most common approach when testing AngularJS applications.

Introducing the Jasmine framework

Jasmine is an opinionated BDD framework developed by the Pivotal organization. Conveniently, Jasmine uses the same terminology as Mocha's BDD interface, including the `describe()`, `it()`, `beforeEach()`, and `afterEach()` methods. However, unlike Mocha, Jasmine comes prebundled with assertion capabilities using the `expect()` method chained with assertion methods called Matchers. Matchers are basically functions that implement a Boolean comparison between an actual object and an expected value. For instance, a simple test using the `toBe()` matcher is as follows:

```
describe('Matchers Example', function() {
  it('Should present the toBe matcher example', function() {
    var a = 1;
    var b = a;

    expect(a).toBe(b);
    expect(a).not.toBe(null);
  });
});
```

The `toBe()` matcher uses the `===` operator to compare objects. Jasmine includes plenty of other matchers and even enables developers to add custom matchers. Jasmine also includes other robust features to allow more advanced test suites. In the next section, we'll focus on how to use Jasmine to easily test your AngularJS components.

 You can learn more about Jasmine's features by visiting the official documentation at `http://jasmine.github.io/2.0/introduction.html`.

AngularJS unit tests

In the past, web developers who wanted to write unit tests to cover their frontend code had to struggle with determining their test scope and properly organizing their test suite. However, the inherent separation of concerns in AngularJS forces the developer to write isolated units of code, making the testing process much simpler. Developers can now quickly identify the units they need to test, and so controllers, services, directives, and any other AngularJS component can be tested as standalone units. Furthermore, the extensive use of dependency injection in AngularJS enables developers to switch contexts and easily cover their code with an extensive test suite. However, before you begin writing tests for your AngularJS application, you will first need to prepare your test environment beginning with the Karma test runner.

Introducing Karma test runner

The Karma test runner is a utility developed by the AngularJS team that helps developers with executing tests in different browsers. It does so by starting a web server that runs source code with test code on selected browsers, reporting the tests result back to the command-line utility. Karma offers real test results for real devices and browsers, flow control for IDEs and the command line, and framework-agnostic testability. It also provides developers with a set of plugins that enables them to run tests with the most popular test frameworks. The team also provides special plugins called browser launchers that enable Karma to run tests on selected browsers.

In our case, we will use the Jasmine test framework along with a PhantomJS browser launcher. However, testing real applications will require you to expand Karma's configuration to include more launchers and execute tests on the browsers you intend to support.

> PhantomJS is a headless WebKit browser often used in programmable scenarios where you don't need a visual output; that's why it fits perfectly for testing purposes. You can learn more about PhantomJS by visiting the official documentation at `http://phantomjs.org/documentation/`.

Installing the Karma command-line tool

The easiest way to start using Karma is to globally install the command-line tool provided using npm. To do so, just issue the following command in your command-line tool:

```
$ npm install -g karma-cli
```

This will install the latest version of Karma's command-line utility in your global `node_modules` folder. When the installation process is successfully finished, you'll be able to use the Karma utility from your command line. Next, you'll need to install Karma's project dependencies.

> You may experience some trouble installing global modules. This is usually a permission issue, so use `sudo` or super user when running the global install command.

Installing Karma's dependencies

Before you can start writing your tests, you will need to install Karma's dependencies using npm. To do so, change your `package.json` file as follows:

```
{
  "name": "MEAN",
  "version": "0.0.10",
  "dependencies": {
    "express": "~4.8.8",
    "morgan": "~1.3.0",
    "compression": "~1.0.11",
    "body-parser": "~1.8.0",
    "method-override": "~2.2.0",
    "express-session": "~1.7.6",
    "ejs": "~1.0.0",
    "connect-flash": "~0.1.1",
    "mongoose": "~3.8.15",
    "passport": "~0.2.1",
```

```
        "passport-local": "~1.0.0",
        "passport-facebook": "~1.0.3",
        "passport-twitter": "~1.0.2",
        "passport-google-oauth": "~0.1.5",
        "socket.io": "~1.1.0",
        "connect-mongo": "~0.4.1",
        "cookie-parser": "~1.3.3"
      },
      "devDependencies": {
        "should": "~4.0.4",
        "supertest": "~0.13.0",
        "karma": "~0.12.23",
        "karma-jasmine": "~0.2.2",
        "karma-phantomjs-launcher": "~0.1.4"
      }
    }
```

As you can see, you added Karma's core package, Karma's Jasmine plugin, and
Karma's PhantomJS launcher to your devDependencies property. To install your
new dependencies, go to your application's root folder and issue the following
command in your command-line tool:

```
$ npm install
```

This will install the specified version of Karma's core package, Karma's Jasmine
plugin, and Karma's PhantomJS launcher in your project's node_modules folder.
When the installation process is successfully finished, you will be able to use these
modules to run your tests. Next, you'll need to configure Karma's execution by
adding a Karma configuration file.

Configuring the Karma test runner

In order to control Karma's test execution, you will need to configure Karma using a
special configuration file placed at the root folder of your application. When executed,
Karma will automatically look for the default configuration file named karma.conf.
js in the application's root folder. You can also indicate your configuration file name
using a command-line flag, but for simplicity reasons we'll use the default filename.
To start configuring Karma, create a new file in your application folder, and name it
karma.conf.js. In your new file, paste the following code snippet:

```
module.exports = function(config) {
  config.set({
    frameworks: ['jasmine'],
    files: [
```

```
        'public/lib/angular/angular.js',
        'public/lib/angular-resource/angular-resource.js',
        'public/lib/angular-route/angular-route.js',
        'public/lib/angular-mocks/angular-mocks.js',
        'public/application.js',
        'public/*[!lib]*/*.js',
        'public/*[!lib]*/*[!tests]*/*.js',
        'public/*[!lib]*/tests/unit/*.js'
    ],
    reporters: ['progress'],
    browsers: ['PhantomJS'],
    captureTimeout: 60000,
    singleRun: true
  });
};
```

As you can see, Karma's configuration file is used to set the way Karma executes tests. In this case, we used the following settings:

- `frameworks`: This tells Karma to use the Jasmine framework.

- `files`: This sets the list of files that Karma will include in its tests. Notice that you can use glob patterns to indicate files pattern. In this case, we included all of our library files and module files, excluding our test files.

- `reporters`: This sets the way Karma reports its tests results.

- `browsers`: This is a list of browsers Karma will test on. Note that we can only use the PhantomJS browser since we haven't installed any other launcher plugin.

- `captureTimeout`: This sets the timeout for Karma tests execution.

- `singleRun`: This forces Karma to quit after it finishes the tests execution.

These properties are project-oriented, which means it will change according to your requirements. For instance, you'll probably include more browser launchers in real-world applications.

 You can learn more about Karma's configuration by visiting the official documentation at `http://karma-runner.github.io/0.12/config/configuration-file.html`.

Mocking AngularJS components

While testing an AngularJS application, it is recommended that unit tests execute quickly and separately from the backend server. This is because we want the unit tests to be as isolated as possible and work in a synchronous manner. This means we need to control the dependency injection process and provide mock components that emulate real components' operation. For instance, most of the components that communicate with the backend server are usually using the $http service or some sort of abstraction layer, such as the $resource service. Furthermore, the $http service sends requests to the server using the $httpBackend service. This means that by injecting a different $httpBackend service, we can send fake HTTP requests that won't hit a real server. As we previously stated, the AngularJS team is very committed to testing, so they already created these tools for us, wrapping these mock components in the ngMock module.

Introducing ngMock

The ngMock module is an external module provided by the AngularJS team. It contains several AngularJS mock utilities that can be used mostly for testing purposes. In essence, the ngMock module provides developers with a couple of important mock methods and a set of mock services. There are two ngMock methods that you'll probably use frequently: the angular.mock.module() method, which you'll use to create mock module instances, and the angular.mock.inject() method, which you'll use to inject mock dependencies. Both of these methods are also published on the window object for ease of use.

The ngMock module also provides developers with a set of mock services, including a mock exception service, timeout service, and log service. In our case, we'll use the $httpBackend mock service to handle HTTP requests in our tests.

The $httpBackend service allows developers to define mock responses to HTTP requests. It does so by providing two methods that enable you to determine the response data returned by the mock backend. The first method is $httpBackend.expect(), which is strictly used for unit testing. It allows developers to make assertions about HTTP requests made by the application, and fails the test if these request are not made by the test and even if they're made in the wrong order. A simple usage of the $httpBackend.expect() method is as follows:

```
$httpBackend.expect('GET', '/user').respond({userId: 'userX'});
```

This will force the AngularJS $http service to return a mock response and will fail the test if a request that fulfill the assertion is not executed. The second method is $httpBackend.when(), which allows developers to loosely define a mock backend without making any assertion about tests requests. A simple usage of the $httpBackend.when() method is as follows:

```
$httpBackend.when('GET', '/user').respond({userId: 'userX'});
```

However, this time, there isn't any assertion made about the tests requests. It simply tells the $http service to return a certain response for any request fulfilling this definition. We'll start using the ngMock module in a moment, but first we'll explain how to install it.

Installing ngMock

Installing the ngMock module is easy; simply go to your bower.json file and change it as follows:

```
{
  "name": "MEAN",
  "version": "0.0.10",
  "dependencies": {
    "angular": "~1.2",
    "angular-route": "~1.2",
    "angular-resource": "~1.2",
    "angular-mocks": "~1.2"
  }
}
```

Now, use your command-line tool to navigate to the MEAN application's root folder, and install the new ngMock module:

```
$ bower update
```

When Bower finishes installing the new dependency, you will see a new folder named angular-mocks in your public/lib folder. If you take a look at your Karma configuration file, you will notice that we already included the ngMock JavaScript file in the files property. Once you're done with the installation process, you can start writing your AngularJS unit tests.

Writing AngularJS unit tests

Once you're done configuring your test environment, writing unit tests becomes an easy task. To do so, you will use the ngMock module's supplied tools to test each component. While the general structure is the same, each entity test is a bit different and involves subtle changes. In this section, you'll learn how to test the major AngularJS entities. Let's begin with testing a module.

Testing modules

Testing a module is very simple. All you have to do is check that the module is properly defined and exists in the test context. The following is an example unit test:

```
describe('Testing MEAN Main Module', function() {
  var mainModule;

  beforeEach(function() {
    mainModule = angular.module('mean');
  });

  it('Should be registered', function() {
    expect(mainModule).toBeDefined();
  });
});
```

Notice how we use the `beforeEach()` and `angular.module()` methods to load the module before we run the test. When the test specification is executed, it will use the `toBeDefined()` Jasmine matcher to validate that the module was actually defined.

Testing controllers

Testing controllers is a bit trickier. In order to test a controller, you will need to use ngMock's `inject()` method and create a controller instance. So, a unit test that minimally covers your `ArticlesController` will be as follows:

```
describe('Testing Articles Controller', function() {
  var _scope, ArticlesController;

  beforeEach(function() {
    module('mean');

    inject(function($rootScope, $controller) {
      _scope = $rootScope.$new();
      ArticlesController = $controller('ArticlesController', {
        $scope: _scope
      });
    });
  });

  it('Should be registered', function() {
    expect(ArticlesController).toBeDefined();
  });

  it('Should include CRUD methods', function() {
```

```
        expect(_scope.find).toBeDefined();
        expect(_scope.findOne).toBeDefined();
        expect(_scope.create).toBeDefined();
        expect(_scope.delete).toBeDefined();
        expect(_scope.update).toBeDefined();
    });
});
```

Again, we used the `beforeEach()` method to create the controller before test specifications were executed. However, this time, we used the `module()` method to register the main application module and the `inject()` method to inject Angular's `$controller` and `$rootScope` services. Then, we used the `$rootScope` service to create a new scope object and the `$controller` service to create a new `ArticlesController` instance. The new controller instance will utilize the mock `_scope` object, so we can use it to validate the existence of controller's properties. In this case, the second spec will validate the existence of the controller's basic CRUD methods.

Testing services

Testing services will be very similar to testing controllers. It is even simpler since we can directly inject the service into our tests. A unit test that minimally covers your `Articles` service will be as follows:

```
describe('Testing Articles Service', function() {
    var _Articles;

    beforeEach(function() {
        module('mean');

        inject(function(Articles) {
            _Articles = Articles;
        });
    });

    it('Should be registered', function() {
        expect(_Articles).toBeDefined();
    });

    it('Should include $resource methods', function() {
        expect(_Articles.get).toBeDefined();
        expect(_Articles.query).toBeDefined();
        expect(_Articles.remove).toBeDefined();
        expect(_Articles.update).toBeDefined();
    });
});
```

We use the `beforeEach()` method to inject the service before running the specs. This, validates the service's existence and confirms that the service includes a set of `$resource` methods.

Testing routes

Testing routes is even simpler. All you have to do is inject the `$route` service and test the routes collection. A unit test that test for an `Articles` route will be as follows:

```
describe('Testing Articles Routing', function() {
  beforeEach(module('mean'));

  it('Should map a "list" route', function() {
    inject(function($route) {
      expect($route.routes['/articles'].templateUrl).
toEqual('articles/views/list-articles.view.html');
    });
  });
});
```

Notice that we're testing a single route and only the `templateUrl` property, so a real test specification will probably be more extensive.

Testing directives

Although we haven't elaborated on directives, they can still be a vital part of an AngularJS application. Testing directives will usually require you to provide an HTML template and use Angular's `$compile` service. A basic unit test that tests the `ngBind` directive will be as follows:

```
describe('Testing The ngBind Directive', function() {
  beforeEach(module('mean'));

  it('Should bind a value to an HTML element', function() {
    inject(function($rootScope, $compile) {
      var _scope = $rootScope.$new();
      element = $compile('<div data-ng-bind="testValue"></div>')(_
scope);

      _scope.testValue = 'Hello World';
      _scope.$digest();

      expect(element.html()).toEqual(_scope.testValue);
    });
  });
});
```

Let's go over this test code. First, we created a new scope object, and then we used the $compile service to compile the HTML template with the scope object. We set the model testValue property and ran a digest cycle using the $digest() method to bind the model with the directive. We finish our test by validating that the model value is indeed rendered.

Testing filters

Like with directives, we didn't discuss filters too much. However, they too can be a vital part of an AngularJS application. Testing filters is very similar to the way we test other AngularJS components. A basic unit test that tests Angular's lowercase filter will be as follows:

```
describe('Testing The Lowercase Filter', function() {
    beforeEach(module('mean'));

    it('Should convert a string characters to lowercase', function() {
        inject(function($filter) {
            var input = 'Hello World';
            var toLowercaseFilter = $filter('lowercase');

            expect(toLowercaseFilter(input)).toEqual(input.toLowerCase());
        });
    });
});
```

As you can see, testing a filter requires the usage of the $filter service to create a filter instance. Then, you just processed your input and validated the filter functionality. In this case, we used JavaScript's toLowerCase() method to validate that the lowercase filter actually works.

While these examples illustrate pretty well the basics of writing AngularJS unit tests, you should keep in mind that the tests can be much more complex. Let's see how we can use the ngMock module to test one of our ArticlesController methods.

Writing your first unit test

A common requirement is testing your controller's methods. Since the ArticlesController methods use the $http service to communicate with the server, it would be appropriate to use the $httpBackend mock service. To begin writing the ArticlesController unit test, you will first need to create a new tests folder inside the public/articles folder. In the public/articles/tests folder, create a new folder for unit tests, called unit. Finally, in your public/articles/tests/unit folder, create a new file named articles.client.controller.unit.tests.js.

In your new file, paste the following code snippet:

```
describe('Testing Articles Controller', function() {
  var _scope, ArticlesController;

  beforeEach(function() {
    module('mean');

    jasmine.addMatchers({
      toEqualData: function(util, customEqualityTesters) {
        return {
          compare: function(actual, expected) {
            return {
              pass: angular.equals(actual, expected)
            };
          }
        };
      }
    });
    inject(function($rootScope, $controller) {
      _scope = $rootScope.$new();
      ArticlesController = $controller('ArticlesController', {
        $scope: _scope
      });
    });
  });

  it('Should have a find method that uses $resource to retrieve a list
of articles', inject(function(Articles) {
    inject(function($httpBackend) {
      var sampleArticle = new Articles({
        title: 'An Article about MEAN',
        content: 'MEAN rocks!'
      });
      var sampleArticles = [sampleArticle];

      $httpBackend.expectGET('api/articles').respond(sampleArticles);

      _scope.find();
      $httpBackend.flush();

      expect(_scope.articles).toEqualData(sampleArticles);
    });
  }));
```

```
    it('Should have a findOne method that uses $resource to retreive a
single of article', inject(function(Articles) {
        inject(function($httpBackend, $routeParams) {
            var sampleArticle = new Articles({
                title: 'An Article about MEAN',
                content: 'MEAN rocks!'
            });

            $routeParams.articleId = 'abcdef123456789012345678';

            $httpBackend.expectGET(/api\/articles\/([0-9a-fA-F]{24})$/).
respond(sampleArticle);

            _scope.findOne();
            $httpBackend.flush();

            expect(_scope.article).toEqualData(sampleArticle);
        });
    }));
});
```

Let's break down the test code. First, you required your module dependencies, and defined your global variables. You started your test using a `describe()` method, which informs the test tool this test is going to examine `ArticlesController`. Inside the `describe` block, we began by creating a new controller and scope objects using the `beforeEach()` method.

Inside the `beforeEach()` method, we created a new custom Jasmine Matcher, called `toEqualData`. This matcher will compare a regular object and a $resource wrapped object using the `angular.equal()` method. We added this matcher because $resource adds quite a few properties to our objects, so the basic comparison matcher will not work.

You then created the first specification that is going to test the controller's `find()` method. The trick here is to use the $httpBackend.expectGET() method, which sets a new backend request assertion. This means that the test expects an HTTP request that fulfills this assertion, and will respond with a certain response. You then used the controller's `find()` method, which will create a pending HTTP request. The cycle ends when you call the $httpBackend.flush() method, which will simulate the server's response. You concluded the test by testing your model's values.

The second specification is almost identical to the first one but will test the controller's `findOne()` method. On top of the $httpBackend service, it also uses the $routeParams service to set the `articleId` route parameter. Now that you have your first unit test, let's see how you can execute it using Karma's command-line utility.

Running your AngularJS unit tests

To run your AngularJS tests, you will need to use Karma's command-line utility you previously installed. To do so, use your command-line tool and navigate to your project's base folder. Then issue the following command:

```
$ NODE_ENV=test karma start
```

Windows users should first execute the following command:

```
> set NODE_ENV=test
```

Then run Karma using the following command:

```
> karma start
```

The preceding command will do a few things. First, it will set the NODE_ENV variable to test, forcing your MEAN application to use the test environment configuration file. Then, it will execute the Karma command-line utility. The test results should be reported in your command-line tool similar to the following screenshot:

Karma's test results

This concludes the unit test coverage of your AngularJS application. It is recommended that you use these methods to expand your test suite and include more components tests. In the next section, you'll learn about AngularJS E2E testing, and to write and run a cross-application E2E test.

AngularJS E2E tests

While unit tests serve as a first layer to keep our applications covered, it is sometimes necessary to write tests that involve several components together that react with a certain interface. The AngularJS team often refers to these tests as E2E tests.

To understand this better, let's say Bob is an excellent frontend developer who keeps his Angular code well tested. Alice is also an excellent developer, but she works on the backend code, making sure her Express controllers and models are all covered. In theory, this team of two does a superb job, but when they finish writing the login feature of their MEAN application, they suddenly discover it's failing. When they dig deeper, they find out that Bob's code is sending a certain JSON object, while Alice's backend controller is expecting a slightly different JSON object. The fact is that both of them did their job, but the code is still failing. You might say this is the team leader's fault, but we've all been there at some point or another, and while this is just a small example, modern applications tend to become very complex. This means that you cannot just trust manual testing or even unit tests. You will need to find a way to test features across the entire application, and this is why E2E tests are so important.

Introducing the Protractor test runner

To execute E2E tests, you will need some sort of tool that emulates user behavior. In the past, the AngularJS team advocated a tool called Angular scenario test runner. However, they decided to abandon this tool and create a new test runner called Protractor. Protractor is a dedicated E2E test runner that simulates human interactions and runs tests using the Jasmine test framework. It is basically a Node.js tool, which uses a neat library called WebDriver. WebDriver is an open source utility that allows programmable control over a web browser behavior. As we stated, Protractor is using Jasmine by default, so tests will look very similar to the unit tests you wrote before, but Protractor also provides you with several global objects as follows:

- `browser`: This is a `WebDriver` instance wrapper, which allows you to communicate with the browser.
- `element`: This is a helper function to manipulate HTML elements.
- `by`: This is a collection of element locator functions. You can use it to find elements by a CSS selector, their ID, or even by the model property they're bound to.
- `protractor`: This is a WebDriver namespace wrapper containing a set of static classes and variables.

Using these utilities, you'll be able to perform browser operations inside your tests' specifications. For instance, the `browser.get()` method will load a page for you to perform tests on. It is important to remember that Protractor is a dedicated tool for AngularJS applications, so the `browser.get()` method will throw an error if the page it tries to load doesn't include the AngularJS library. You'll write your first E2E test in a moment, but first let's install Protractor.

Protractor is a very young tool, so things are bound to change rapidly. It is recommended that you learn more about Protractor by visiting the official repository page at `https://github.com/angular/protractor`.

Installing the Protractor test runner

Protractor is a command-line tool, so you'll need to globally install it using npm. To do so, just issue the following command in your command-line tool:

```
$ npm install -g protractor
```

This will install the latest version of Protractor command-line utilities in your global `node_modules` folder. When the installation process is successfully finished, you'll be able to use Protractor from your command line.

 You may experience some trouble installing global modules. This is usually a permission issue, so use `sudo` or super user when running the global install command.

Since Protractor will need a working WebDriver server, you will either need to use a Selenium server or install a standalone WebDriver server. You can download and install a standalone server by issuing the following command in your command-line tool:

```
$ webdriver-manager update
```

This will install the Selenium standalone server, which you'll later use to handle Protractor's tests. The next step would be to configure Protractor's execution options.

 You can learn more about WebDriver by visiting the official project page at `https://code.google.com/p/selenium/wiki/WebDriverJs`.

Configuring the Protractor test runner

In order to control Protractor's test execution, you will need to create a Protractor configuration file in the root folder of your application. When executed, Protractor will automatically look for a configuration file named `protractor.conf.js` in your application's root folder. You can also indicate your configuration filename using a command-line flag, but for simplicity reasons, we'll use the default filename. So begin by creating a new file named `protractor.conf.js` in your application's root folder. In your new file, paste the following lines of code:

```
exports.config = {
    specs: ['public/*[!lib]*/tests/e2e/*.js']
}
```

Our Protractor's configuration file is very basic and only includes one property. The `specs` property basically tells Protractor where to find the test files. This configuration is project-oriented, which means that it will change according to your requirements. For instance, you'll probably change the list of browsers you want your tests to run on.

 You can learn more about Protractor's configuration by going over the example configuration file at https://github.com/angular/protractor/blob/master/docs/referenceConf.js.

Writing your first E2E test

Since E2E tests are quite complicated to write and read, we'll begin with a simple example. In our example, we'll test the **Create Article** page and try to create a new article. Since we didn't log in first, an error should occur and be presented to the user. To implement this test, go to your `public/articles/tests` folder and create a new folder named e2e. Inside your new folder, create a new file named `articles.client.e2e.tests.js`. Finally, in your new file, paste the following code snippet:

```
describe('Articles E2E Tests:', function() {
  describe('New Article Page', function() {
    it('Should not be able to create a new article', function() {
      browser.get('http://localhost:3000/#!/articles/create');
      element(by.css('input[type=submit]')).click();
      element(by.binding('error')).getText().then(function(errorText)
{
        expect(errorText).toBe('User is not logged in');
      });
    });
  });
});
```

The general test structure should already be familiar to you; however, the test itself is quite different. We began by requesting the **Create Article** page using the `browser.get()` method. Then, we used the `element()` and `by.css()` methods to submit the form. Finally, we found the error message element using `by.binding()` and validated the error text. While this is a simple example, it illustrates well the way E2E tests work. Next we'll use Protractor to run this test.

Running your AngularJS E2E tests

Running Protractor is a bit different than using Karma and Mocha. Protractor needs your application to run so that it can access it just like a real user does. So let's begin by running the application; navigate to your application's root folder and use your command-line tool to start the MEAN application as follows:

```
$ NODE_ENV=test node server
```

Windows users should first execute the following command:

```
> set NODE_ENV=test
```

Then run their application using the following command:

```
> node server
```

This will start your MEAN application using the test environment configuration file. Now, open a new command-line window and navigate to your application's root folder. Then, start the Protractor test runner by issuing the following command:

```
$ protractor
```

Protractor should run your tests and report the results in your command-line window as shown in the following screenshot:

Protractor's test results

Congratulations! You now know how to cover your application code with E2E tests. It is recommended that you use these methods to expand your test suite and include extensive E2E tests.

Summary

In this chapter, you learned to test your MEAN application. You learned about testing in general and the common TDD/BDD testing paradigms. You then used the Mocha test framework and created controller and model unit tests, where you utilized different assertion libraries. Then, we discussed the methods of testing AngularJS, where you learned the difference between unit and E2E testing. We then proceeded to unit test your AngularJS application using the Jasmine test framework and the Karma test runner. Then, you learned how to create and run E2E tests using Protractor. After you've built and tested your real-time MEAN application, in the next chapter, you'll learn how to dramatically improve your development cycle time using some popular automation tools.

11
Automating and Debugging MEAN Applications

In the previous chapters, you learned how to build and test your real-time MEAN application. You learned how to connect all the MEAN components and how to use test frameworks to test your application. While you can continue developing your application using the same methods used in the previous chapters, you can also speed up development cycles by using supportive tools and frameworks. These tools will provide you with a solid development environment through automation and abstraction. In this chapter, you'll learn how to use different community tools to expedite your MEAN application's development. We'll cover the following topics:

- Introduction to Grunt
- Using Grunt tasks and community tasks
- Debugging your Express application using node-inspector
- Debugging your AngularJS application's internals using Batarang

Introducing the Grunt task runner

MEAN application development, and any other software development in general, often involves redundant repetition. Daily operations such as running, testing, debugging, and preparing your application for the production environment becomes monotonous and should be abstracted by some sort of an automation layer. You may be familiar with Ant or Rake, but in JavaScript projects, the automation of repetitive tasks can be easily done using the Grunt task runner. Grunt is a Node.js command-line tool that uses custom and third-party tasks to automate a project's build process. This means you can either write your own automated tasks, or better yet, take advantage of the growing Grunt eco-system and automate common operations using third-party Grunt tasks. In this section, you'll learn how to install, configure, and use Grunt. The examples in this chapter will continue directly from those in previous chapters, so copy the final example from *Chapter 10, Testing MEAN Applications*, and let's take it from there.

Installing the Grunt task runner

The easiest way to get started with Grunt is by using the Grunt command-line utility. To do so, you will need to globally install the grunt-cli package by issuing the following command in your command-line tool:

```
$ npm install -g grunt-cli
```

This will install the latest version of Grunt CLI in your global node_modules folder. When the installation process is successfully finished, you'll be able to use the Grunt utility from your command line.

> You may experience some troubles installing global modules. This is usually a permission issue, so use sudo or super user when running the global install command.

To use Grunt in your project, you will need to install a local Grunt module using npm. Furthermore, third-party tasks are also installed as packages using npm. For instance, a common third-party task is the grunt-env task, which lets developers set Node's environment variables. This task is installed as a node module, which Grunt can later use as a task. Let's locally install the grunt and grunt-env modules. To do so, change your project's package.json file as follows:

```
{
  "name": "MEAN",
  "version": "0.0.11",
  "dependencies": {
```

```
        "express": "~4.8.8",
        "morgan": "~1.3.0",
        "compression": "~1.0.11",
        "body-parser": "~1.8.0",
        "method-override": "~2.2.0",
        "express-session": "~1.7.6",
        "ejs": "~1.0.0",
        "connect-flash": "~0.1.1",
        "mongoose": "~3.8.15",
        "passport": "~0.2.1",
        "passport-local": "~1.0.0",
        "passport-facebook": "~1.0.3",
        "passport-twitter": "~1.0.2",
        "passport-google-oauth": "~0.1.5",
        "socket.io": "~1.1.0",
        "connect-mongo": "~0.4.1",
        "cookie-parser": "~1.3.3"
    },
    "devDependencies": {
        "should": "~4.0.4",
        "supertest": "~0.13.0",
        "karma": "~0.12.23",
        "karma-jasmine": "~0.2.2",
        "karma-phantomjs-launcher": "~0.1.4",
        "grunt": "~0.4.5",
        "grunt-env": "~0.4.1"
    }
}
```

To install your new dependencies, go to your application's root folder and issue the following command in your command-line tool:

```
$ npm install
```

This will install the specified versions of the grunt and grunt-env modules in your project's node_modules folder. When the installation process is successfully finished, you'll be able to use Grunt in your project. However, first you'll need to configure Grunt using the Gruntfile.js configuration file.

Configuring Grunt

In order to configure Grunt's operation, you will need to create a special
configuration file placed at the root folder of your application. When Grunt
is executed, it will automatically look for the default configuration file named
Gruntfile.js in the application's root folder. You can also indicate your
configuration filename using a command-line flag, but we'll use the default
filename for simplicity.

To configure Grunt and use the grunt-env task, create a new file in your
application's root folder and name it Gruntfile.js. In your new file, paste the
following code snippet:

```
module.exports = function(grunt) {
  grunt.initConfig({
    env: {
      dev: {
        NODE_ENV: 'development'
      },
      test: {
        NODE_ENV: 'test'
      }
    }
  });

  grunt.loadNpmTasks('grunt-env');

  grunt.registerTask('default', ['env:dev']);
};
```

As you can see, the grunt configuration file uses a single module function to inject
the grunt object. Then, you used the grunt.initConfig() method to configure
your third-party tasks. Notice how you configured the grunt-env task in the
configuration object, where you basically created two environment variables
sets: one for testing and the other for development. Next, you used the grunt.
loadNpmTasks() method to load the grunt-env module. Be aware that you will
need to call this method for any new third-party task you add to the project. Finally,
you created a default grunt task using the grunt.registerTask() method. Notice
how the grunt.registerTask() method accepts two arguments: the first one sets
the task name and the second argument is a collection of other grunt tasks that will
be executed when the parent task is used. This is a common pattern of grouping
different tasks together to easily automate several operations. In this case, the
default task will only run the grunt-env tasks to set the NODE_ENV variable for your
development environment.

To use the default task, navigate to your application's root folder and issue the following command in your command-line tool:

```
$ grunt
```

This will run the `grunt-env` task and set the `NODE_ENV` variable for your development environment. This is just a simple example, so let's see how we can use grunt to automate more complex operations.

> You can learn more about Grunt's configuration by visiting the official documentation page at `http://gruntjs.com/configuring-tasks`.

Running your application using Grunt

Running your application using the node command-line tool may not seem like a redundant task. However, when continuously developing your application, you will soon notice that you stop and start your application server quite often. To help with this task, there is unique tool called Nodemon. Nodemon is a Node.js command-line tool that functions as a wrapper to the simple node command-line tool, but watches for changes in your application files. When Nodemon detects file changes, it automatically restarts the node server to update the application. Although Nodemon can be used directly, it is also possible to use it as a Grunt task. To do so, you will need to install the third-party `grunt-nodemon` task and then configure it in your Grunt configuration file. Let's begin by installing the `grunt-nodemon` module. Start by changing your project's `package.json` file as follows:

```
{
  "name": "MEAN",
  "version": "0.0.11",
  "dependencies": {
    "express": "~4.8.8",
    "morgan": "~1.3.0",
    "compression": "~1.0.11",
    "body-parser": "~1.8.0",
    "method-override": "~2.2.0",
    "express-session": "~1.7.6",
    "ejs": "~1.0.0",
    "connect-flash": "~0.1.1",
    "mongoose": "~3.8.15",
    "passport": "~0.2.1",
    "passport-local": "~1.0.0",
```

```
      "passport-facebook": "~1.0.3",
      "passport-twitter": "~1.0.2",
      "passport-google-oauth": "~0.1.5",
      "socket.io": "~1.1.0",
      "connect-mongo": "~0.4.1",
      "cookie-parser": "~1.3.3"
    },
    "devDependencies": {
      "should": "~4.0.4",
      "supertest": "~0.13.0",
      "karma": "~0.12.23",
      "karma-jasmine": "~0.2.2",
      "karma-phantomjs-launcher": "~0.1.4",
      "grunt": "~0.4.5",
      "grunt-env": "~0.4.1",
      "grunt-nodemon": "~0.3.0"
    }
}
```

To install your new dependencies, go to your application's root folder and issue the following command in your command-line tool:

```
$ npm install
```

This will install the specified version of the grunt-nodemon module in your project's node_modules folder. When the installation process is successfully finished, you will need to configure the Nodemon Grunt task. To do so, change your project's Gruntfile.js file as follows:

```
module.exports = function(grunt) {
  grunt.initConfig({
    env: {
      test: {
        NODE_ENV: 'test'
      },
      dev: {
        NODE_ENV: 'development'
      }
    },
    nodemon: {
      dev: {
        script: 'server.js',
        options: {
          ext: 'js,html',
```

```
          watch: ['server.js', 'config/**/*.js', 'app/**/*.js']
        }
      }
    }
  });

  grunt.loadNpmTasks('grunt-env');
  grunt.loadNpmTasks('grunt-nodemon');

  grunt.registerTask('default', ['env:dev', 'nodemon']);
};
```

Let's go over these changes. First, you changed the configuration object passed to the grunt.initConfig() method. You added a new nodemon property and created a development environment configuration. The script property is used to define the main script file, in this case, the server.js file. The options property configures Nodemon's operation and tells it to watch both the HTML and JavaScript files that are placed in your config and app folders. The last changes you've made load the grunt-nodemon module and add the nodemon task as a subtask of the default task.

To use your modified default task, go to your application's root folder and issue the following command in your command-line tool:

```
$ grunt
```

This will run both the grunt-env and grunt-nodemon tasks and start your application server.

 You can learn more about Nodemon's configuration by visiting the official documentation page at https://github.com/remy/nodemon.

Testing your application using Grunt

Since you have to run three different test tools, running your tests can also be a tedious task. However, Grunt can assist you by running Mocha, Karma, and Protractor for you. To do so, you will need to install the grunt-karma, grunt-mocha-test, and grunt-protractor-runner modules and then configure them in your Grunt's configuration file. Start by changing your project's package.json file as follows:

```
{
  "name": "MEAN",
  "version": "0.0.11",
```

```json
        "dependencies": {
          "express": "~4.8.8",
          "morgan": "~1.3.0",
          "compression": "~1.0.11",
          "body-parser": "~1.8.0",
          "method-override": "~2.2.0",
          "express-session": "~1.7.6",
          "ejs": "~1.0.0",
          "connect-flash": "~0.1.1",
          "mongoose": "~3.8.15",
          "passport": "~0.2.1",
          "passport-local": "~1.0.0",
          "passport-facebook": "~1.0.3",
          "passport-twitter": "~1.0.2",
          "passport-google-oauth": "~0.1.5",
          "socket.io": "~1.1.0",
          "connect-mongo": "~0.4.1",
          "cookie-parser": "~1.3.3"
        },
        "devDependencies": {
          "should": "~4.0.4",
          "supertest": "~0.13.0",
          "karma": "~0.12.23",
          "karma-jasmine": "~0.2.2",
          "karma-phantomjs-launcher": "~0.1.4",
          "grunt": "~0.4.5",
          "grunt-env": "~0.4.1",
          "grunt-nodemon": "~0.3.0",
          "grunt-mocha-test": "~0.11.0",
          "grunt-karma": "~0.9.0",
          "grunt-protractor-runner": "~1.1.4"
        }
      }
```

To install your new dependencies, go to your application's root folder and issue the following command in your command-line tool:

```
$ npm install
```

This will install the specified versions of the `grunt-karma`, `grunt-mocha-test`, and `grunt-protractor-runner` modules in your project's `node_modules` folder. However, you'll also need to download and install Protractor's standalone `WebDriver` server by issuing the following command in your command-line tool:

```
$ node_modules/grunt-protractor-runner/node_modules/protractor/bin/
webdriver-manager update
```

When the installation process is successfully finished, your will need to configure your new Grunt tasks. To do so, change your project's `Gruntfile.js` file as follows:

```javascript
module.exports = function(grunt) {
  grunt.initConfig({
    env: {
      test: {
        NODE_ENV: 'test'
      },
      dev: {
        NODE_ENV: 'development'
      }
    },
    nodemon: {
      dev: {
        script: 'server.js',
        options: {
          ext: 'js,html',
          watch: ['server.js', 'config/**/*.js', 'app/**/*.js']
        }
      }
    },
    mochaTest: {
      src: 'app/tests/**/*.js',
      options: {
        reporter: 'spec'
      }
    },
    karma: {
      unit: {
        configFile: 'karma.conf.js'
      }
    },
    protractor: {
      e2e: {
```

```
        options: {
          configFile: 'protractor.conf.js'
        }
      }
    }
  });

  grunt.loadNpmTasks('grunt-env');
  grunt.loadNpmTasks('grunt-nodemon');
  grunt.loadNpmTasks('grunt-mocha-test');
  grunt.loadNpmTasks('grunt-karma');
  grunt.loadNpmTasks('grunt-protractor-runner');

  grunt.registerTask('default', ['env:dev', 'nodemon']);
  grunt.registerTask('test', ['env:test', 'mochaTest', 'karma',
'protractor']);
};
```

Let's go over these changes. First, you changed the configuration object passed to the grunt.initConfig() method. You added a new mochaTest configuration property with a src property that tells the Mocha task where to look for the test files and an options property that sets Mocha's reporter. You also added a new karma configuration property that uses the configFile property to set Karma's configuration filename and a new protractor configuration property that uses the configFile property to set Protractor's configuration file name. You finished by loading the grunt-karma, grunt-mocha-test, and grunt-protractor-runner modules and creating a new test task containing mochaTest, karma, and protractor as subtasks.

To use your new test task, go to your application's root folder and issue the following command in your command-line tool:

```
$ grunt test
```

This will run the grunt-env, mochaTest, karma, and protractor tasks and will run your application tests.

Linting your application using Grunt

In software development, linting is the identification of suspicious code usage using dedicated tools. In a MEAN application, linting can help you avoid common mistakes and coding errors in your daily development cycles. Let's see how you can use Grunt to lint your project's CSS and JavaScript files. To do so, you will need to install and configure the `grunt-contrib-csslint` module, which lints CSS files, and the `grunt-contrib-jshint` modules, which lints JavaScript files. Start by changing your project's `package.json` file as follows:

```
{
    "name": "MEAN",
    "version": "0.0.11",
    "dependencies": {
        "express": "~4.8.8",
        "morgan": "~1.3.0",
        "compression": "~1.0.11",
        "body-parser": "~1.8.0",
        "method-override": "~2.2.0",
        "express-session": "~1.7.6",
        "ejs": "~1.0.0",
        "connect-flash": "~0.1.1",
        "mongoose": "~3.8.15",
        "passport": "~0.2.1",
        "passport-local": "~1.0.0",
        "passport-facebook": "~1.0.3",
        "passport-twitter": "~1.0.2",
        "passport-google-oauth": "~0.1.5",
        "socket.io": "~1.1.0",
        "connect-mongo": "~0.4.1",
        "cookie-parser": "~1.3.3"
    },
    "devDependencies": {
        "should": "~4.0.4",
        "supertest": "~0.13.0",
        "karma": "~0.12.23",
        "karma-jasmine": "~0.2.2",
        "karma-phantomjs-launcher": "~0.1.4",
        "grunt": "~0.4.5",
        "grunt-env": "~0.4.1",
        "grunt-nodemon": "~0.3.0",
```

```
    "grunt-mocha-test": "~0.11.0",
    "grunt-karma": "~0.9.0",
    "grunt-protractor-runner": "~1.1.4",
    "grunt-contrib-jshint": "~0.10.0",
    "grunt-contrib-csslint": "~0.2.0"
  }
}
```

To install your new dependencies, go to your application's root folder and issue the following command in your command-line tool:

```
$ npm install
```

This will install the specified versions of the grunt-contrib-csslint and grunt-contrib-jshint modules in your project's node_modules folder. When the installation process is successfully finished, your will need to configure your new Grunt tasks. To do so, change your project's Gruntfile.js file as follows:

```
module.exports = function(grunt) {
  grunt.initConfig({
    env: {
      test: {
        NODE_ENV: 'test'
      },
      dev: {
        NODE_ENV: 'development'
      }
    },
    nodemon: {
      dev: {
        script: 'server.js',
        options: {
          ext: 'js,html',
          watch: ['server.js', 'config/**/*.js', 'app/**/*.js']
        }
      }
    },
    mochaTest: {
      src: 'app/tests/**/*.js',
      options: {
        reporter: 'spec'
      }
    },
```

```
      karma: {
        unit: {
          configFile: 'karma.conf.js'
        }
      },
      jshint: {
        all: {
          src: ['server.js', 'config/**/*.js', 'app/**/*.js', 'public/
  js/*.js', 'public/modules/**/*.js']
        }
      },
      csslint: {
        all: {
          src: 'public/modules/**/*.css'
        }
      }
    });

    grunt.loadNpmTasks('grunt-env');
    grunt.loadNpmTasks('grunt-nodemon');
    grunt.loadNpmTasks('grunt-mocha-test');
    grunt.loadNpmTasks('grunt-karma');
    grunt.loadNpmTasks('grunt-contrib-jshint');
    grunt.loadNpmTasks('grunt-contrib-csslint');

    grunt.registerTask('default', ['env:dev', 'nodemon']);
    grunt.registerTask('test', ['env:test', 'mochaTest', 'karma']);
    grunt.registerTask('lint', ['jshint', 'csslint']);
  };
```

Let's go over these changes. First, you changed the configuration object passed
to the grunt.initConfig() method. You added a new jshint configuration
with an src property that tells the linter task which JavaScript files to test. You also
added a new csslint configuration with an src property that tells the linter task
which CSS files to test. You finished by loading the grunt-contrib-jshint and
grunt-contrib-csslint modules, and creating a new lint task containing jshint
and csslint as subtasks.

To use your new lint task, go to your application's root folder and issue the following
command in your command-line tool:

```
$ grunt lint
```

This will run the jshint and csslint tasks and will report the results in your command-line tool. Linters are great tools to validate your code; however, in this form, you would need to run the lint task manually. A better approach would be to automatically run the lint task whenever you modify a file.

Watching file changes using Grunt

Using the current Grunt configuration, Nodemon will restart your application whenever certain files change. However, what if you want to run other tasks when files change? For this, you will need to install the grunt-contrib-watch module, which will be used to watch for file changes, and the grunt-concurrent module that is used to run multiple Grunt tasks concurrently. Start by changing your project's package.json file as follows:

```
{
  "name": "MEAN",
  "version": "0.0.11",
  "dependencies": {
    "express": "~4.8.8",
    "morgan": "~1.3.0",
    "compression": "~1.0.11",
    "body-parser": "~1.8.0",
    "method-override": "~2.2.0",
    "express-session": "~1.7.6",
    "ejs": "~1.0.0",
    "connect-flash": "~0.1.1",
    "mongoose": "~3.8.15",
    "passport": "~0.2.1",
    "passport-local": "~1.0.0",
    "passport-facebook": "~1.0.3",
    "passport-twitter": "~1.0.2",
    "passport-google-oauth": "~0.1.5",
    "socket.io": "~1.1.0",
    "connect-mongo": "~0.4.1",
    "cookie-parser": "~1.3.3"
  },
  "devDependencies": {
    "should": "~4.0.4",
    "supertest": "~0.13.0",
    "karma": "~0.12.23",
    "karma-jasmine": "~0.2.2",
    "karma-phantomjs-launcher": "~0.1.4",
```

```
    "grunt": "~0.4.5",
    "grunt-env": "~0.4.1",
    "grunt-nodemon": "~0.3.0",
    "grunt-mocha-test": "~0.11.0",
    "grunt-karma": "~0.9.0",
    "grunt-protractor-runner": "~1.1.4",
    "grunt-contrib-jshint": "~0.10.0",
    "grunt-contrib-csslint": "~0.2.0",
    "grunt-contrib-watch": "~0.6.1",
    "grunt-concurrent": "~1.0.0"
  }
}
```

To install your new dependencies, go to your application's root folder and issue the following command in your command-line tool:

```
$ npm install
```

This will install the specified versions of the `grunt-contrib-watch` and `grunt-concurrent` modules in your project's `node_modules` folder. When the installation process is successfully finished, your will need to configure your new `grunt` tasks. To do so, change your project's `Gruntfile.js` file as follows:

```
module.exports = function(grunt) {
  grunt.initConfig({
    env: {
      test: {
        NODE_ENV: 'test'
      },
      dev: {
        NODE_ENV: 'development'
      }
    },
    nodemon: {
      dev: {
        script: 'server.js',
        options: {
          ext: 'js,html',
          watch: ['server.js', 'config/**/*.js', 'app/**/*.js']
        }
      }
    },
    mochaTest: {
```

```
        src: 'app/tests/**/*.js',
        options: {
          reporter: 'spec'
        }
      },
      karma: {
        unit: {
          configFile: 'karma.conf.js'
        }
      },
      protractor: {
        e2e: {
          options: {
            configFile: 'protractor.conf.js'
          }
        }
      },
      jshint: {
        all: {
          src: ['server.js', 'config/**/*.js', 'app/**/*.js', 'public/
js/*.js', 'public/modules/**/*.js']
        }
      },
      csslint: {
        all: {
          src: 'public/modules/**/*.css'
        }
      },
      watch: {
        js: {
          files: ['server.js', 'config/**/*.js', 'app/**/*.js', 'public/
js/*.js', 'public/modules/**/*.js'],
          tasks: ['jshint']
        },
        css: {
          files: 'public/modules/**/*.css',
          tasks: ['csslint']
        }
      },
      concurrent: {
        dev: {
          tasks: ['nodemon', 'watch'],
          options: {
```

```
            logConcurrentOutput: true
        }
      }
    }
  });

  grunt.loadNpmTasks('grunt-env');
  grunt.loadNpmTasks('grunt-nodemon');
  grunt.loadNpmTasks('grunt-mocha-test');
  grunt.loadNpmTasks('grunt-karma');
  grunt.loadNpmTasks('grunt-protractor-runner');
  grunt.loadNpmTasks('grunt-contrib-jshint');
  grunt.loadNpmTasks('grunt-contrib-csslint');
  grunt.loadNpmTasks('grunt-contrib-watch');
  grunt.loadNpmTasks('grunt-concurrent');


  grunt.registerTask('default', ['env:dev', 'lint', 'concurrent']);
  grunt.registerTask('test', ['env:test', 'mochaTest', 'karma',
  'protractor']);
  grunt.registerTask('lint', ['jshint', 'csslint']);
};
```

First, you changed the configuration object passed to the `grunt.initConfig()` method. You added a new `watch` configuration property with two subconfigurations. The first one is to watch the JavaScript files and the second is to watch the CSS files. These watch configurations will automatically run the `jshint` and `csslint` tasks whenever file changes are detected. Then, you created a new configuration for the `concurrent` task that will run both the `nodemon` and `watch` tasks concurrently. Notice that the `concurrent` task will log the console output of these tasks since you set the `logConcurrentOutput` option to `true`. You finished by loading the `grunt-contrib-watch` and `grunt-concurrent` modules and modifying your `default` task to use the `concurrent` task.

To use your modified `default` task, navigate to your application's root folder and issue the following command in your command-line tool:

```
$ grunt
```

This will run the `lint` and `concurrent` tasks that will start your application and report the results in your command-line tool.

Grunt is a powerful tool with a growing ecosystem of third-party tasks to perform any task from minimizing files to project deployment. Grunt also encouraged the community to create new types of task runners, which are also gaining popularity such as Gulp. So, it is highly recommended that you visit Grunt's home page at `http://gruntjs.com/` to find the best automation tools suitable for your needs.

Debugging Express with node-inspector

Debugging the Express part of your MEAN application can be a complicated task. Fortunately, there is a great tool that solves this issue called node-inspector. Node-inspector is a debugging tool for Node.js applications that use the Blink (a WebKit Fork) Developer Tools. In fact, developers using Google's Chrome browser will notice that node-inspector's interface is very similar to the Chrome Developer Tools' interface. Node-inspector supports some pretty powerful debugging features:

- Source code files navigation
- Breakpoints manipulation
- Stepping over, stepping in, stepping out, and resuming execution
- Variable and properties inspection
- Live code editing

When running node-inspector, it will create a new web server and attach to your running MEAN application source code. To debug your application, you will need to access the node-inspector interface using a compatible web browser. You will then be able to use node-inspector to debug your application code using node-inspector's interface. Before you begin, you'll need to install and configure node-inspector and make a few small changes in the way you run your application. You can use node-inspector independently or by using the node-inspector Grunt task. Since your application is already configured to use Grunt, we'll go with the Grunt task solution.

Installing node-inspector's grunt task

To use node-inspector, you will need to install the `grunt-node-inspector` module. To do so, change your project's `package.json` file as follows:

```
{
  "name": "MEAN",
  "version": "0.0.11",
  "dependencies": {
    "express": "~4.8.8",
```

```
    "morgan": "~1.3.0",
    "compression": "~1.0.11",
    "body-parser": "~1.8.0",
    "method-override": "~2.2.0",
    "express-session": "~1.7.6",
    "ejs": "~1.0.0",
    "connect-flash": "~0.1.1",
    "mongoose": "~3.8.15",
    "passport": "~0.2.1",
    "passport-local": "~1.0.0",
    "passport-facebook": "~1.0.3",
    "passport-twitter": "~1.0.2",
    "passport-google-oauth": "~0.1.5",
    "socket.io": "~1.1.0",
    "connect-mongo": "~0.4.1",
    "cookie-parser": "~1.3.3"
  },
  "devDependencies": {
    "should": "~4.0.4",
    "supertest": "~0.13.0",
    "karma": "~0.12.23",
    "karma-jasmine": "~0.2.2",
    "karma-phantomjs-launcher": "~0.1.4",
    "grunt": "~0.4.5",
    "grunt-env": "~0.4.1",
    "grunt-nodemon": "~0.3.0",
    "grunt-mocha-test": "~0.11.0",
    "grunt-karma": "~0.9.0",
    "grunt-protractor-runner": "~1.1.4",
    "grunt-contrib-jshint": "~0.10.0",
    "grunt-contrib-csslint": "~0.2.0",
    "grunt-contrib-watch": "~0.6.1",
    "grunt-concurrent": "~1.0.0",
    "grunt-node-inspector": "~0.1.5"
  }
}
```

To install your new dependencies, go to your application's root folder and issue the following command in your command-line tool:

```
$ npm install
```

This will install the specified version of the grunt-node-inspector module in your project's node_modules folder. When the installation process is successfully finished, your will need to configure your new grunt task.

Configuring node-inspector's grunt task

The node-inspector's `grunt` task configuration is very similar to other tasks' configuration. However, it will also force you to make a few changes in other tasks as well. To configure the `node-inspector` task, change your project's `Gruntfile.js` file as follows:

```
module.exports = function(grunt) {
  grunt.initConfig({
    env: {
      test: {
        NODE_ENV: 'test'
      },
      dev: {
        NODE_ENV: 'development'
      }
    },
    nodemon: {
      dev: {
        script: 'server.js',
        options: {
          ext: 'js,html',
          watch: ['server.js', 'config/**/*.js', 'app/**/*.js']
        }
      },
      debug: {
        script: 'server.js',
        options: {
          nodeArgs: ['--debug'],
          ext: 'js,html',
          watch: ['server.js', 'config/**/*.js', 'app/**/*.js']
        }
      }
    },
    mochaTest: {
      src: 'app/tests/**/*.js',
      options: {
        reporter: 'spec'
      }
    },
    karma: {
      unit: {
        configFile: 'karma.conf.js'
      }
    },
```

```
    protractor: {
      e2e: {
        options: {
          configFile: 'protractor.conf.js'
        }
      }
    },
    jshint: {
      all: {
        src: ['server.js', 'config/**/*.js', 'app/**/*.js', 'public/
js/*.js', 'public/modules/**/*.js']
      }
    },
    csslint: {
      all: {
        src: 'public/modules/**/*.css'
      }
    },
    watch: {
      js: {
        files: ['server.js', 'config/**/*.js', 'app/**/*.js', 'public/
js/*.js', 'public/modules/**/*.js'],
        tasks: ['jshint']
      },
      css: {
        files: 'public/modules/**/*.css',
        tasks: ['csslint']
      }
    },
    concurrent: {
      dev: {
        tasks: ['nodemon', 'watch'],
        options: {
          logConcurrentOutput: true
        }
      },
      debug: {
        tasks: ['nodemon:debug', 'watch', 'node-inspector'],
        options: {
          logConcurrentOutput: true
        }
      }
    },
    'node-inspector': {
```

```
      debug: {}
    }
  });

  grunt.loadNpmTasks('grunt-env');
  grunt.loadNpmTasks('grunt-nodemon');
  grunt.loadNpmTasks('grunt-mocha-test');
  grunt.loadNpmTasks('grunt-karma');
  grunt.loadNpmTasks('grunt-protractor-runner');
  grunt.loadNpmTasks('grunt-contrib-jshint');
  grunt.loadNpmTasks('grunt-contrib-csslint');
  grunt.loadNpmTasks('grunt-contrib-watch');
  grunt.loadNpmTasks('grunt-concurrent');
  grunt.loadNpmTasks('grunt-node-inspector');

  grunt.registerTask('default', ['env:dev', 'lint',
'concurrent:dev']);
  grunt.registerTask('debug', ['env:dev', 'lint',
'concurrent:debug']);
  grunt.registerTask('test', ['env:test', 'mochaTest', 'karma',
'protractor']);
  grunt.registerTask('lint', ['jshint', 'csslint']);
};
```

Let's go over these changes. First, you changed the configuration object passed to the `grunt.initConfig()` method. You began by modifying the `nodemon` task by adding a new `debug` subtask. The `debug` subtask will use the `nodeArgs` property to start your application in debug mode. Then, you modified the concurrent task by adding a new `debug` subtask as well. This time, the `debug` subtask is simply using the `nodemon:debug` task and the new `node-inspector` task. Near the end of the configuration object, you minimally configured the new `node-inspector` task and then loaded the `grunt-node-inspector` module. You finished by creating a `debug` task and modifying your `default` task.

> You can learn more about node-inspector's configuration by visiting the official project at `https://github.com/node-inspector/node-inspector`.

Running the debug grunt task

To use your new `debug` task, navigate to your application's root folder and issue the following command in your command-line tool:

```
$ grunt debug
```

This will run your application in a debug mode and start the node-inspector server. The output in your command-line tool should be similar to the following screenshot:

As you can see, the `node-inspector` task invites you to start debugging the application by visiting `http://127.0.0.1:8080/debug?port=5858` using a compatible browser. Open this URL in Google Chrome and you should see an interface similar to the following screenshot:

Debugging with node-inspector

As you can see, you'll get a list of your project files on the left-hand side panel, a file content viewer in the middle panel, and a debug panel on the right-hand side panel. This means your `node-inspector` task is running properly and identifies your Express project. You can start debugging your project by setting some breakpoints and testing your components' behavior.

> Node-inspector will only work on browsers that use the Blink engine, such as Google Chrome or Opera.

Debugging AngularJS with Batarang

Debugging most of the AngularJS part of your MEAN application is usually done in the browser. However, debugging the internal operations of AngularJS can be a bit trickier. For this purpose, the AngularJS team created a Chrome extension called Batarang. Batarang extends the Chrome Developer Tools with a new tab where you can debug different aspects of your AngularJS application. Installing Batarang is quite straightforward; all you have to is to visit the Chrome web store at `https://chrome.google.com/webstore/detail/angularjs-batarang/ighdmehidhipcmcojjgiloacoafjmpfk` and install the Chrome extension.

> Batarang will only work on the Google Chrome browser.

Using Batarang

Once you're done installing Batarang, use Chrome to navigate to your application URL. Then, open the Chrome Developer Tools panel and you should see an **AngularJS** tab. Click on it and a panel similar to the following screenshot should open:

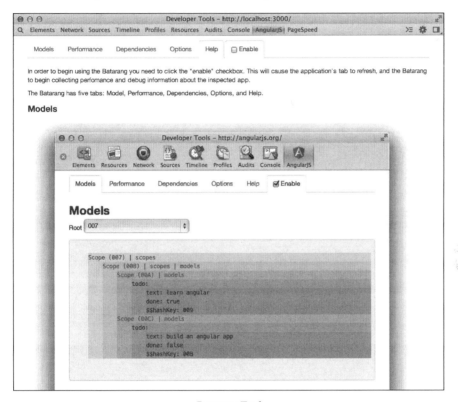

Batarang Tool

Note that you need to enable Batarang using the **Enable** checkbox at the top of the panel. Batarang has four tabs you can use: **Models**, **Performance**, **Dependencies**, and **Options**. The last tab is the **Help** section where you can learn more about Batarang.

Batarang Models

To explore your AngularJS application models, make sure you've enabled Batarang and click on the **Models** tab. You should see a panel similar to the following screenshot:

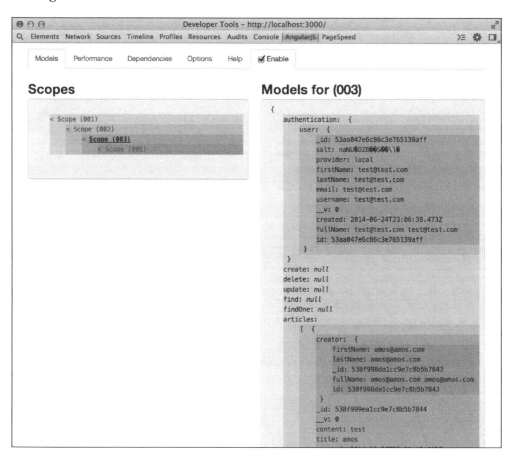

Batarang models

On the left side of the panel, you'll be able to see the page scopes hierarchy. When selecting a scope, you'll be able to see the scope model on the right. In the preceding screenshot, you can see the scope model for the articles example from the previous chapters.

Batarang Performance

To explore your AngularJS application performance, make sure you enabled Batarang and click on the **Performance** tab. You should see a panel similar to the following screenshot:

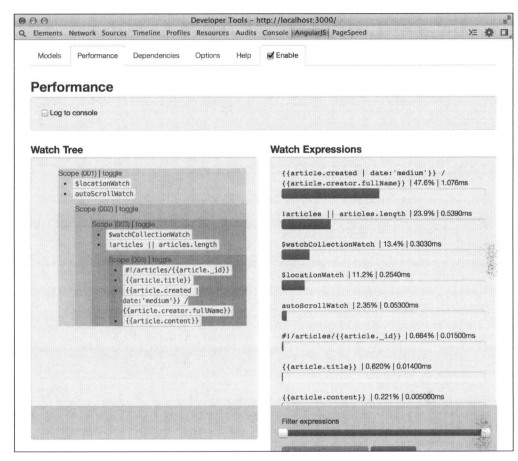

Batarang performance

On the left side of the panel, you'll be able to see a tree of your application's watched expressions. On the right-hand side of the panel, you'll be able to see the relative and absolute performance status of all of your application's watched expressions. In the preceding screenshot, you'll be able to see the performance report for the articles example from the previous chapters.

Batarang Dependencies

To explore your AngularJS services' dependencies, make sure you enabled Batarang and then click on the **Dependencies** tab. You should see a panel similar to the following screenshot:

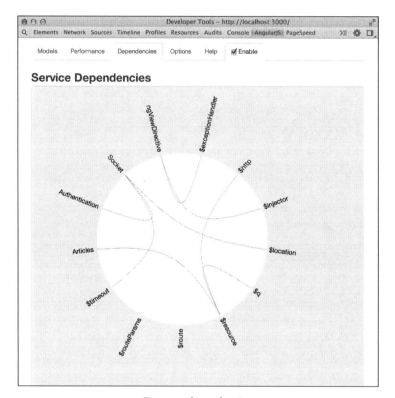

Batarang dependencies

In the **Dependencies** tab, you'll be able to see a visualization of the application's services dependencies. When hovering with your mouse over one of the services, the selected service will be colored green and the selected service dependencies will turn red.

Batarang options

To highlight your AngularJS components' elements, make sure you've enabled Batarang and then click on the **Options** tab. You should see a panel similar to the following screenshot:

Batarang options

When you enable one of the options, Batarang will highlight the respective feature of the application. Scopes will have a red outline, bindings will have a blue outline, and applications will have a green outline.

Batarang is a simple yet powerful tool. Used right, it can save you a lot of time of endlessly looking around and using console logging. Make sure you understand each tab and try to explore your application yourself.

Summary

In this chapter, you learned how to automate your MEAN application's development. You also learned how to debug the Express and AngularJS parts of your application. We discussed Grunt and its powerful ecosystem of third-party tasks. You learned how to implement common tasks and how to group them together in your own custom tasks. Then, you installed and configured the node-inspector tool and learned how to use Grunt and node-inspector to debug your Express code. Near the end of this chapter, you learned about the Batarang Chrome extension. You went through Batarang's features and found out how to debug your AngularJS internals.

Since it's the last chapter of this book, you should now know how to build, run, test, debug, and automate your MEAN application.

The next step is up to you.

Index

Symbols

$http service 207
$resource service
  using 210, 211
$resource factory method, arguments
  Actions 210
  Options 210
  ParamDefaults 210
  Url 210
$routeProvider object 185
.bowerrc configuration file 170
--dbpath command-line flag 12
--logpath command-line flag 13

A

ad hoc queries, MongoDB 84
after(callback) method 260
afterEach(callback) method 260
AND/OR queries
  building 93
angular.bootstrap() method
  config argument 169
  element argument 169
  modules argument 169
angular global object 162
AngularJS
  about 162
  application structure 172-175
  configuring 171
  debugging, with Batarang 314
  installing 169
  installing, Bower used 171
  key concepts 162
  MVC entities 177, 178

  routing 182
  services 187
  URL, for core directives 168
AngularJS application
  bootstrapping 176
  E2E tests 284, 285
  testing 271
  testing, with Jasmine 271, 272
  unit tests 272
AngularJS application bootstrap
  about 168
  automatic bootstrap 168
  manual bootstrap 169
AngularJS application routes
  defining 185-187
AngularJS authentication
  Authentication service, adding 191-193
  Authentication service, using 193
  managing 189
  user object, rendering 190, 191
AngularJS components
  mocking 276
AngularJS core directives
  about 167, 168
  ng-app directive 167
  ng-controller directive 167
  ng-hide directive 168
  ng-model directive 167
  ng-repeat directive 168
  ng-show directive 168
AngularJS custom directives 168
AngularJS custom services
  URL, for documentation 189
AngularJS directives
  about 167
  core directives 167, 168

E

E2E tests **256**
E2E tests, AngularJS application
  about 284, 285
  executing 288, 289
  Protractor test runner 285, 286
  Protractor test runner, configuring 287
  Protractor test runner, installing 286
  writing 287, 288
edit-article view **218, 219**
EJS views
  rendering 72, 73
emit() method **232, 233**
end() method **41**
end-to-end tests. *See* E2E tests
equality statement
  using 92
error handling method
  creating 198
event handlers, Socket.io chat
  setting up 244-246
existing documents
  updating 93
expect() method **261**
Express
  about 49, 50
  application object 52
  debugging, with node-inspector 308
  installing 50, 51
  request object 53
  response object 54
Express application
  configuration system 66-68
  configuring 206, 207
  creating 51
  executing 52
  Mocha test, writing 264
  test environment, configuring 263
  testing 259
  testing, with Mocha 259, 260
  testing, with Should.js 260
  testing, with SuperTest 261
Express components
  Express application, configuring 206, 207
  Express controller, setting 198
  Express routes, setting 204-206

Mongoose model, creating 196, 197
  setting 196
Express controller
  authorization middleware 204
  create() method 199
  creating 63
  delete() method 202, 203
  error handling method 198
  list() method 199, 200
  read() method 200, 201
  setting 198
  update() method 201
  users controller authentication
    middleware 203
Express framework
  MVC pattern, implementing 55
express.js file **65**
Express middleware
  about 55
  body-parser 55
  Compression 55
  cookie-parser 55
  express.static 55
  method-override 55
  Morgan 55
  Session 55
  URL 55
Express routes
  setting 204-206
express-session module
  installing 75
express.static() middleware **74**
Express view system
  configuring 71, 72
Express web framework **50**
external modules **163**

F

Facebook's developer
  URL 148
factory method **188**
failureFlash property **143**
failureRedirect property **143**
file changes
  monitoring, Grunt used 304-307
file modules **39**

Thank you for buying
MEAN Web Development

About Packt Publishing

Packt, pronounced 'packed', published its first book "*Mastering phpMyAdmin for Effective MySQL Management*" in April 2004 and subsequently continued to specialize in publishing highly focused books on specific technologies and solutions.

Our books and publications share the experiences of your fellow IT professionals in adapting and customizing today's systems, applications, and frameworks. Our solution based books give you the knowledge and power to customize the software and technologies you're using to get the job done. Packt books are more specific and less general than the IT books you have seen in the past. Our unique business model allows us to bring you more focused information, giving you more of what you need to know, and less of what you don't.

Packt is a modern, yet unique publishing company, which focuses on producing quality, cutting-edge books for communities of developers, administrators, and newbies alike. For more information, please visit our website: www.packtpub.com.

About Packt Open Source

In 2010, Packt launched two new brands, Packt Open Source and Packt Enterprise, in order to continue its focus on specialization. This book is part of the Packt Open Source brand, home to books published on software built around Open Source licenses, and offering information to anybody from advanced developers to budding web designers. The Open Source brand also runs Packt's Open Source Royalty Scheme, by which Packt gives a royalty to each Open Source project about whose software a book is sold.

Writing for Packt

We welcome all inquiries from people who are interested in authoring. Book proposals should be sent to author@packtpub.com. If your book idea is still at an early stage and you would like to discuss it first before writing a formal book proposal, contact us; one of our commissioning editors will get in touch with you.

We're not just looking for published authors; if you have strong technical skills but no writing experience, our experienced editors can help you develop a writing career, or simply get some additional reward for your expertise.

Mastering Node.js

ISBN: 978-1-78216-632-0   Paperback: 346 pages

Expert techniques for building fast servers and scalable, real-time network applications with minimal effort

1. Master the latest techniques for building real-time, Big Data applications, integrating Facebook, Twitter, and other network services.

2. Tame asynchronous programming, the event loop, and parallel data processing.

3. Use the Express and Path frameworks to speed up development and deliver scalable, higher quality software more quickly.

Mastering Web Application Development with AngularJS

ISBN: 978-1-78216-182-0   Paperback: 372 pages

Build single-page web applications using the power of AngularJS

1. Make the most out of AngularJS by understanding the AngularJS philosophy and applying it to real-life development tasks.

2. Effectively structure, write, test, and finally deploy your application.

3. Add security and optimization features to your AngularJS applications.

Please check **www.PacktPub.com** for information on our titles

PHP and MongoDB Web Development Beginner's Guide

ISBN: 978-1-84951-362-3   Paperback: 292 pages

Combine the power of PHP and MongoDB to build dynamic web 2.0 applications

1. Learn to build PHP-powered dynamic web applications using MongoDB as the data backend.

2. Handle user sessions, store real-time site analytics, build location-aware web apps, and much more, all using MongoDB and PHP.

3. Full of step-by-step instructions and practical examples, along with challenges to test and improve your knowledge.

Getting Started with Grunt: The JavaScript Task Runner

ISBN: 978-1-78398-062-8   Paperback: 132 pages

A hands-on approach to mastering the fundamentals of Grunt

1. Gain insight on the core concepts of Grunt, Node.js, and npm to get started with Grunt.

2. Learn how to install, configure, run, and customize Grunt.

3. Example driven and filled with tips to help you create custom Grunt tasks.

Please check **www.PacktPub.com** for information on our titles

Made in the USA
Middletown, DE
18 February 2016